Jasmuheen •

The information in this book is applicable to all
individuals who have an interest in self-mastery and global harmony.

We dedicate this book
»Ambassadors of Light«
to the Angelics and the Arcturians for their teachings of
the Higher Light Science,
and to the Ambassadors of Light for their commitment to
discovering their potential and also for
their courage to challenge the status quo.
I wish to also thank the Ascended Ones,
who I call the Master Alchemists, for their vision,
their inspiration, and their pragmatic solutions
to the challenges faced by our modern-day world.

»I can't believe that,« said Alice.
»Can't you?« said the Queen in a pitying tone.
»Try again. Draw a long breath and shut your eyes.«
Alice laughed. »There's no use trying,« she said. »One can't believe
impossible things.«
»I dare say you haven't had much practice« said the Queen. »When
I was your age, I always did it for half an hour a day. Why sometimes
I've believed as many as six impossible things before breakfast.«
quote from Lewis Carroll's
»Alice in Wonderland«

Thanks to Helen and Jeff at S.E.A.,
for all your help with editing and research.
Thanks to all the Ambassadors of Light
who took part in our research.

Sources of Research:
The United Nation's Agencies
Encyclopedia Britannica
The World Wide Web

Jasmuheen

Ambassadors of Light

To the Angel within all

Self Empowerment Academy
PO Box 737
Brisbane 4069 Australia
Ph: + 61 7 3878 2446
Fax: +61 7 3878 2564
www.selfempowermentacademy.com.au
Published January 2000
ISBN 3-929512-70-x

Front cover by ChiaraDina Cerweny - Austria
chiaradina@magnet.at
Copyright © KOHA Publishing

KOHA-Verlag GmbH
Almstrasse 4
84424 Burgrain
Germany
e-mail: koha-verlag@t-online.de

Distributed by:

United Staates
KOHA Publishing
Angelika Kalem
P.O. Box 5564
Pagossa Springs, Co 81147
e mail: heart@frontier.net

UK
Airlift Book Company
8 The Arena, Mollison Ave.
Enfield, Middlesex, EN3 7NJ, UK
Tel: (+44) 181-8040400
Fax: (+4) 181-804044

Contents

Introduction

»The known is a prison. It is the unknown which is the
field of pure potentiality, the field we need to step into.«
Dr Deepak Chopra

It is interesting to sit and write this introduction for this, the
follow-on book to »Living on Light – Nutrition for the New Millennium«, as when I was initially guided to share my personal journey of
being free from the need to eat food through the power of the Divine,
I had no idea that it would become so popular and be published in so
many languages. Nor was I aware of the potential impact that the
lifestyles that allow us to be nourished in this way, could have on world
health and world hunger issues or the controversy that this ›food free
journey‹ would cause.

As time goes by, more and more people are now sharing their
experiences on the higher possibilities that come from connecting with
the Divine One Within (DOW) – including being able to exist purely
on Its energy. My work also continues to expand and change due to
my own DOW connection, and for the last few years I have been
focused on the M.A.P.S. Ambassadry, and more recently, writing the
Camelot Trilogy with Saint Germain.

Nonetheless, what seems to grab people's attention is that there
are now ›everyday type‹ individuals who are completely free to choose
whether they wish to eat or not – without fear of starvation and death.
Apart from supporting the effective redistribution of resources to
address world hunger issues, people can also learn to free themselves
from their addiction to eating food if they so desire.

As long as an individual chooses a lifestyle that promotes then
achieves physical fitness, emotional fitness, mental fitness AND spiritual fitness, then living free from the need of nourishment from food
is within their grasp if they desire it. One of the main benefits of self
mastery is freedom from perceived or self-imposed limitations. As we
have continued to stress, the living on light journey is purely about
freedom of choice.

It is our desire in this book to provide not just up to date information and stories of my own continued experience in this field of
research, but to also look at how we can apply this knowledge on a

pragmatic level globally. Not all of my stories are provable, as some are told by people about people who have since passed on. Some stories come with great research like the work of Dr. Karl Graninger or the Qigong phenomena called ›Bigu‹, and we provide contacts for you to investigate this further if you are someone who needs this type of proof.

Rather than labor the point that living free from the need from food is possible by sharing detailed test studies, we would like to move on to other issues like our »World Health, World Hunger Project« and what this really means. Our research has shown that there is a recipe or set lifestyle that both individuals and governments can apply to address personal health and happiness, plus global issues such as long-term resource sustainability, poverty and famine. So the purpose of this book is to offer viable solutions to these challenges in a way that supports the M.A.P.S. Declaration of Inter-Dependence (see chapter 33).

Under the guidance of the Ascended Masters Kuthumi and Saint Germain, in 1996 the Australian-based Self Empowerment Academy (S.E.A.) created M.A.P.S. – the Movement of an Awakened Positive Society. (see the MAPS Visions and Agendas article at the back of this book) The focus of M.A.P.S. is to offer pragmatic solutions to some of the challenges faced by many people and countries in our modern-day world by unifying people under common visions.

Working with specific social, educational, economic and political agendas, the M.A.P.S. Ambassadors are committed to positive personal and planetary progression. In 2000 we will have published the »M.A.P.S. Alliance Manifesto« to offer facts, figures and feedback on some of the current global ›hotspots‹, apart from world health and world hunger problems.

Not all M.A.P.S. Ambassadors choose to live on light as it is not part of their blueprint at this time. The knowledge of how to obtain an alternative form of nourishment to food, is the specialized field of expertise of the M.A.P.S. Ambassadors of Light. It is our project, our ›divinely inspired‹ assignment to share how this is possible, so that more people can have real freedom of choice.

The global benefits of this choice have enormous ramifications to our resource sustainability, our health care programs and even our personal happiness as an evolving species. What the world chooses to do with our research is really up to them.

This book is possibly my final testimonial on this topic, as I feel that my research in this field and writing about it is nearly complete, and I have other projects to fulfill within the M.AP.S. Ambassadry. An educational cartoon series from the book »Our Camelot – the Game of Divine Alchemy« is on the agenda, as are other projects« with the Masters that really make my heart sing.

I am so honored to have shared this journey with you all, no matter how controversial it has been. Are we here to challenge the status quo? It seems like that's a game some of us have been destined to play, and it is our desire to do this as graciously and impeccably as possible.

When people make noise it draws our attention – sometimes it is an offer for us to get caught up in another's movie – if we stop, watch, listen and choose to hear their message. Yet if we stop our busy lives, be in silence and meditate and listen to the inner voice, we will hear the most brilliant message of all. It is the voice of the Divine One Within us inviting us to move beyond our limitations and enter into the experience of personal and then global paradise.

For the Ambassadors of Light, it is time to be more pragmatic, and via the redirection of vital resources on our planet we will eliminate all world health and world hunger challenges and eventually create global paradise for all and not just for the few.

No doubt we will attract a lot more controversy as we discuss our reasons for:
- holistic education
- the proper utilization of the human resource factor
- tithing and service
- global disarmament
- the dissolution of prohibition
- the forgiveness of third world debt and raising money for social welfare.

Still, challenging the ›powers that be‹ who currently hold the purse strings of the planet, has never been a popular way to go! Money of the mighty versus unity where all have enough food, shelter and a decent education? It's an interesting challenge and one that many of the Ambassadors of Light feel is worthy of pursuit.

As Henry Ford once said; »If money is your hope for independence you will never have it. The only real security that a man will have in this world is a reserve of knowledge, experience and ability.«

So the purpose of this book is to present our experience and our knowledge from nearly three decades of training in the field of metaphysics and apply it to some of our current global challenges. Information is available to everyone; yet retrieving it, assembling it and utilizing it positively is another game – as is experiencing it.

As Brigham Young said: »True independence and freedom can only exist in doing what's right.« In unity and sharing intelligent alternatives, we can do what's right for all and shift the balance of power back into the hands of the people so that true democracy can reign.

We trust that the wealth of information contained within these pages will provide both answers and insights. As with all our work, we ask you to hold an open, yet discerning heart and mind as we share more of our own, and others, research into the lifestyles of the Ambassadors of Light and what this can mean to the world.

Namaste,
Jasmuheen

O N E

The Supreme Splendour – DOW Power

»The more you depend on forces outside of yourself
the more you are dominated by them.«
Harold Sherman

We live in an age of magnificence – of prosperity and true joy, and it only takes a recipe to tune us all in. What miracles are these that we have been given so much love, wisdom and power to use at our discretion? Many of the Ambassadors of Light believe that we come as Gods to find the Gods that we are in physical earth form. Some say that God is like the sun. It feeds us, and keeps all our movies alive and its nature can be nirvanic and tender. When we swim in It, merge with It, feel It, allow It to love us as we remember It, miracles happen. Some call living without the need of food, a miracle.

Yet, simplistically put, the ability to live on light is a result of an initiation into the Presence of the God Within which then feeds us by the power of Its radiation. I prefer to call this the Divine One Within or our DOW.

In the experience of the Ambassadors of Light, DOW Power is a limitless and never-ending source of pure energy that dwells within everything, whether it is animate or not. It is the Power or Presence of what some call the Supreme Splendour of OH-OM, the One Heart and One Mind that exists within all.

Some call the DOW Power of OH-OM: God's power, Allah's power, Brahma's power, the force of Supreme Intelligence, the radiation from the Singularity; or other labels depending on their culture and beliefs. As the beings of light that I work with have often said: »We don't care what you call your God, just so long as you call It«, for experiencing It will bring love, wisdom, passion and purpose to our lives. Talk without experience perpetuates separatism as our minds always filter knowledge to mirror our own beliefs.

The living on light journey has never been about eating or not eating, it has always been about DOW Power. Everyone has this power available to them – in the same quantities – we just access It with different regularity and in different quantities. DOW Power is not restricted by our races, religions, cultures or our beliefs. It is like a hidden source of energy that when recognized, connected with, experienced and allowed to flow unimpeded through our bodies, brings many miracles to our lives. Being free from the need to take our nourishment from food is one very small benefit of this.

There are a myriad of ways to experience this Divine Power and the 21 day initiation that we talk about in my first book on this topic, is just one. As a consequence of this initiation that is designed to connect us further with the power of the Divine One Within, an individual finds freedom on many levels and yes, it is true that for many this means being free from the need to take nourishment from food. This is fact.

How this occurs has been detailed in our first book called »Living on Light – Nutrition for the New Millennium – A Personal Journey«. The success of this initiation, and the Light Ambassador's ability to maintain and sustain being fed by prana is dependant on a very disciplined lifestyle choice. This is where the individual involved focuses their time on maintaining a high level of physical, emotional, mental and spiritual fitness.

We call the individual who chooses this path, an Ambassador of Light or the spiritual warrior, for undergoing the process of conversion to pranic nourishment often demands both discipline and courage. To be successfully nourished by prana for over a long period of time, requires a clear commitment to experience DOW Power as It radiates Its Presence through us all on Earth. Many who undergo this journey have realized that the Holy Grail can be found within and that the physical body is also a temple to house the Presence of this Divine Force of Creation.

Throughout millennia, spiritual warriors have been undergoing initiations that allow them to radiate the light, love and wisdom of the Divine One Within. Obviously there are those who believe that the Divine Force of Creation is an external force – rather than a Force that permeates everything – and therefore they may not feel as though they can experience this Supreme Power personally.

The Oxford Dictionary describes ›God‹ as a »superhuman being worshipped as having power over nature and human fortunes.« In the ancient Vedas, it is said that we are to God as sunshine is to sun. In fact the Vedas have more information on prana and Its power than any other source of literature.

Debating about the way we think the Divine expresses Itself is not the issue of focus here. We all know that personal experience speaks volumes and surpasses theory and postulation, and often people may have experiences of ›higher powers‹ that defy both medical and scientific explanation. This is true in the case of the Ambassadors of Light.

In essence, the ability to live on prana alone is a natural by-product of allowing our DOW to feed us as we invite It to radiate through us. This is what the Christians would call living from God's light – literally. Religious texts and scriptures are filled with references as to the power of this divine radiation.

Are all who live from light religious? Not necessarily – at least not in the way that is commonly accepted, yet over 80% of the Ambassadors of Light have both a very deep understanding of metaphysics and have been long-term meditators. It is my belief that one cannot live from light unless one has the intrinsic understanding and experience in the existence of a Higher Intelligence – a cosmic order behind the chaos. For if we cease to take nourishment from food and yet we do not believe in, or have no experience of the Divine Force, then what will feed us in the place of food?

Human beings need nourishment to survive or else the physical body will feed off itself and eventually die, which is what happens to those with anorexia, or those who exist in situations with food scarcity, or those who are involved in hunger strikes. While we have plenty of research about what happens to people denied food, there has been virtually no precedence in the West of people being fed by prana.

Prana in Sanskrit means primal energy and is sometimes translated as breath of vital force; though it is more than these. The subject of prana is common in yogic thought and we talk more of this in the chapter called Prana Power. To me, prana is the essence of our DOW, and living healthily without food requires the ability to tap into DOW Power to obtain this alternative form of nutrition. And, as living purely on light is an exercise in self-mastery, it is not possible to do this without knowledge and experience of our Divine Self. Not the

14

ego/personality/culturally influenced self, but the Self that inspires us to explore and understand our true human potential.

Some call this desire to experience the Divine Self, the journey of enlightenment. According to the »Dictionary of Symbols«, enlightenment is a »Symbol of a condition experienced by candidates during rites of initiation. The known pattern of these rites involves death, a journey to the spirit world and a rebirth.«

Those who have experienced the 21 day process have found it to be an initiation that takes courage and commitment and great trust. All the Light Ambassadors who have chosen to stay with the experience of being fed by DOW Power have held a long-term interest in esoteric matters and initiations that allow them to be more »light filled«.

Albert Einstein once said: »The most beautiful thing we can experience is the mysterious. It is the source of true art and science. He to whom the emotion is stranger, who can no longer pause to wonder and stand wrapped in awe, is as good as dead; his eyes are closed. The insight into the mystery of life, coupled though it be with fear, has also given rise to religion.

»To know what is impenetrable to us really exists, manifesting itself as the highest wisdom and the most radiant beauty, which our dull faculties can comprehend only in their most primitive forms – this knowledge, this feeling is at the centre of true religiousness.«

To the Ambassadors of Light, radiation of the Supreme Splendour of the DOW is of paramount importance for we understand that this one focus alone has the power to transform our world. As has been the way since linear time began on Earth, every single human being is at choice as to how they wish to live their life, moment by moment. Choosing to focus on self-responsibility and self-refinement and getting to know our DOW will fulfil the prophecy of the »Second Coming«.

This is something that all who breathe can do right here, right now, rather than anticipating miracles or the return of the ›Messiah‹ to save us. Focusing on the Divine Perfection that dwells within us will release an experience of the Christed consciousness or the Buddhic consciousness within our hearts and minds and bring the world and her people into a state of true harmony and grace.

There are many ways to radiate the Supreme Splendour and these are well covered in our previous book titled »In Resonance«, and also throughout esoteric and metaphysical material and the scriptures of many religions. The knowledge of these paths is always revealed to the sincere seeker, for our DOW is always looking for opportunities to reveal Its Presence in our lives when invited to do so.

Yes, radiating the Supreme Splendour is about en›light‹enment – and to many of the Ambassadors of Light, this means being filled with Light. The four attributes of en›light‹enment are said to be: a) discrimination; b) desirelessness; c) good conduct and d) love. These are issues that the Light Ambassadors feel are worthy of experiencing.

As ancient texts have always said, we hold all the knowledge and all the keys to universal wisdom within us. Nothing is new and all will unfold on earth eventually in accordance with the Divine Plan. This Plan is a field of possibility that all who believe in grace and magic can play within. The wizards call what occurs within this field, the game of Divine Alchemy which we cover in detail in the Camelot Trilogy.

To the beings of light that I call the MA (or Master Alchemists), the lifestyles of the Ambassadors of Light who choose to be fed by their DOW, offer a more civilized alternative to the continual slaughter of both animal and human life at this time.

For me it is wonderful being able to be part of a small group of people who are able to offer this alternative to the world even though we accept that it is challenging to many people's belief systems. For those who intuitively respond to this lifestyle choice, Living on Light seems a very natural alternative.

While the »Exactly how is this possible?« question still needs a lot of scientific and medical research, the fact is that people can be nourished by liquid light, chi or prana, if they are physically fit, emotionally fit, mentally fit and spiritually fit AND desire this lifestyle, as yogis have done this for millennia.

In more recent times, studies have been done on the state of ›bigu‹ which is attained via qi emissions which are the radiation of a qigong master. After this exposure, many report a loss of appetite and maintain this desire to not eat, and practice of not eating, for days, months and years.

Our journey into pranic nourishment is somewhat different yet the results are the same. How well we are fed by prana and how well we can sustain this form of nourishment long-term, is directly related to how powerfully we allow the DOW to radiate through our body. We control the level of this emission daily by the quality of our thoughts, words and deeds.

As my friend and colleague, Louix Dor Dempriey says in his book »Dawn of Enlightenment«: »Divinity reveals itself from within the self, where it lies dormant until such time as the soul is ready and willing to externalize it. There are four qualities necessary to liberate the soul: desire, faith, willingness and obedience. Of the four, obedience is the last to which the ego personality will succumb. It is not enough to read all the right books and quote all the great sages. The divine laws of cause and effect must be obeyed.«

The evidence of these laws is everywhere on our planet if only we choose to look. So is the evidence of Holiness which appears in different ways to different people. And yet it is not our different beliefs that stop us from experiencing Holiness – it is our lack of deep desire. Without desire, without intention and without vision, the evidence of the Supreme Splendour remains hidden from us all. Those who have found and experienced the evidence of Holiness often become the Ambassadors of Light.

TWO

The Ambassadors of Light

»You cannot weaken the strong in order to strengthen the weak.«
Abraham Lincoln, 16th President of the United States

»Be such a man, and live such a life, that if every man were
such as you, and every life a life like yours,
this earth would be God's Paradise.«
Phillip Brooks, U.S. clergyman

I have come to call those choosing to be fed by the light of the
DOW, the Ambassadors of Light, and they come from many fields of
experience and many backgrounds. Not all who choose this path would
call themselves religious and many do not share my personal movie of
reality where telepathy is common, as is communication with, and
being in the Presence of, beings of light.

Probably the most wonderful, and better known, examples of
Ambassadors of Light are Jesus, Buddha, Mohammed, Krishna, Mother
Mary, Kwan Yin and all the inspiring teachers who have graced our
earth through time sharing their light, love and wisdom. To me these
beings exist still, they guide and aid many in their quest to experience
human potential in a way that honors life.

The Oxford Dictionary says that an Ambassador is a »diplomat
sent by one sovereign State on mission to another; diplomat of highest rank permanently representing sovereign or State at foreign court
or government.« Yes, it is true that many of the Ambassadors of Light
feel that they exist to fulfil and experience some higher, more divine
purpose. Many also feel that the ›State‹ they represent is the Divine
State of Grace and that the ›foreign court‹ is planet earth.

As I have traveled the globe, I have met many Ambassadors of
Light who see themselves as Buddhists, Christians, Jews, Catholics, Sai
Baba devotees, Babaji devotees, devotees of countless Indian gurus, plus
those with few religious ideologies who just wish to improve their fitness and health. Generally all are people who wish to experience qual-

ity living for themselves and also for others. Some are devoted to environmental issues or support the cessation of slaughter of animal life and promote the moral viewpoint, or the health benefits, or the long-term resource sustainability advantages of either a vegetarian diet or a food-free life style. I have researched both.

In the last few years, we have spoken to media, scientists and medical practitioners and watched something that was initially rejected by many, become a choice that is now tolerated and even understood. This is the power of focused re-education which can bring the elimination of fear through the elimination of ignorance.

While the Ambassadors may not have a step by step specific process to deal with every challenge on the planet as it enters the new millennium, we do have enough simple and practical information and tools that will create very powerful personal and global changes – assuming that what we are suggesting is adopted and practised. It may not happen overnight, but it will happen.

Through changing some of our very basic lifestyle choices, the Ambassadors of Light envisage the elimination of societal dis-ease which will allow for the redirection of billions of dollars into social welfare programs.

Under the M.A.P.S. Agenda we have established the Ambassadry of Light for those who Merlin calls the Light Knights so that we can continue to share of our personal journeys with DOW Power and living on Its Light. My last book, »Our Camelot – the Game of Divine Alchemy«, autobiographically details my experiences with these Cosmic Light Ambassadors that I have come to call the Master Alchemists (the MA).

In this book, Merlin describes the Light Ambassadors on earth as »Kosmic Knights on assignment for OH-OM, (One Heart One Mind) whose role is to pave the way for pranic nourishment as new millennium nutrition for humankind. They are often inspired to aid in the cessation of slaughter of all life on earth, particularly the animal kingdom. Beyond the moral benefits of a vegan lifestyle, they are also often environmentalists interested in long-term planetary resource sustainability«.

Later in the book, looking backwards in time Merlin talks more about the difference between those He calls the Nirvana Knights and the Knights of Light, saying:

»The Nirvana Knights were inspiring all to seek to know their DOW, to be ›light-filled‹ and they promoted the ecstasy of enlightenment. Their slogan was »E is for ecstasy, the power not the drug!« which somehow seemed appropriate in the ›quick hit‹ time of pills and potions that mesmerized the less disciplined on earth.

»The Light Knights were the fitness fanatics, like cosmic aerobic teachers. They were the ones who had found a solution to health and hunger-related problems at the end of the millennium before the big change. Many had become part of the Ambassadry of Light and were advocates of what some had come to call »prana nirvana«. To be successfully nourished by their DOW required being fit on all levels.«

Apart from being fit on all levels, one of the biggest challenges for the Knights of Light is in the area of environmental field control. Being able to exist in this world and yet be detached from it enough to be unaffected by our environment – except by choice – is another skill of mastery and one that many of the Ambassadors of Light are still developing.

To achieve the experience of the nirvana of prana, much preparation has to be done. To many of the Light Ambassadors this includes a daily schedule of focused attention to diet, exercise, solitude and time for contemplation and alignment with our DOW. In other words, we need to make basic lifestyle choices that support sustainable fitness on all levels of our being. Those who do not have, and maintain, a strong ›spiritual‹ practice find it impossible to be nourished by just prana.

Since beginning my research for this book, other methods of living without the intake of food have come to light. As they are unfamiliar to me personally, I can only share about the experiences and research of those who have converted the bodies to light food as outlined in my first book on this subject. People in the qigong state of ›bigu‹ seem to have a different experience, and what I am sharing here may have no relevance to their methodology.

What many Ambassadors have experienced is that being fit on all levels creates a strong vehicle for the Divine to radiate from within. A less fit vehicle can only attract, hold and emit certain levels of DOW Power that may not be enough to allow the vehicle to be sustained by just prana for long periods of time.

Also if a person is not fit enough on all levels, then during the 21 day process they may encounter problems with the body's electromagnetic circuitry. Mind mastery must be practised by each Ambassador of Light as they learn to be free from the influences of limiting beliefs based on past experiences and future fears.

The benefits of total fitness are far too numerous to mention here, suffice to say that it is an experience that once enjoyed you become addicted to. No illness, total joy, feelings of purpose and passion in life, great relationships, abundance on all levels – these are some of the attributes that many enjoy from this type of mastery.

I remember a recent conversation I had with Saint Germain where He said that:

»Mastery is being conscious of choice and the intelligent application of that choice. Choice of quality thinking, quality feeling and quality feeding, will bring a quality lifestyle. Regardless of cultures, rituals or religion – you all have choice – no one tells you what to think, what to say or what to eat. Even where there is little food, if a being expects to be healthy, commands their body to be nourished by prana and the God within them and believes, then they will be. And yet there is much that a Knight of Light can do to strengthen and support this process of revelation.«

»Revelation?« I asked.

»The revelation of the power of their DOW, dear one« He responded. »The revelation does much more than provide food for the body. It brings food for the soul, purpose and vision to the heart and mind. Spiritual fulfillment and magic. The revelation of your DOW is something you can all witness and experience. As you allow yourself to radiate The Presence more each day, more magic, grace and synchronicity are magnetised to your field; and soon you will live constantly within this zone of purpose and pleasure.«

»It sounds like the best addiction to have?« I responded questioningly to which He answered,

»And so it is dear one, for human beings are constantly becoming addicted – to food, to love, to purpose. Yet being addicted to their DOW will satisfy all other addictions simultaneously.«

Until I underwent this transformational process, I never thought that people were addicted to food. Like many of the Light Ambassadors, I assumed that we all needed to eat to live, although I had met many people who lived to eat. However, over the last six years I have realized that many of us are addicted to our taste sensations, while others are still addicted to the social pleasure of eating.

Like recovering alcoholics, we probably always will be. The point we need to ask is are our addictions – whatever they may be – healthy and supporting who we wish to be in life? To this question many would have to say no. A study of obesity conducted by the British Nutrition Foundation said that more than 40% of the population of Britain are obese or overweight. According to this report, the level of obesity from dietary choices has reached epidemic proportions. They mentioned that the associated health risks of obesity are heart disease, diabetes, stroke and some cancers, and so they are urging people to eat lots of fresh fruit and vegetables and take more exercise. Similar reports have been issued in many other countries.

Many of the Light Ambassadors relationship to food changed substantially after the 21 day process. Some loosened up from being long term »food purists« and, experiencing that they only wanted food to satisfy taste cravings, would only ever eat ice cream or chocolate until they didn't want any more. For some this took days or weeks. Others returned to eating every few days but only ate raw food, or took a little fruit and juice. Others would eat a small meal once a week just for the social pleasure of it all.

Before, during and after the 21 day conversion process, people are confronted with their addiction to, and relationship with, food. Everyone handles this in a different way. Some sound like junkies going through withdrawal and can become quite ›boring‹ to be around. As a friend of mine once said to me, »For people who are choosing not to eat, you sure all spend a lot of time talking about food!« And she was right – this is a normal stage that many go through, analyzing and discussing their relationship to food.

To some, there is nothing else as absorbing on the planet as food. Its production, cultivation and distribution employs millions and supports millions. As author and chef James Beard once said: »Food is our common ground, a universal experience.«

Its benefits when correctly used, or disadvantages when abused, preoccupy many nutritionists and doctors and researchers globally. Organic or not? Raw or cooked? Supplement your diet with vitamins of not? To diet or not? To eat junk food or healthy or not? To genetically engineer or not?

Being free from diets, vitamin issues and all of the above can be extremely liberating without even looking at the other benefits that the Ambassadors of Light enjoy. No food shopping, no cooking, and no dishes are also a bonus in life and, as we have often shared, is excellent time management.

Not all those attracted to the work of the Light Ambassadry are interested in self-mastery, solutions to world hunger challenges or even the reality of telepathic communication with »beings of light«. In fact we have found from our interactions with those contributing to the Living on Light Forum in the Cosmic Internet Academy (C.I.A.) website and from those completing our questionnaire, that the lifestyle choices, backgrounds and personality profiles of the Ambassadors of Light are amazingly varied.
Briefly:

   85% meditate regularly
   83% know they create their own reality
   68% are fit and strong
   71% have been long term vegetarians
   25% were living on raw food
   25% were celibate by choice
   47% regularly go to church, temple or synagogue
   61% are in full-time service – that is they are committed to enhancing the planet and not abusing it.

Ambassadors of Light come from all religious backgrounds. Among them are doctors, alternative practitioners, musicians, artists, writers, lecturers, public servants, business men and women, blue collar workers, housewives, the retired and even the unemployed. Of those who participated in our survey, their average age is 47 and 51% are women. The oldest is 93 and the youngest is 18.

Finally I would like to clarify the term Ambassador of Light. If used in the context that through daily spiritual experience, people have become more ›light'-filled and connected to DOW Power, then millions of people could be termed Ambassadors of Light. Anyone who is committed to service in the unfoldment of Divine Will, Love and Wisdom on earth can be called an Ambassador of Light. In the context of this book, we use this term specifically to discuss those who choose to let DOW Power feed them. The visual aspect of DOW Power of light.

So in summary, the Light Ambassadors invite you all to:

- Open up to higher possibilities, as if we can imagine it then it's possible.
- Get fit and healthy by refining your lifestyle choice.
- Get to know your DOW and feel the benefits of Its power. Increased clairvoyance, clairaudience and clairsentience are common.

THREE

The M.A.P.S. Ambassadors
»World Health, World Hunger Project«

»Thousands of candles can be lighted from a single candle,
and the life of the candle will not be shortened.
Happiness never decreases by being shared.«
The teaching of Buddha

As more individuals commit to a lifestyle choice that promotes fitness on all levels, they begin to not just enjoy the personal benefits of this choice but can often see the global benefits as well. For me personally, it took some three years of experimenting with living without food until I began to clearly see how pranic nourishment and the lifestyle it requires, could be applied to many of our world health and world hunger-related challenges.

To the Light Ambassadors, hunger means hunger for love, hunger for health, hunger for happiness, hunger for meaningful work, hunger for wealth, as well as hunger that arises from lack of food. As many are now aware, lack of food and poverty comes from the unequal distribution of the world's resources and not from any actual lack of resources on this planet.

We also know that the hunger that many have for deep and lasting happiness and also for meaning in life and purpose, cannot be satisfied by material gain – although many western entrepreneurs have said that they would rather be unhappy with money than without. Personal happiness comes from feeling abundant on many levels and means many things to different people. Happiness is linked to our genetic structure plus our environmental and even past life influences. Financial wealth alone does not guarantee personal happiness. An old Greek proverb says: »First secure an income, then practise virtue.«

When we satisfy our deep hunger for life purpose, true love and happiness via the path of true Self-awareness, then we shift from our own self-absorption and become more altruistic, service-minded and concerned for the welfare of others. Hence the ›haves‹ can effectively address, and then provide for, the needs of the ›have nots‹.

I remember 25 years ago an Eastern guru said that you don't give spirituality to the east because they have lots of that, you give them food and you give them shelter and a decent education. What you do is give the Westerners who have absolutely everything and are still often miserable – spiritually; and hopefully they will then become more focused on selfless service and altruism. Then they can support the re-distribution of the resources around the planet so that the people who are in need can be taken care of.

In our »World Health, World Hunger Project«, health means health of mind, health of emotions and health of spirit as well as health of body. All these things we address at the Self Empowerment Academy via our website, books, newsletters and published articles.

Global health education is also now supported by a complex system of teamwork among holistic educators such as alternative therapists and medical practitioners. This is a group of individuals who recognize the power of the mind/body connection and are focused on re-educating people into lifestyle choices that promote wellness.

Many of these are individuals who are also committed to the idealism of M.A.P.S., and comprise aware media representatives, doctors, nutritionists, alternative therapists, research centres and all are people who are dedicated to their particular field of service. As such, the M.A.P.S. »World Health, World Hunger Project« is already well-supported by those who wish for health and happiness for all.

Lifestyle practices normally associated with the ›new age‹ community have moved into mainstream awareness as many have become aware that it is time for each of us to take complete responsibility in life. In order to create positive relationships with others we must first learn to love and honor ourselves. To some of the Ambassadors of Light, allowing the DOW to feed us is the ultimate sign of trust and respect for who we really are.

A signpost of this change in attitudes to our health and happiness in the world is the increase in the media focus on healthy living via the promotion in many magazines of the benefits of yoga or meditation or a vegetarian diet and regular exercise.

Even the World Health Organization (WHO) defines health as »a state of complete physical, mental and social wellbeing, and not merely the absence of disease and infirmity«, and they also state that good health is held to be fundamental to world peace and security.

Health is a choice and one each person makes every day by what we choose to eat, how we choose to feel, what we choose to think and how we choose to treat our bodies. In the West, people enjoying good health is not the sole responsibility of our governments, although education in lifestyle choice should definitely be part of all school curriculums.

Research shows that we are living longer and are in fact eating better and exercising, which are major factors supporting this trend. This in itself adds further complications. In 1998 there were 66 million over the age of 80. By the year 2050 it is expected that the number of over 80's will rise to 370 million.

Although the population is only growing at 1.3% per annum, it still will effect our long-term resource sustainability. We will look at this in more detail in later chapters for it is no longer enough to make choices that just suit us, it is time to also be aware of how our personal lifestyle choices impact upon our planet.

Solutions to both health and hunger-related challenges will not come out of magic or wizardry but by the intelligent application of choice in each moment of each day. Choice of quality thinking, quality feeling and quality feeding will go a long way to bringing health of our spirit, mind, emotions and body.

Unfortunately some people perceive the work of the Ambassadors of Light in the field of pranic nourishment to be in conflict with the medical profession and many nutritionists. Our work actually honors these professions, supports and complements accepted research in these fields and then takes it to another level. Our focus in health is on the power of preventative medicine and the promotion of luscious lifestyles that allow many to be permanently free from dis-ease.

Pranic nourishment and learning to create realities that serve us all effectively, is the result of a very particular and disciplined lifestyle choice by people who, for many decades, have actually followed the advice of both doctors and nutritionists. Having added meditation and mind mastery to sensible nutritional food and exercise, we have moved on to discover an alternative and viable source of nourishment.

Our commitment as Light Ambassadors, is to work in conjunction with alternative practitioners and doctors who practise holistic methods of medicine, not in competition. Nor do we dispute that which is traditionally found to be true, we simply ask that people keep an open mind to the field of the Higher Light Science as it reveals to us some more civilized possibilities.

Prana is being offered as an additional form of nourishment to the world, not as a »must«. Why? Because we need it. Yes, there are programs that address world health and hunger issues, yet they too face their challenges.

So we look at the global application of world health and world hunger programs and the funding of these in section 3 of this book. In the meantime we as individuals, regardless of our situations, can begin to take personal responsibility for our own health and hunger issues by being open to other alternatives.

It is our hope that eventually enough credible research will have been released to the world on past studies in this field that some doctors call »inedia paradoxa«, so that the idea of being nourished by DOW Power – or prana power – becomes more acceptable.

Obviously many of the Light Ambassadors would also like more research to be done to find out what happens to the body when a person lives on prana for years. What we do know is that living on DOW Power allows us to be healthier and happier and this is a great revelation in itself.

In the meantime we recommend that you:
1. Be aware of your lifestyle choice and how you choose to fill each moment of each day. Research more and understand that all disease comes from inner dis-ease.
2. Utilize and apply the knowledge of your holistic health practitioner. Become a vegetarian.
3. Take responsibility for your own health and hunger issues.
4. Are your thoughts, words and actions supporting your health and feeding all your hungers?
5. Be prepared to break old habits that no longer serve you and the planet. For example, ask yourself: »Why do I eat meat?« Because you like it? Or because it is a habit that you have never questioned? Continuing to do something because you like it or out of habit when it has negative personal and global repercussions

is illogical. This is what we mean by breaking habits that no longer serve you or the planet as a whole.

In section 2 and 3 we will cover more on:
1.   Our own and other people's research into living free from the need of food
2.   Current world hunger solutions and programs
3.   The health benefits of a vegetarian lifestyle
4.   Long term global resource sustainability, plus
5.   Fund raising for social welfare and holistic educational programs.

FOUR

Media Misconceptions

»If you attack apparent negativity, you merely feed and inflame the
source. It's always best to take the positive in any conflict.
If you genuinely love, or at least send kind thoughts to a thing,
it will change before your eyes.«
John & Lyn St. Clair, »Eyes of the Beholder«

In this chapter we begin with an excerpt from the C.I.A. website Media section as it addresses many issues that have been constantly
raised among the Light Ambassadors and in my own dealing with the
global media. Where applicable we have made up to date additions.

In the next few pages we look at issues of anorexia, the experts,
proof, world hunger, responsible reporting, challenging medical
beliefs, and our position of influence. We assume that these are key
issues that concern many.

In 1996 the Ascended Master Kuthumi telepathically provided
me with the global vision of M.A.P.S., and over the next 2 years
together we carefully laid the foundation for the International M.A.P.S.
Ambassadry. At the time I was still holding the self-image that I was
an author living a yogic lifestyle who chose to be living on light purely
because it suited me. As editor and publisher of »The ELRAANIS
Voice«, disseminating information and the vision of the M.A.P.S.
Ambassadry did not present any challenge, as we were in the field of
re-education anyway.

Shortly after this, Saint Germain manifested His presence and
asked if I was prepared to also work as one of the Ascended Masters'
representatives with the global media. He advised me that in this age
of technology, the media is one of our planet's most powerful tools of
education. He said that the masters wished to utilize the fact that I
did not need to eat food to attract media attention to the ideals of the
M.A.P.S. Ambassadry.

I realized that »coming out of the closet« would: (a) mean my
loss of privacy, which as a yogic warrior was most precious, and (b) be

a huge challenge as, for over two decades, I had already experienced the Western world's reluctance to fully embrace the benefits of holistic medicine and vegetarianism.

I had also already experienced the disbelief and fear – bred by ignorance – towards my more recent lifestyle choice. Educating my holistic therapy friends and acquaintances, and even family took a great deal of patience as their beliefs around surviving without food were often challenged by my presence.

To say that I was somewhat reluctant to tackle the job of »media public relations/education officer« in the almost »unbelievable« practice of pranic nourishment would be a gigantic understatement. Still, Saint Germain's logic prevailed, and eventually I agreed. I did stipulate however that if He was to be my etheric »press officer« then He was only to send me open minded journalists. To date He has kept His part of the bargain and I have met some amazingly »switched on« journalists, interviewers and film crews.

I have often experienced the world's press to be quite relentless in their questioning – which is their job after all. I also consider that while skepticism is natural and also healthy for any discerning mind, fear mongering bred from ignorance is not. Nor is the reporting of unsubstantiated rumors as if they were fact, which is a journalistic practice devoid of integrity. I do tend to remind the skeptical that there was a time when people thought that the earth was flat, that the sun circled the earth and that the idea of people walking on the moon was also absurd.

Prana Power has been well-covered in the ancient Vedas and the Upanishads but not in western literature and the idea that people can live without nourishment from what the Western world knows as »food«, is also seen by some to be absurd. I know that there will come a time in our future history when being sustained from prana will be as widely acceptable as vegetarianism is becoming today. Both for health and resource sustainability reasons.

So there are a few issues to do with media representation that need clarification. These are either commonly asked questions by the public and/or media, or what I term »media misconceptions« that are in need of rectification.

ISSUE 1 – ANOREXIA

One of the first issues that we feel is important to look at, regarding concerns of the media and select public, is anorexia. Those associated with, and affected by this challenge, have commented that it is morally irresponsible for us to publicly talk about not eating food. We have, in fact, had scheduled television appearances cancelled when those working in the field of anorexia have found out the topic that was to be discussed on air.

On this we would like to share that the dis-ease called anorexia can only be spread or encouraged by our public discussions on living on light if :

- We fail to get the message across that this is a spiritual initiation that provides a by-product of obtaining nourishment from another source. This is highly unlikely, as we are well aware of the need to share this research in a responsible manner and also of the danger that could occur by the untrained attempting this,

and/or secondly if:

- The media are irresponsible in reporting the full picture and hence fail to address the issue correctly. This can be a bit of a challenge and some journalists have stated that their magazine/newspaper cannot get into the religious/spiritual aspects of our journey with this as it could »switch off their readers«.

Back to anorexia. The facts are:

1.   The ability to live without nourishment from food is the result of a highly complex spiritual initiation. Initiates prepare for decades and even lifetimes for this and it is not to be taken lightly. It can also be a very dangerous journey for the unprepared. For the well trained it is a most joyous initiation.
2.   Living on light has nothing to do with dieting or the practice of fasting. In Christian terms, if one does not have a strong connection with their God, it is impossible to sustain living on light. For it is our belief in the existence of this Supreme Force of Intelligence and our experience of Its power that allows us to be nourished in this way. Without this, not eating becomes fasting, and without the conscious willing our DOW to feed the vehicle, the

vehicle will eventually die from lack of nourishment. In this matter, everything the nutritionists and medical practitioners share is 100 per cent correct.

3.   Anorexia is an emotionally-based imbalance that also has associated mind sets that are damaging to the physical vehicle and general welfare of the one with this affliction. In our newsletter The ELRAANIS Voice, volume 3 issue 1, (available free from our website) we have an article of an interview with Peggy Claude Pierre in Canada. This came from the Share International web site (www.shareintl.org) and Peggy seems to be providing some great research in this field. Her article is well worth reading and rather than comment further on anorexia, we will let you deal directly with the experts in this field.

So while we hear some say that it is irresponsible for us to talk about not eating when there is the problem with anorexia in the world, what we would like to say is that we feel it would be irresponsible to not share of our research findings in light of the fact that every second second, according to UNICEF statistics, a child dies of hunger-related diseases.

Assuming that what we are claiming is correct, we consider that it would be morally unacceptable for us to discover this source of nourishment, keep it to ourselves and not share the benefits of this with the world. It is interesting to note that the average age of the Light Ambassador is 52, and the oldest one is 93 and the youngest 20.

I recommend to anyone who suffers from anorexia or bulimia that you:

1.   Learn to meditate with the intention of having the experience of »who« you really are. Knowing that you are more than just your mind, body and emotions is a very liberating experience.

2.   Focus on becoming physically fit, emotionally fit, mentally fit and spiritually fit.

3.   Learn mind mastery and how thoughts create reality.

4.   Learn how to love your self and others more fully.

5.   Heal your relationships with yourself and others by doing courses on self-esteem building and communication.

6.   Find something creative to do that you love and do it daily –
      painting, dancing, music, gardening etc.

7.   Spend time serving others less fortunate than yourself – selfless
      service is the fastest way to move beyond self-absorption, self-
      pity or lack of self-love.

8.   Begin to experience the preciousness of life by spending time
      each day giving thanks and feeling gratitude for everything that
      works in your life no matter how trivial e.g. »Thank you
      God/universe/spirit for those who love me, thank you for my
      warm bed, thank you for the sun that shines, thank you for my
      talent in ....; thank you for ....« Know that the more
      we act with sincere gratitude the more we will be given to be
      grateful for – this is Universal Law.

9.   Ask the Divine One Within you: »I now ask my DOW to allow
      me to complete all my karmic learning around this issue in joy
      and ease and grace, so that I may be free to express my Divine
      Self fully in every moment.«

10.   Use this program: »I now ask that my life be filled with mean-
      ing and purpose and that all discord within my mental, emo-
      tional and physical bodies be brought into perfect harmony with
      my DOW.«

11.   Ask the universe to bring you the right healers and teachers to
      help you move back into a state of wellness.

For more information on using programming, the power of our
emotions and mind mastery, read my book »In Resonance«.

ISSUE 2 – THE EXPERTS

One thing that I find a little »trying« is the media game of »let's
interview Jasmuheen, together or separately, with an expert doctor, biol-
ogist, nutritionist« or whatever. The expert says: »It is impossible for
a body to survive without nourishment«, and I say: »I agree«. The
expert says: »Bodies must have good nourishing food«, and I say: »I
agree«. I cannot see that this makes for interesting television. Firstly
because I cannot disagree as they are quite correct with what they know

own field and I have had to apply all that to move into the next phase. Secondly, it keeps the subject matter curtailed by the belief system of the program host and »expert', rather than allowing us to have an intelligent conversation to share further details of our research so that people can find out how, rather than stay in the »you couldn't possibly« mode.

Having someone keep insisting that something is impossible when you have personally experienced the opposite is really strange. Still it makes us patient as we realize that many people initially go into »disbelief« when first exposed to something that challenges their belief systems as this lifestyle choice can do.

To the media interested in serious, informative journalism, who want to move beyond sensationalism and the »he/she says, she says, lets try to have a heated discussion and make some interesting television game, we ask them to please at least get an »expert« who is familiar with the work of individuals like Dr. Deepak Chopra. Deepak has done some powerful research on the mind/body connection and the miracle of the human system and I recommend his books to everyone.

Ideally to compare apples with apples, the »expert« will need to also have a good grasp and experience of the mind/body connection understanding, and be someone who is also theoretically and experientially trained in the benefits of meditation. To me, a credible »expert« is also someone who is aware of the power of mind mastery and is a good example of applied dietary refinement and a regular exercise proponent. Then maybe we can have an informative discussion.

The number of »experts« I have met in these situations, who are overweight, unhealthy and unexercised is amazing! Nearly all have never heard about prana or chi, don't believe in the existence of a universal life force and still are at odds about reincarnation and the indestructibility of energy and its properties. Rarely do I meet an expert on radio or television who is well read in the field of metaphysics, who understands that we are creative beings with the power to manifest any reality that we choose. This does not discredit their expertise in the field of nutrition or medicine, however the ability to live on light is the result of many other factors, outside of these fields.

We do not say this to sound elitist (to use another media label for our work) but because we would really like to be able to provide a more suitable comparison. Otherwise to me this is like asking a general practitioner (doctor) to provide a detailed analysis on the work of a highly specialized heart surgeon and to comment on his/her research and field of expertise – it just doesn't make sense. Both have undergone basic study that is complimentary, but one has then branched out and specialized. We do not dispute what doctors or nutritionists say, we just have additional information that they have not yet had the opportunity to experience or research.

To the media, we only make three claims:
1.   Firstly, that for many of the Light Ambassadors of M.A.P.S., if we never had food again, we would not die. Do we snack for pleasure now and then? Some do, some don't. It's no big deal. The big deal is the freedom of choice that this specific lifestyle can bring. Also being free from another limiting belief is a field of interest for all those committed to exploring human potential.
2.   Secondly, we claim that there is an alternative source of nourishment available to human beings – right here, right now. In Eastern terms, it is called prana, in religious terms we are fed by the light of God. Pure and simple. Being fed in this manner means no fuss and no waste. Prana is a never-ending source of civilized nutrition that has huge positive global ramifications to our societies as a whole. Unequivocally, yes – the Ascended Masters, as my colleagues, offer the lifestyles that allow us to be nourished in this way, to the world as a long-term solution to world hunger. However, we are realistic enough to realize that in order for this to be implemented as we envision, a massive global re-education program needs to be entered into. Hence their interest in those in the media who act in integrity and wish to use their craft for planetary progression in a positive manner.
3.   We also claim that by the beginning of the new millennium we aim to have shared our research with the appropriate individuals in the medical, scientific, social and political communities globally. What the world chooses to do with this information, will then be up to each individual and each organization and/or government.

We also wish to state our purpose:

Our real work here is to encourage individuals to create their personal paradise and aid in the creation of a harmonious and unified global paradise.

The M.A.P.S. Ambassadors all have very specific projects. These are assignments for bringing pragmatic and positive change to the planet. Our first project is re-education, and I personally choose to do this in four ways:

a)   via the Self Empowerment Academy's »Cosmic Internet Academy« (C.I.A.) at: www.selfempowermentacademy.com.au,
b)   via our international newsletter The ELRAANIS Voice (TEV),
c)   via our global media interviews and documentaries,
d)   the sharing of our books, videos, CD, tapes, and
d)   via our international tours of lectures and training seminars for the potential M.A.P.S. Ambassadors.

All the above – except (c) – is funded by both myself personally as part of my commitment to the creation of paradise and also from the Universal Bank of Abundance. There's another mind twister for many – »cosmic banking« – where credits and debits are governed by Universal Law. My sub-assignment, or assignment as a Light Ambassador is also in the field of re-education.

In Christian terms, it is said that God is everywhere, and therefore – 35 years ago – I began my spiritual journey with the assumption that »It« is inside me. I have spent my whole life desiring and experiencing this God. And now I choose to prove Its power by allowing It and trusting It enough, to nourish my body.

ISSUE 3 – PROOF

As I began to elaborate on our research in response to the often asked »prove it to me!« question, it soon became obvious that we needed to make it a separate chapter which we have called »Facts and Faith – Prove it to me!«. We have placed this just before we begin section 2 where we share more of our own, and others', research with this phenomena.

ISSUE 4 – WORLD HUNGER

This brings us to the next question. »How can we make a leap from a personal spiritual journey that has allowed some people to live on light, to its application to eliminate world hunger?«

The answer is of course – our lifestyles are the key. Still this is also too in depth a topic to consider here, so we cover it in more detail in section 3.

ISSUE 5 – RESPONSIBLE REPORTING

The next media misconception we would like to address is the constant plethora of headlines around the world that generally run like this: »Woman claims she has not eaten for 6 years«. This is perhaps one of the biggest misconceptions perpetuated by the media, as far as sensationalism and attention-grabbing headlines are concerned. While we understand the need for the sale of copy, this is a very misleading statement.

We always share that what we have done is to have lived without taking any nourishment from food for as long as was needed to prove to ourselves that it is prana that is nourishing us. For some it is months, for others years. This proof has come as we live day by day without taking vitamins, without taking food, and finding:

1. Our weight has stabilised.
2. That our energy levels have increased.
3. Our requirement for sleep has decreased.

These are the three signposts to prove to an individual that they are being sustained by prana. Once this has been achieved, what occurs is that some individuals may choose to taste food for pleasure. This may range from a chocolate biscuit once a week, or a packet of potato crisps if that is their choosing once a week, to eating once a fortnight or even once a month.

It is entirely the choice of the individual. Some individuals choose to eat in social situations with family once a month or once a week. Again, it is purely personal choice. The claim that the Light Ambassadors make, once we have proved to our own satisfaction that we do not need food to live, is that if we never had food again, we know that we would not die.

Footnote July 1999: I now find myself appealing to the media that if they wish to report on this lifestyle choice from purely a dietary angle then please don't. So often I have said that the ability to live on light is a result of a certain level of physical fitness, emotional fitness, mental fitness and spiritual fitness only to find the media say that: »Jasmuheen says this is possible as a result of physical, emotional and mental fitness.« For many reasons TV interviews edit out words such as »spiritual fitness« or »in religious terms we are fed by the light of God«. It certainly makes live radio and television more appealing.

Similarly we also discourage media from printing partial details on the exact procedure of the 21 day process as, for people to proceed without doing full research and having complete facts, is highly dangerous. As long as the media indulge in responsible reporting, then the continued sharing of our research and personal spiritual practices can only have a positive effect in this world.

- Do we wish to »convert all« to living on light and not food? No.
- Do we wish for people to have freedom of choice? Yes.
- Would it please many of the Light Ambassadors to see the cessation of the senseless slaughter of animal life on earth? Definitely.
- If we can live healthily without food, then surely others can begin to seriously embrace vegetarianism – not just for issues of morality and civility but also for reasons of global resource sustainability.
- Would we like to see more responsible reporting on the personal and global benefits of the cessation of slaughter of all life?
- Definitely.

As our work is now beginning to be taken more seriously, increased attempts are made to discredit our experiences. Journalists are often not bothering to investigate rumors and are therefore perpetuating the dissemination of incorrect data. Again we encourage the media to be involved in responsible reporting and not spread fear and disbelief through ignorance and lack of journalistic integrity.

ISSUE 6 – CHALLENGING BELIEFS

The first thing we would like to address is the fallacy that people will die if they go for more than six days without fluid. Some sources say four days without fluid brings death. Many people now have successfully completed the 21 day process which requires an initial seven day period of non-eating and non-drinking. One Light Ambassador in Bogota in South America successfully went for 36 days without food or fluid and experienced no negative effects.

Over the last few years, I have discovered many areas that I would like clarified and researched so that we can understand what occurs within the physical body as a result of this ability to live on light. These questions and guideposts will be given to our researchers at the appropriate time so that they can do the correct testing that is required.

We would also now like to elaborate on what my personal journey has been with this, for it was never my intention to seek publicity for this. Personally, I chose to undergo the process discussed in my first book »Living on Light« as it was the next step in my own journey and personal spiritual initiations and my total focus at the time was my ascension to the light.

Had I realized what lay ahead, I may not have chosen this path. However, in my model of reality, all human life is on earth to give and to receive, to learn about being in dense physical matter, to remember that we are spiritual beings having a human experience, and to also serve the greater good simply because we can. I have also come to realize that personal reality is just a movie that can be rescripted anytime at will.

Part of my assignment, my role, that I have chosen to fulfil in this embodiment, was to create both the Light Ambassadry and the M.A.P.S. Ambassadry as vehicles for positive change. As mentioned, I became public with this work at the request of the Ascended Master Saint Germain who manifested before me in 1996 and asked if I was prepared to work with the media as their messenger.

The Ascended Masters reasoned that because I do not need food to exist, that this would attract media attention and hence spread the message about the need on our planet for individual self-responsibility and self-refinement. The main benefits of encouraging these attributes – self-responsibility and self-refinement – will be the cessation of dis-ease and the discovery of inner peace which will create personal and planetary harmony and unity. So these attributes are well worth pursuing.

I would like to reiterate here – the work of the Light Ambassadry is about hunger and health-related issues and not about proposing that everyone learn to live on light. Learning how to create positive personal and global community lifestyles that work for all, is far more important at this time. Without positive lifestyles, living on light for long periods of time appears to be virtually impossible, at least according to our research.

If we are to fulfil our desire for unification and provide the basic living standards that all beings are entitled to, we need to also realize that our planet does not lack resources, it simply lacks the intelligent application of these resources.

In May 1999, Thomas A. Hirschl and his Washington University collaborator Mark R. Rank, published a report called »The Likelihood of Poverty Across the American Lifespan« which states that almost 60% of all Americans will live below the poverty line for at least one year of their lives. »What surprised us is that poverty in America is a very common experience,« said Cornell Professor Hirschl, »yet is not part of the popular consciousness.«

Statistics confirm the inefficiency about the way that the wealth on the planet is distributed. Regardless of the reasons for this, with a little emotional intelligence, with personal discipline and commitment to working in harmony as a team, many of the challenges that face our modern-day world can be addressed and solved.

My personal lifestyle choice is to live as a yogi, to spend my days in solitude and meditation, to exercise my physical vehicle to keep it strong, and to write as I am guided – that is my preference. Consequently, there is an interesting adjustment that needs to be made every time I am »out on the road«, as to go from living like a yogi to touring extensively in situations under the constant public gaze at lectures and seminars is quite challenging.

Some come to meet me as they have heard these strange »rumors« about a woman who claims she doesn't need to eat food. Others come because they are fascinated by the subject of self- mastery and others come to offer their support. However, as students and as masters we are all committed to serve and to serve graciously.

Often I have found when dealing with journalists, that they go into what may be seen as »attack mode', and I understand that this is done because they are looking for holes in the story, or what we call schisms in the field. And they feel that the deeper and harder they push and probe, the more likely they are to unveil discrepancies.

The Masters' response to this is that if we as Ambassadors of Light and M.A.P.S. Ambassadors make the commitment to live our life in impeccability, with integrity, then we have nothing to hide and nor will we have any schisms in our field. The elimination of schisms in our field is covered in depth in the second book of the Camelot Trilogy – »The Wizard's Tool Box«.

ISSUE 7 – THE POSITION OF INFLUENCE

Some journalists have asked if I am concerned about my influence over people because of the way I look…models, movie stars and political figures are just some who influence people every day. If people say »wow Jasmuheen looks great and she says it comes from daily meditation, regular exercise, eating really healthy food for decades before eventually getting to the point that she now has no need of food, so I might« begin to follow these practices as well« then fantastic. Here it is the job of the media to not just focus on the fact that I look »so good for my age« (to use media words), but to say that I have achieved this through the conscious daily application of the above which entails a very specific lifestyle choice. And if this inspires people to be more responsible with their thinking, feeling and feeding habits then we are achieving something.

To the media we say, your work is about responsible reporting, and my work is about encouraging people to be all that they can be and not be limited by their cultures, conditioning or beliefs. The very end result of this may be – if they chose – to eventually live on light which can be achieved through a very intense physical, emotional, mental and spiritual training schedule.

Sharing gossip and spreading unsubstantiated rumors are two of the most powerful tools people use without thought, that carry the potential to destroy good in the world. The cessation of both would be most beneficial to us all.

FIVE

My Home, My Laboratory –
My Body, My Experiment

»Each player must accept the cards life deals him or her.
But once they are in hand, he or she alone must decide
how to play the cards in order to win the game.«
Francois Voltaire, French philosopher and author

Working with the media regarding the »living on light« phenomena, has been been most fascinating for me. In an interview with the London Daily Telegraph in November 1998 – Barbie Dutter wrote: »Her home, with its sunshine-yellow walls and pungent scent of incense, overflows with ancient and new-age icons. A gallery of ›the Ascended Ones‹ – Christ, Krishna, Babaji, Saint Germain, the Dalai Lama and more – adorn the walls. Their presence seems awkward alongside the material trappings of a fully-equipped gym, sauna and dance room. But Jasmuheen attributes her glowing health not only to lack of toxicity in her body, but to a daily routine of meditation and exercise involving hour upon hour of work-outs, weight-training and aerobics.«

Well, with twenty or more hours a day to play with, there's more than enough time for all this, and work, and family. Also, does Barbie mean that we can't be ›spiritual‹ and also be fit and healthy and choose to spend our time and money creating a lifestyle to support all this? Interesting statement, and one very reminiscent of the idea that spiritual people must all take vows of poverty, chastity and obedience. Thankfully this is no longer a reality for most of us in the nineties!

What many have not understood is that in order to attract the presence of these wonderful masters, one has to acknowledge their existence. This can only be done to the individual's personal satisfaction via research, and a set lifestyle which then allows us to enjoy a personal experience with them. All the great teachers and masters are available to all who seek their presence.

In the field of bio-energetics – which is my latest passion – the gallery of masters in my home provides an energy vortex. Each icon in our house acts as a bio-conductor of energy, a doorway to the energy field of the one that the image represents. Each object can be programmed to attract specific frequencies for specific reasons.

Bio-energetics provides techniques for self-healing and tuning the physical body, and all our energy fields. It utilizes energy grids which can be revealed or created, then activated, but which generally remain inert until programmed. This is done via our thoughts, will and intention, and the last section of »The Wizard's Tool Box« focuses on this in greater detail.

By combining these techniques in a fun way with dance, intuitive yoga and isometrics, we can exercise the physical body, become much stronger, self-heal and do much more. This is all part of our Luscious Lifestyles Program.

Hence our house is our laboratory. It is filled with specific objects and tools to support us in the radiation of The Divine Presence. The gym equipment and sauna my husband and I have had for over twenty years are there for our daily usage to keep the physical vehicle – as the temple – for the Divine, in prime condition. Also when God becomes our employer, the Ambassadors of Light in full-time service receive a ›cosmic pay packet‹ that includes many benefits to support us in our work here. How much financial abundance we are given depends on the work we have come to do. The following has been one of our most powerful realizations in the past few years:

When all we wish to do is serve and allow our temples to radiate Divine Will in all Its glory – we cannot be denied, and everything we need to do this will come to us. Guaranteed! Our DOW must support us on all levels if this is our heartfelt desire – this is Universal Law!

So not only have I chosen to make our home, my laboratory, but my body has been my continual experiment – at least since I became aware of the benefits that ›Luscious Lifestyles‹ can bring. Before a person even considers living on light, they need to be well- trained and prepared, and we cover this in the next chapter. By prepared, we mean daily action that allows them to attain a high level of physical, emotional, mental and spiritual fitness.

I would now like to briefly list chronologically what has occurred in my own life, and how it resulted in my ability to be nourished by prana. Hopefully this will elaborate on basic things like my choice of my lifestyle, training, and also some of my experiments.

From Then 'till Now...

1959: I began to fight with my mother about eating meat. Intuitively, eating most animal products did not sit well with me. My mother was, like many, concerned about feeding her children a balanced diet. This struggle to gain control over my own diet continued for the next 13 years.

During this time I was extremely athletic – running, swimming, diving, playing all sports. From ages 13 to 15 I often lived for months on as little as an apple a day with no detrimental effects. No, I was not anorexic, and yes, I had a very loving and supportive childhood with excellent parents; it was more that I had no real interest in food.

In **1972** I began to switch to a complete vegetarian diet with the compromise that if I got sick from lack of protein etc, my mother could step in. It was then that I discovered alternate protein sources like legumes and nuts.

In **1973** I began the long process of mastering my emotional dependency on food. Like with many, this had come from both my childhood conditioning and my predominantly European background (my parents are Norwegian). I also began to notice how stress and emotional upset seemed to increase my desire for food types such as cake, chocolate and ice-cream.

1974: Began to research all that I could find on vegetarianism, which led me to the study of Eastern philosophy as vegetarianism was a common lifestyle choice for the yogis.

1974: Met an Indian Mahatma and was initiated into the art of meditation using ancient techniques that dated back to the Vedas. Began to learn about the power of service, satsang (being in the company of truth) and meditation, and since that time I have continued to meditate daily. Thank you Maharaji. The Rig-Veda is the earliest of sacred literature that describes creation and extols the virtues of the early deities. Written in Sanskrit, the hymns contained in the Vedas were written around 1700-1800 B.C.

1974: Did my first 11 day water only fast. Felt fantastic. Energy levels increased, found that I needed less sleep. So much has been written about the benefits of fasting, I truly recommend this practice and that you research this for yourself.

1975-76: Over 6 months, I began a regular process of colonic irrigation. These were designed to clear out the bowel and intestines from ›old dietary remnants‹ that, according to some research, are known to putrefy for years in our colons – particularly meat.

1975: Bored with study and fascinated by Eastern philosophy, I left university and moved interstate with the intention of dedicating my life to yogic living. I applied to move into the ashram immediately upon my arrival and was asked to wait and become more involved in community service. While waiting for acceptance into the ashram, I decided to travel to India and into the Himalayas, and began to work in various jobs to raise the capital required for the journey.

1975-1992: Over the next 17 years, I developed a strong experiential understanding of my mind/body connection (as discussed in Dr Deepak Chopra's work – which I had not read at that time). I was intuitively also guided to begin a series of personal experiments using basic »trial and error«. For a year after my first fast, I stayed mainly with raw food and fresh juices.

At 15, I had begun the process of selective eating which meant only eating small amounts of food when I was hungry, rather than having set meal times, and also the practice of ceasing to eat before I became full. Over the next 15 years, I looked at a variety of vegetarian diets – macrobiotics, vegan, raw food, and pure juice fasts and water only fasts. I also set out to experience the difference of being well exercised compared to not exercised, while maintaining a very healthy and pure diet.

In **1975** I also began to notice how easily meditation could ›state change‹ me emotionally – from reacting to acting, from being upset to being calm. I discovered the wonderful physical benefits and the calming power of doing daily conscious, deep, connected breathing. My 2nd book »In Resonance« covers personal mastery and fine tuning, using such tools, in great detail.

1976: My first daughter was born. Throughout my pregnancy I found that I could only eat raw food. Anytime I tried to eat something cooked I would feel nauseous. As I was travelling throughout most of this pregnancy, I became incredibly strong, fit and healthy. Because of this lifestyle choice and my natural body reaction to cooked food, I found that at the end of this pregnancy I was 54 kgs and weighed only 2 kilos more than when I first fell pregnant. This was also due to the high level of exercise as well as my strictly raw food diet. My body shape and condition was fantastic 2 weeks after delivery, which was an easy home birth and after 3 weeks my body weight stabilized at 48 kgs. I am 165cm tall.

1978: My second daughter was born. This was a quick, but difficult birth. My diet and fitness levels at the time of this birth were nowhere near as good as with the first. Although I was in a ›natural childbirth‹ hospital, I personally experienced this to be far more stressful than the first ›home‹ birth.

Due to ill health from giardia – which I contracted overseas when travelling with both children – by early 1979, my weight dropped to nearly 45 kilos. In a bid to regain weight I began to eat more cooked food and adopted a macrobiotic style diet. Over the next decade my body weight eventually stabilized at between 50-51 kgs.

1978-1992: Throughout this period, I remained on a mainly vegan diet, with a raw food intake of 60-80%. I also took the vitamins B6 and B12, spirulina, nuts and occasionally very small amounts of cheese in social situations when vegan food was often unavailable, and a little milk in tea.

Over the years of continuing to refine my diet, I developed the mind-set that food to me was just fuel. With other personal experiments, I soon found that my body felt sluggish if I ate heavier, cooked foods and more energized again when I ate raw foods. I also noticed I slept a lot less when I stayed on a raw food diet.

Probably two of the best proponents of raw food today in the U.S.A. are the ›Nature's First Law‹ people who are based in San Diego. Stephen Arlin has written a wonderful book called »Raw Power« for body-builders. He says »Listening to and acting upon your own body's natural instincts, desires, and needs is the way to Paradise Health, not by listening to someone else's dietary dogma.« David Wolfe's new book »The Sunfood Diet Success System« is also well worth reading as a preparation manual for living on light.

From **1974** to **1992** I continued to experiment with different physical exercise routines – swimming, cycling, hatha yoga, dance, aerobics, weight training and jogging. I was also guided to experiment with increasing and decreasing the time spent doing daily meditation and to note the effects this had on my physical, emotional and mental bodies. Some days I would meditate in stillness for periods of up to 3 hours. Other days I would do no ›formal‹ meditation but would spend all day in one long conscious meditation focused on my breathing patterns.

During the first few years after childbirth, I was preoccupied with family issues and had less personal time for meditation and exercise. As a result, my ability to handle stressful situations decreased, my immune system was affected and from 1980 to 1985, I found myself afflicted with the flu and colds. In retrospect I could not have classified myself as someone who was physically, or emotionally fit over that period. I functioned like many other young mothers with financial concerns and a marriage that was breaking down.

1972-1992: Over this 20 year period, my interest in esoteric matters continued to grow. For 15 years, via the practice of regular meditation, I experienced much of what is discussed in Eastern philosophy, including brief states of Samahdi. From 1986, I researched metaphysics by reading everything I was intuitively guided to read. I also began to keep more detailed journals and collect notes for what would eventually become the book »In Resonance«.

From **1976**, I raised my children and worked in various careers. In 1984 I became a sole parent and finally found my career path as a financial consultant and computer programmer. Between 1983 and 1992 I played the corporate game and was absorbed with working mother/single parent issues. My lifestyle choice was still to meditate, exercise regularly and maintain a vegetarian diet as it allowed me to cope much better as a single parent with a demanding career.

I would also like to add that like many, I come from a bloodline with a few genetic weaknesses yet although this has influenced the rest of my family, personally I have not experienced any problems with this. I truly believe that this is due to my general lifestyle. I am convinced by my own experience and research that the combination of daily meditation, daily exercise and a vegan or raw food diet are imperative for the experience of healthy living.

1987: After years of sporadically receiving messages from ›dead people‹ for their loved ones, I also began to receive increased telepathic communication from various ›guides‹ – usually directing me to read a particular book, or attend a particular self-help seminar.

1990: After nearly a decade in the fields of finance and insurance, I began to receive strong, clear inner guidance to pursue something more creative. I chose to ignore this guidance as I was concerned about how I would manage financially while still educating my daughters.

1992: The company I was working with folded, and I found myself unable to gain immediate employment in the same field. I subsequently decided to take 6 months off, to paint again and find work that made my heart sing. Over the next year I enjoyed the luxury of a less busy lifestyle, increased my daily meditation time, began to exercise more intensely and also enjoy more of the role of motherhood.

1992: I began conscious telepathic contact with the Ascended Masters and received information on living on light. From here much of my journey with this has been outlined in the book »Living on Light – A Personal Journey.«

Briefly:

With the sole intention of merging with my DOW, in May 1993, I underwent the 21 day process and then immediately went into a six month period of intense solitude. I went out only as required, began to hold weekly meditation classes and was guided to write »In Resonance« as a self-empowerment manual for those interested in esoteric matters. I had also begun to channel and wrote the first book of the »Inspirations« Trilogy.

As a result of doing the 21 day conversion process, my weight went down from 50-51kg to 45kg then to 47kg as I slowly learnt how to effectively reprogram my body and deal with my own doubts about it being possible to live purely from prana. This time to gain weight I relied solely on mind mastery and visualization techniques.

1993-1995: Over the next two years I began to understand the emotional body's addiction to the private and social pleasure that came from eating food. I was also being personally challenged by my own repetitive boredom from the lack of flavor.

During this time, I went for extended periods, months at a time, of ingesting only three glasses (approx. half a litre) of water, tea and water – non-vitamin and non-nourishing fluids a day. I would air fast for 16 hours straight each day – from 11 p.m. each evening until 4.00 p.m. the next day – before having my first drink. These three drinks I would take in the late afternoon and before bedtime. I found myself drinking simply because I felt I needed a tea break from my work routine. For over two years my weight remained stable at between 48 and 49 kg.

June 1993-August 1998: During this time due to personal experimentation, I became convinced that I received all my nourishment from prana. By 1996, I found the boredom from lack of flavor to be an ongoing issue. At this point, I had practiced various techniques to overcome this, but still found myself wanting the pleasure of certain taste sensations. After a little inner turmoil, I decided that I had proven to myself that I was being nourished by light and decided to loosen up and enjoy the odd mouthful for fun. At the time I was also a little weary of being constantly challenged by people's disbelief in my ability to do this and the attitude of »Why would you? I love my food!« that boomed out from many. I was doing it because I had been guided to and had learnt NEVER to ignore my inner voice.

1996-1997: Over the next period, once a month or sometimes once a week, I experimented with different food flavours and began to experience their different effects on my body. I found chocolate and chocolate biscuits disruptive to my system. From this and tea, I had various physical reactions from itching, acidity and general discomfort and I learnt the ability of transmutation.

I found during this time that the food that the body had minimum reaction to was potato. I also found that spending a little time once a month cooking a delicious pumpkin soup was more emotionally nurturing than physically nourishing. Soup or a baked potato shared with my family soon became a feast to be savored!

During this time it became obvious to me that I was still emotionally addicted to food and like an alcoholic, may always be. Also like any addict, even though they may love the drug of their choice, they usually chose to be without it as they find life preferable without the side effects of their addiction.

I now feel the same way about food. While my emotional body enjoys flavor, my physical body prefers to get its nourishment direct from Source. It enjoys being able to by-pass the process of digestion and the consequent process of the elimination of waste. To be free of such things really is personally preferable.

Throughout this period, I always kept the experimentation to minimum amounts of food – a mouthful here and there. Nothing in this period that was ever taken, could be said to have given the body the full range of vitamins and minerals that nutritionists would expect it would require to maintain the health that I did.

In fact many of the Light Ambassadors, when they assess exactly what and how much they have consumed over the years, are amazed they have not developed scurvy and other problems normally associated with lack of proper nourishment. This in itself helps to convince us that we are receiving nourishment from an alternative source.

Throughout this time, I underwent various medical testing with doctors for health check-ups, and also alternative health practitioners. The results always proved that my body was extremely healthy and in fact healthier than it had ever been, which was great confirmation that I too was being pranically nourished.

The main benefits that I gained from this period of experimentation was:
- Learning about the power of transmutation, and
- Creating the program for the body elementals (both of these are covered in our first book)

- Another benefit was realizing how natural it is for me to live without regular food consumption and how much better my body feels being fed by DOW Power.

August 1998: At the end of my European tour in June 1998, I began to get the urge to eat something approximately every second day – some nuts, a packet of salty crisps or a small piece of fruit. As I had had no interest in nuts, fruit or vegetables for over 5 years, I found this very interesting. My inner guidance concurred that I was to try to resume regular ingestion of food so that I could re-undergo the 21 day process with a test group at the Research retreat we were planning.

I intuitively felt that the next experiment was set to achieve the following:
- To make my body more »normal« so that the medical and scientific testing that we were to do would have specific results.
- I would discover a specific formula or daily program of preparation that we could then recommend for those interested in the beginning the journey into pranic nourishment, and lastly,
- I also wanted to see if my physical body's strength, tone and energy levels would improve even more with the addition of good nutritional food. I wanted to experience if being actually fed from both prana and healthy food would have a ›double whammy‹ effect.

With my will, intention and action, in July 1998 I used a particular program to reactivate my system to take nourishment from food as well as prana. On the 16 August I felt a profound energetic shift within my body and realized that the two systems were now operational simultaneously. At this point I was intuitively guided to keep the flow of nourishment from prana so that while my body would continue to be sustained by liquid light, it would also begin to digest any food ingested and absorb any nourishment from this rather than just transmute it as I had been doing previously.

The first thing that I noticed was that I was no longer interested in having food for the mere flavor, and instead became conscious of the type of food I wished to eat for its nutritional content. This was a resumption of my understanding of the need for correct nutrition from my previous decades of training. I found that I was no longer interested in sweet things like chocolate, which had been my main taste hit while I was predominantly only being nourished by prana.

It is important to understand here that people who are being pranically nourished are free from the need to absorb nutrition from food stuffs because all their vitamins, minerals and nutrition comes via their DOW. Hence, we are free to indulge in the odd mouthful of flavor if we choose, purely for the taste sensation and, provided we use transmutation techniques, we suffer no detrimental effects.

September 1998: Further information was given to me by the Ascended Masters about the Research Retreat, and we began to gather the questionnaires from all those who had already undergone the 21 day process.

Phase 1 began with approximately 22 people in late 1992 to mid-1993. From this, the information of the 21 day process went underground and was propagated by the issuance of Charmaine Harley's 21 day guidelines.

After this time, I was guided by the Masters to add our research to these guidelines and hence in 1995, we wrote the book »Living on Light – A Personal Journey«. This book detailed our experiences of this spiritual initiation, our current understanding of it at the time, plus it included Charmaine's own research which produced the 21 day guidelines. I continued to update this book as more material came to hand. This book has now been translated into more than half a dozen languages globally.

Phase 2 was the sharing of this information on a global level and the gathering of others who would be part of this project. It was the laying of the foundation for our retreat and the Light Ambassadry's Global Research Project no. 2. The details of our research projects 1 and 2, the questionnaire and the retreat are covered throughout this book.

Phase 3 will be the release of all our research via the MAPS Alliance Manifesto, to the relevant international governments and organizations. This Manifesto focuses on solutions to many global challenges as we enter a new millennium.

From here we would like to see phase 4 in place. This is where the relevant organizations and governments implement the logic of this Manifesto. By our media work and our »World Health / World Hunger

Project«, we will continue to encourage individuals to get healthier and happier by applying personal discipline and logic, and refining their daily lifestyle choices.

As many of the Ambassadors of Light have backgrounds in holistic therapy, we would like to see the hospitals emptied as the wellness, mind mastery and M.A.P.S. programs work as applied and attended. I also like to envisage that the billions of dollars spent on pharmaceuticals such as headache tablets, Prozac and all the other drugs that treat symptoms of both societal and personal dis-ease, can be redirected into other areas, as individuals self heal and become happy. Same for dietary aids, weight loss programs and pills and potions.

This can easily occur as more individuals combine a lifestyle choice of :

- A predominantly raw food diet – I personally recommend a 60% raw food, 40% cooked (grains) vegetarian diet initially, then vegan, then totally raw food. (then eventually fruit, then liquids, then pure prana)
- Daily exercise that is enjoyable.
- Daily meditation – a time of silence and solitude to talk to and experience your DOW.
- Daily personal creative activity.
- Selfless service – helping others where possible.
- The elimination of personal toxic thinking, toxic feeling and toxic feeding.

It is my personal belief that if the above is practised, with the commitment to only engage in relationships with the intention to create mutual pleasure and mutual empowerment, then all dis-ease in society will disappear.

In October 1998, I came to the conclusion that my physical body really prefers to be without food. My emotional body may enjoy the pleasure – as it has always done – of taste, but my physical body feels bloated and does not enjoy the process of elimination every few days. My food intake during this month had to be done gradually as my stomach had shrunk and my metabolic rate had changed.

I found that the most that I could take is a small handful of nuts after a cup of tea or water every morning, and maybe more tea or water during the day. After I had completed my dance, exercise and sauna routine each evening, trying to eat more than a little bit of potato, would make me feel unwell. The more that I tried to eat, the more tired I became, the more dense I felt and the more bloated I became.

Of course it is what I expected, as I have found in my research with pranic nourishment that the more I allowed my body to be nourished by prana, and the more I commanded the radiation of the Divine through my whole being, the lighter I became, the freer I became, the less I needed sleep, the more alert, the more active I became.

For me, going back into the journey of existence from food created tiredness and the very symptoms that most people think would occur with the body from not eating. This misconception that many have comes because they do not realize that prana is actually a supreme nourishment source, and is far more easy for the physical body to deal with than actually going through the whole process of digestion of food and absorption of vitamins and nutrients from food.

November 1998: After two months of trying to get back to a »normal« diet, then after enjoying the freedom of a month on prana only as I toured, I decided that my preference, and addiction one could say, is to the feeling of being fed by light. I also found that for the first time in seven years I came down with a raging fever at the end of the tour as my system had been weakened by my pre-tour experiment. Yes, I was in Germany in minus 15 degree temperatures and being hugged by many who had the flu, however, it is most unusual for those of us who are fed by DOW Power alone to get sick IF we are properly connected.

Yes, the experiment was valuable as I proved to myself again how easily I can switch off and on my system of digestion without any negative effects. At the time the Masters had said to me that we could just as well be addicted to not eating as we are to eating, and that mastery is about freedom from all addictions.

Personally, I like the lama diet that is discussed in the book of the Five Tibetan Rites and I have no desire to return to a normal food intake as it no longer suits my being. To me, having tried both systems, being nourished purely by prana is like riding in a Porsche, and getting energy via food and digestion is like riding in an old jalopy. One ride is just so much smoother than the other.

The second focus of this experiment was to find a good recipe for pre-process preparation for people who desire to be free to eat for pleasure and not need, yet are unsure how to prepare for this. We will share more on this in the next chapters.

The third focus of the experiment was to experience the difference in my body after adding nourishment from particular food groups such as nuts, carbohydrates, and fresh fruit and vegetables. I wished to see if I could gain better form and higher energy levels when going through my exercise program than what I was currently achieving by just being sustained by prana alone.

What I found from this was that while I immediately put on weight – three kilograms to be exact – and gave the appearance of looking more muscular, my stamina levels decreased rapidly. I found it difficult to do my usual two or three hours of exercise per day, whereas prior to the ingesting of any food I could easily do isometrics, yoga, calisthenics, light weights – and treadmill work – then heavier weights and a dance routine all in one session. This was often followed by a sauna with no physical detriment to the body at all other than the desire to increase my water intake while doing the routine.

After one month on greater food intake of a few very small snacks per day, I began to feel enormously tired and listless. My bowels began more regular elimination and my skin was breaking out. My breath which had been odor-free for years was becoming stale and I noticed my body odor changing as well.

Unfortunately, all of the above had no appeal and I decided to end the experiment and return to being solely nourished by prana. Like all previous experiments, my findings from this period of research have been very instructional and it was good to loosen up my lifestyle a little. It was fun to enjoy the pleasure of food with my vegan husband and to allow him to prepare interesting tit bits for me, but even though I was not able to have ›normal‹ size meals, I did enjoy the flavor of fruit again – particularly paw paw and watermelon.

As I have shared with the media, the amount of food that I have personally taken over the last six years is probably the same amount that someone would live on in a normal month. Generally nothing that I have had has had the nutritional value to maintain the level of health that I have enjoyed. It has been obvious to me for the last six years from my personal experience that some other source of nourishment has been in operation. Regardless of this, eventual medical and scientific research should give evidence of the fact that something is happening within our bodies that defies accepted thinking in this field.

Another thing that I found during this experiment over those two months, was that I slept a lot more, yawned a lot more, felt tired, felt full, and felt dense instead of light and weightless. The one constant thing I have noticed is that I still never get hungry, regardless of any experiment I may be doing and I never feel the desire to eat because of hunger.

So I have enjoyed taking advantage of being more relaxed around the idea of food because yes, it does take discipline initially to be around people and choose not to eat, when they are obviously enjoying the whole social game around food. Social interaction still remains one of the most difficult things for the Light Ambassadors to deal with.

Through my decision to not go back to normal dietary consumption, I felt like I was given a reprieve. To follow my preference for a light lifestyle is such a blessing. I will possibly still continue to indulge my desire for flavor on the odd occasion, and I enjoy the flavor and texture of a banana soya milk smoothie. I am also now armed with a hundred questions for the research team!

August 1999: My current »diet« consists of non-caffeine ginger tea plus water and a smoothie for taste every few days. Simple but suitable. My exercise routine has increased again to include weights, dance, bioenergetics and the dance of the whirling dervish.

Probably the one issue that annoys the ›watchers‹ of this movement more than anything is the fact that we keep professing that this is all about freedom of choice and is not a black and white issue about whether we eat or not.

I remember speaking with Wiley Brooks about this issue in America when we first met a few years ago. For those of you unfamiliar with Wiley, he was probably the West's forerunner to the breatharian movement in the 1970s. After an enlightening experience on a mountain top where he found he no longer needed to eat or drink, Wiley was guided to share of this in the world, and via the TV talk show circuit went on to make some amazing claims. He lifted 10 times his body weight on TV to show that you don't need food to maintain strength, and generally he built up quite a following in the USA. I concur with his findings as I am also now stronger and fitter.

Wiley told me that after a period of time back in the pollution of the cities he began to eat now and then as he found it hard to stabilize his weight as he traveled constantly doing seminars. Dr. Barbara Ann Moore, a 1950s breatharian repeated the same thing and he began to experiment as he also began to feel sick and extremely sensitive now and then from being in the pollution.

I also have had the same problem with extreme sensitivity and noted that it is easy to maintain full pranic nourishment in my sanctuary called home but more difficult to do this when »on the road«. I always lose 2 to 3 kilos when I travel. Another friend of mine in Sweden said that every time he went to the doctor for medical tests when he first began to live from prana, he noticed that his weight would drop. That is how sensitive we can become where pollution and also other people's thought projections can actually interfere with our being fed from prana properly. Obviously this is just another step to address in our own mastery.

Back to Wiley... at some point Wiley was ›sprung‹ coming out of an all night convenience store and/or a Macdonald's, which of course the newspapers loved! His supporters disbanded and Wiley's ministry obviously lost its momentum having been built on the idea that he never ate or drank. As Wiley said to me recently, »I traveled with group of people who ate so of course I would be seen coming in and out of such places. Also like you, I was continually experimenting.« I know what he means for once you have had the experience of going for long periods of time without nourishment from food, many begin to treat their bodies as a laboratory to find out more such as what happens if we do eat again.

Personally I find the focus on ›not eating‹ rather than being free from the need to eat – ridiculous, and I have encouraged the Light Ambassadors to be completely honest regarding all claims. None of us claim to be saints, rather we are people who are daring to push ourselves beyond accepted limits in society by exploring our potential on all levels. Have we mastered this fully yet? I haven't.

I remember an in-depth conversation that I once had with Saint Germain when I felt compelled to nibble something now and then. My immediate reaction was that I could no longer continue to talk about living on light for in the strictest sense I did ›eat‹ now and then. This was the basis of the conversation...

Saint Germain: »Have you proven to yourself 100% that you are free from the need to eat food?«

Me: »Yes.«

S.G.: »And do you feel that all of your research and experimentation in this field is invalid if you nibble now and then?«

Me: »Of course not!«

S.G.: »Precisely. An inventor may invent a plane but may choose to drive a car instead now and then. That is the inventor's choice. Just because s/he decides to drive rather than always fly will not invalidate their invention and its benefits in the world!«

Suffice to say I got the point. Now prana has not been invented, it is universal life force or qi or God or whatever we wish to call it. What the Ambassadors of Light have invented is a way of living day to day that allows us to keep this delicate connection to DOW Power. I say delicate because many vibrations bombard us all constantly, and it is easy to be influenced to the degree that some cannot maintain this pranic flow enough to stay healthy for very long periods of time without taking nutrition from food. DOW Power works and will feed us – what doesn't always work are our chosen lifestyles and belief systems about who we really are. These both seem to need constant refining.

So yes, I encourage the Ambassadors of Light to say that they are ›free from the need to eat food‹ rather than they never eat food. As while it may be true that they are not eating anything today, what about in a few months or years if they feel to enjoy flavor then? Should all our work and what we have achieved be discounted so easily as it was with Wiley Brooks just because we may choose to enjoy flavor now and then?

There is so much I am still learning every day about human potential, including my own. The more I dance with the Divine, the more divine the dance becomes. Some days I feel as though ›why am I doing all this?‹ and the more I learn, the more I realize how little I know. Other days, the beauty of it all astounds and overwhelms me, as tears of gratitude and joy flow at the miracle of being given the chance to even play the game and freely learn this dance with my DOW.

We mention this as it is so easy to judge and dismiss what we don't fully understand and so easy for those being judged to give up. If you see a Light Ambassador having a snack, it's no big deal, they are just learning how to break their emotional body's addiction to food and this can take years. Remember that we have had lifetimes of believing we needed food to survive!

I also met people who have done the process and then after three weeks when their hair loss increases or when their weight hasn't stabilized, they say »it's obviously not working« and so they go back to eating again. This process of learning to live on light can take years of preparation and months of trial and error afterwards.

So in summary we recommend that you: Loosen up, be flexible, experiment. Remember there is no ›one way‹ to create a lifestyle that works for you, trust in your DOW and find a way that is perfect for you. Enjoy every step of the journey and don't just focus on the goal and result; Learn to listen more to your body; sometimes you may take two steps forward and one back. It's all OK. There is no such thing as failure, just opportunities to learn and grow. If at first you don't succeed, try and try again. Dare to dream and rise above the mediocrity in life.

SIX

Precious Preparation

»Listen to your conscience, for you may be listening to God.«
J.H. Rhodes

When I wrote the first book »Living on Light«, it was done as a service for those who were being drawn to undergo the 21 day process, to make their journey easier. As I was guided to maintain this lifestyle choice, over the next few years I began to deal with the day to day living with this and to also experiment with the many different issues that came up.

I assumed when I wrote this book, that everyone who was drawn to undergo the process would have understood the importance of being fit on all levels. I have since discovered that this is not always the case.

As I have often said, being healthy and ›fit‹ means physically fit, emotionally fit, mentally fit and spiritually fit. The fitter you are the easier the conversion to pranic nourishment is going to be. I call this the 4 »F's«.

I had personally taken two and a half decades to become fit enough to be able to live without the nourishment of food. Our research data has since proven that those with a longer, stronger history of self-care and nurturing, have had more success in being pranically nourished than those who have given very minimum attention to their personal care.

By care we mean the things covered in our book »In Resonance« which are the things that support us being healthy and happy. Care also means living each day enhancing not just our own lives, but also in a way that means our existence here enhances the planet.

So it is important to spend precious time in preparation before undergoing the 21 day process. As we have often discussed, it is a highly scientific initiation for the spiritual warrior and a person needs to be trained well prior to undergoing this. The better the preparation, the better the results. Simple.

If you are drawn to living on light, then ask your DOW – the

Divine One Within you, to bring you all the necessary information and techniques and people that can teach you so that you may be as fit as possible on all levels. Remember you have all the time in the world, just not a moment to waste. The process of absolute fitness can take lifetimes or decades or months. It all depends on what each person's current lifestyle choices are today.

Can someone die while doing this? That's like asking can someone die if they run a 100 km marathon. If they are unprepared, definitely – if they are well-prepared, then no. Anyone who does something that is physically challenging could encounter problems and die if they are not well-prepared, particularly if it is their time to die. As all in esoteric fields have come to realize – the time of our birth and death is controlled by our DOW and Its contract with the One who created us, yet sensible preparation will allow us to enjoy all that we set out to achieve.

This brings us to another fallacy. Many people say that because it took me decades to get to a level of fitness to sustain pranic nourishment, then it will take all people decades. That is not necessarily true. I have seen people become fit in less than a year because of their ›previous lives‹ training.

Our first book on pranic living was written and published in English after our book »In Resonance« which is an in-depth manual that covers preparation for tuning into DOW Power. However, as people have asked for more on this, we also recommend that you do make sure you detox prior to undergoing the process using fasting or other methods and that you apply the guidelines we offer in the next chapters.

The reason that doing this slowly and going via raw foods then to fruit then liquids over a LONG period of time is that it helps us release our addiction to variety in food. Living on raw foods for at least six months is a wonderful way to prepare for the process and most of those who have existed on raw foods for some time pre-process find the post-process journey easier. This is because they have already dealt with their emotional body's attachment to food.

So if an individual is well-prepared they should breeze through the 21 day process and be problem-free and hence not require the services of a caregiver as was mentioned in book 1 by Charmaine Harley. The best caregiver we have is our DOW.

The 21 day process is an initiation about self-mastery, and to go without food or water for seven days can be very extreme. To do so without adequate training could bring negative results. Yes, I have heard a story of a man in Germany who died (before my book was published there) after reading the guidelines that had somehow found their way into Europe. This is why I wrote the first book, to give more information on what the initiation was about.

Yes, a woman died in Australia while undergoing the process with Jim Pesnak. He and his wife – as caregivers – have been charged with negligence and may also face a manslaughter charge. Again our organization was not involved, and when this occurred we reissued new guidelines for caregivers and these can be found in our website. Still as a Light Ambassador said to me recently, there is a far greater risk that you will die of cancer from cigarette smoking or from a car accident than you will from attempting to plug into DOW power and live off light – particularly if you are well-prepared.

Every step of the way we have been honest and open in our sharing with our experience and research and we hope that those of you choosing this journey will do the same. Living our lives in truth and impeccability is part of this journey of mastery.

Be aware also that:

- The decision to even go through the process is step one of an initiation about clarity and courage.
- Step two is having clear enough inner guidance to KNOW without doubt that it is the next step for you. If your heart really sings at the idea of doing it then pay attention, as the singing heart is the voice of the God within. If you are in doubt do nothing – no singing heart, no process. So this second initiation is about personal clarity, discernment and self assurance.
- Initiation three is the level of preparation an individual elects to partake in before undergoing the process, which then will also directly determine the outcome of their experience. Step three is also about the intelligent application of knowledge – that is the correct use of wisdom. This means also the active re-education of family and friends so that they can form a strong support system for a person in their post process time. If an individual is well prepared, the process itself can be most joy-

ous and easy. It is after the process where many have difficulty with social reaction and family pressure.

Completing these three initiations qualifies one to be their own caregiver and hence for the past few years we have strongly discouraged anyone from undergoing the process if they feel the need for a caregiver. Our advice to them is to wait until they have no doubt and are tuned enough to require no assistance. That way no one but them can be responsible for their experience.

Some Light Ambassadors elect to undergo the 21 day process with others and have someone who has done this facilitate their journey, like Chris Schneider has done in Germany for the past few years – his details are in the back of this book.

Remember that the people who have elected to undergo the 21 day process are warriors. They are often tough non conformist individuals whose current focus is positive personal and planetary progression. The 21 day process is a spiritual initiation for these yogis who, as Ambassadors of Light, demonstrate the power of light by living on it. This light is the visual aspect of the Creative Force.

We repeat that the 21 day process is not necessary to undergo as we have discovered through our research that there are gentler ways to condition the body to obtain nourishment from light e.g. reprogramming, dietary discipline etc. However, if an individual is determined that this is the correct course of action for them, then they must also be prepared to take full responsibility for both their preparation and subsequent experience.

As the 21 day process is very extreme and should not be entered into lightly, make sure that you are well-trained, spiritually aware and understand that you create your own reality and understand the power and vision of Oneness. You should be dedicated to self-mastery and have a long background in spiritual practices and be as fit as you can be on all levels.

Yes, some people are drawn to this who see it as a ›quick fix‹ solution to all their problems. We recommend that they fix all health, emotional, dietary, mental or family problems before they undergo the process. If these things are not attended to they may be exacerbated by the process leading to hospitalization for physical or mental reasons and even death.

If you are interested in living on light as a future possibility for yourself, then set a few programs in place like:

- »I now ask my DOW to support my transition into living on light with joy and ease and grace.«
- »I ask that my weight stabilize at the perfect level to express my full divinity now.«
- »I ask to be nourished by my DOW on all levels of my being.« Then follow some of the recipes in this book. Have an open mind, do some intelligent research, use your discernment and be more disciplined, for then we as individuals can achieve great things.

The Light Ambassadors know that when we connect with our DOW, It guides us into the fulfillment of our purpose and passion in life, and living on the light of Its power is just a very small by-product of being in tune with this aspect of our Self.

For those who have chosen to live on prana, we recommend that you learn how to switch your system on and off. Remember we can be as addicted to not eating as we are to eating. So experiment, find a lifestyle and program that works for you. Most of all stay open and enjoy each step along the way.

So without repeating a lot of information contained in »In Resonance«, which we recommend you read, we would like to share the simple ›Luscious Lifestyles Program‹ that can be applied whether you are interested in living on prana or not. Then apply our ›DOW Match – Get Fit for Prana‹ recommendations.

SEVEN

Luscious Lifestyles

Part 1 – A Daily Recipe for Physical Mastery

»Men become bad and guilty because they speak and act
without foreseeing the results of their words and deeds.«
Franz Kafka, German language novelist born in Prague

Creating a lifestyle that you deem to be ›luscious‹ is really a matter of personal choice and basic trial and error; however I'd like to offer a few suggestions for this that anyone can apply and soon feel the benefits of. On one level, personal mastery for getting the 4 »F's« – physical, emotional, mental and spiritual fitness – is like baking a cake and there is a personal formula for perfection that we each can discover. Some say that it takes a minimum of 21 days to form a new habit, so we recommend that you apply the following suggestions for a period of either 22 days or 33 days. Then if you experience the benefits continue with them daily.

While our previous books and articles go into great detail on personal mastery and retuning, for me, the most simple and effective program for personal mastery has been summarized as follows:

- Know that you are a system of energy and prove this idea to yourself intellectually and experientially, then ...
- Learn to tune yourself in a fun, inspiring and enjoyable manner. This means getting physically, emotionally, mentally and spiritually fit. (See next chapter)
- Meditate each morning and each evening: Pamper yourself daily with a minimum of 22 minutes of meditation on your breath – there are a myriad of breath techniques to choose from, find one that works for you as our breath is one of the most powerful tuning techniques.
- Include energy work of light rays and sound waves with breath work and creative visualizations.

- Listen to music – one CD/tape every day of Buddhist chants, indigenous music, angelic music – listen to what you are guided, but only ud also in our new book »The Wizard's Tool Box«) and apply specific programming for environmental field control.
- Develop mind mastery – meditation allows you to be detached and be the »witness«. Watch your thoughts and have the courage to change outmoded or personally limiting belief systems. Our mind is our database and only WE can reprogram it effectively to perform well enough to create the life we want.
- Be in silence each day. Sit in your garden and feel the devic energy of nature. Develop your garden to encourage the energy of the devas to flourish. Silence stimulates the revelation of self-knowledge.
- Experience the benefits of regular fasting AFTER you have researched this subject thoroughly.
- Eat live and light food. Seriously consider pranic nourishment or at least research it and see if it could be a viable future option for you. Go vego then vegan then raw. Be aware of the humane and also global benefits of being vegetarian.
- Use acupuncture and other alternative therapies to treat your addictions.
- Bring all your relationships into completion by creating pleasure and empowerment that is mutual.
- Aim to drink a minimum of 1 to 2 litres of pure water a day to keep your system flushed and clean. If you have been living on light and obtaining pranic nourishment, look at cutting out liquid at some stage altogether – do this joyously and effortlessly; if it is a struggle then wait as perhaps the time is not right. Air fast for a day or two a week, do this gradually.
- Exercise the body daily – dancing, sport, stretching, weight lifting, yoga – again do what you are drawn to and what makes you feel enough joy so that you will do it daily.
- Learn simple self-healing techniques to reclaim your full health and vitality – self-healing is an essential part of self-mastery.
- Enjoy long, hot showers or baths daily to tune the auric field. Sit by an open fire regularly if possible.

- Create an electromagnetic force field around the body – (as in the Wizard's Shield Meditation – this is on the website in the C.I.A. Library an
- Learn to listen to, and communicate with, your DOW – the Divine One Within. This is the most important thing you can do.
- Ask for proof of your higher potential so you can be free of doubt and really discover your true Self.
- Ask and you will receive ...
- Remember that one does not necessarily become a concert pianist overnight, it takes practice and discipline, so ...
- Always be gentle, loving and compassionate with yourself and others but also exercise joyful discipline.
- And most importantly, learn to laugh a lot and do what makes your heart sing!
- Remember, quality thinking, quality feeling and quality feeding create a quality life.

I would also like to include the following information by Jeff, my colleague at the Academy who has also been training for nearly three decades in creating successful metaphysical lifestyles. He writes:

»The essential goal in lifestyle is impeccability. Impeccability is probably best defined as perfect alignment and timing in all thoughts, feelings, words and actions in life. That is, as the Japanese culture has ritualized the tea ceremony to now being an art form, so we should think of every action in our life in the same sense and try to fill it with as much content and meaning. Apart from daily meditation, having a purpose in life, utilizing programming, plus breathing – diet and exercise are the main points of interest that should be considered.

Purpose in life – a purpose about which you are passionate – a burning desire. It's not difficult to tell people to look for a purpose in life. What is difficult is to access it. Many people feel that they have a reason for existence, something that is just beyond their grasp currently, that they are often vaguely aware of, but they are unable to exactly focus on it. Something that they feel they have been destined to do, something they feel they were meant to achieve, without being able to quite identify the matter. This is a frequent concern, and the answer to the problem is to program to be given your purpose – that is, to locate and to put into effect the purpose about which you are passionate.

Programming is quite a substantial subject in its own right and is something to addressed separately. (See chapter 33 – Progeny's Pearls and Programs)

Breathing is the next major issue. There's a cleaning aspect of the deep breathing in meditation which eliminates negative and toxic cellular residue. Many teachers stress the importance of balanced breathing by breathing in the left nostril, then out the right nostril, back in the right nostril, out the left nostril, and trying to exercise balance in this regard. Most people are not aware that they normally are only using one nostril at a time to breathe, switching over from one to the other nostril every so often. In an ideal life, breathing is completely balanced. Meditation is the exercise that leads to that ideal breathing situation. In fact, 70 per cent of nourishment for living for the average person comes from breathing. It's traditionally referred to as the ›first food‹.

Regarding diet, this is a tricky subject to discuss because there is such a wide variety of cultural backgrounds to be addressed. Firstly, certainly in Western cultures, most people eat far too much and research proves that overeating effects both the quality and quantity of life. Reduction by half of the individual's current calorie intake increases their life expectancy by one-third of what it was, from the time that they made the change. Scientific studies to establish this fact have now been satisfactorily concluded and the evidence is available for any of those who are skeptical of this matter. A light, vegetarian diet has long been recommended for all serious esoteric students.«

The Ambassadors of Light work on the premise that our world is filled with loving, caring and intelligent human beings who, if provided with logical information, will use their discernment to create positive change in their lives and in this world. It is not information that is powerful but what we choose to do with it.

EIGHT

DOW Match – Our Perfect Match

Luscious Lifestyles Part 2 – Getting Fit for Prana

»Goodness is the only investment that never fails.«
Henry David Thoreau, US Author and naturalist

Many individuals are attracted to the idea of being free from the need to eat food. Others desire to be free from all external attachments and seeking enlightenment, willingly begin to make adjustments to their lifestyles so that this is achieved.

As we have often shared, there is nothing mysterious about living on light, it is a natural by-product of connection with DOW Power. How to hook into the DOW Power channel or frequency is another issue and the purpose of this chapter.

When I wrote the first book, it was a simple story of a personal initiation. It has taken me years to understand what this is all truly about, and longer still to find a way that I can express it simply.

We call the process of connecting with DOW Power, DOW matching. How well we match depends on the lifestyles we live. Matching is about tuning two complimentary channels. The DOW dims itself and we get brighter. Then boom! We are hooked up – just like making a telephone call.

This is basically what occurs during the 21 day process. A DOW match. A DOW match comes automatically at a certain level of fitness. Our desire to hook up allows a process of metamorphosis to begin that we can control the speed of. We control the speed through diet, meditation and through physical, emotional, mental and spiritual exercise.

Mental exercise involves programming and mind mastery. Emotional exercise occurs through the way we co-exist in our relationships with each other. Spiritual exercise is the path all initiates take when they want to experience the ›enlightening‹ qualities of their DOW.

As we have often stated, the 21 day process is a placebo for living on light. It is instead a powerful spiritual initiation that is not to be taken lightly. This initiation, if prepared for well, can leave you in a state of grace and wonder at the majesty of life – its sole purpose is to connect you consciously on a much deeper level with your DOW. When a deep connection has been made, you will find that you will be free from the need to eat for long periods of time. Some never return to food again, preferring to be pranically nourished for its obvious benefits. Some don't connect deeply enough to sustain being nourished in this way without a few negative side effects.

Connecting more deeply to our DOW via this initiation results in different things for different people. For those of you drawn to spending 21 days in solitude and silent contemplation with the Divine, know that the less you are preoccupied with toxic dumping, aches and pains, doubts and fears, the more open you are to enjoy Its power and this process of frequency matching.

Connecting with your DOW can be very addictive and brings both positive and powerful rewards. You can do it anytime without any process. Remember it is not necessary to undergo the 21 day process to experience DOW power and live on prana. Remember also that your desire, devotion, discipline, discernment, and dedication all determine how well you connect. Getting fit on all levels also makes this connection so much easier.

So, if you wish to undergo the 21 day process, and have researched all you can on the matter, and read my book »Living on Light« (also titled »Pranic Nourishment«) then the next step is to ask yourself and answer honestly:

Are you physically fit?
- Are you able to do at least one solid hour of exercise each day without a problem?
- I recommend a cross-training program for strength, grace, flexibility and stamina such as: weight lifting, walking, yoga, isometrics, swimming, dance, martial arts etc
- Have you been a vegetarian for at least a few years?
- Prior to the process are you prepared to become vegan for 6 months, then raw food, then liquids for up to another 6 months before beginning the 21 day process?

- Have you done all you can do to detox your physical body system?
- Have you learnt about fasting and fasted on juice and/or water for over 7 days before?
- Over the years have you learnt to listen to the voice of your body and treat it like a temple?

Are you emotionally fit?
- Do you have positive relationships with family and friends? Do you feel content in life and happy with who you are?
- Have you worked through your personal agendas and are now wishing to only serve and have your life here make a positive difference to the planet?
- Have you sat down and asked yourself why you wish to do this?
- Have you looked at your emotional attachments to food?
- Are you disciplined enough to slowly eliminate everything but raw food from your diet?
- If so are you disciplined enough to then eliminate everything but fruit?
- Then everything but liquids? Are you aware how boring this limited flavor intake is for many?
- Are you aware how this lifestyle choice will impact on your social life? Does it matter?

Are you mentally fit?
- Do you KNOW and experience that you create your own reality?
- Do you exercise mind mastery and thus feel the benefits of applied positive thoughts and programming in creating a life that you feel is well worth living and that honors all life?
- Do you have a strong mind body connection?
- Do you listen to your body's guidance on physical matters?

Are you spiritually fit?
- Have you been meditating regularly enough to feel the presence of the Divine One Within (DOW) you?, and
- Have you experienced the benefits of daily meditation in your life?

- Have you learnt to listen to and trust the voice of the Divine Within you as it guides you in life?
- Are you prepared to be flexible and open and experiment with this new lifestyle regardless of what others think?
- Are you prepared to do this until you have convinced yourself that you are free from the need to eat food again? Even if this takes months?
- Do you realize that the 21 day process will not ›fix all your problems‹ and that the opposite may occur where all your problems are highlighted and can appear to be worse?
- Lastly did your heart really sing when you discovered information about this process – to the point where you just ›know‹ it is for you?

Unless you can say ›yes‹ to all of the above, we recommend that you wait to do the 21 day process. Remember it is a high level initiation and the success of being nourished continually from prana after the process is totally dependant on the above issues. The continuation of this lifestyle choice takes both daily discipline, commitment and courage.

Over the last 5 years in my research, I have heard so many stories about individuals who were physically fit from exercise, raw food diets etc who were not able to be sustained by prana even though they underwent the process exactly as outlined in our first book on this as they did not have a strong spiritual practice.

I have also met many who were very spiritually fit and had a long history of meditation but encountered many difficulties as they were not physically fit. I have also met many who were physically fit and had meditated for many years but who didn't apply mind mastery in their lives and hence were unconvinced that they create their own reality. I have also met many people who are fit on all levels but have absolutely no desire to cease eating food.

Some ask me »does that mean I can't do the process if I have some health problems?« Only in some cases do people who are not fit on all levels receive amazing healing from undergoing the process and yes, while some have been healed, others have experienced their problems becoming worse. Why it works for some and not others seems to be a matter of divine grace.

While we understand that the type of person attracted to this is often very strong and not the type who needs to be »told what to do«, we do stress that all who undergo this process, exercise common sense and caution and listen to their body and their DOW every step of the way. Hence we offer the above questions to ensure that you are well-prepared and may enjoy this journey without unnecessary problems.

Listening to, and trusting, our DOW is an imperative pre-requisite prior to undergoing the process and the following story is one of many that explains why. I have a very dear friend in Croatia who is a Light Ambassador. A strong, fit and healthy man, he was an expert in martial arts, a focused and connected meditator, a shaman and a healer. When I first met him, I thought that he would make a perfect example of a good Ambassador who was well-tuned to undergo the process.

After he had completed the initiation, he met his Reiki master who, noticing a change in his energy fields, asked what he had been doing. My friend excitedly told him and the next day the Reiki master rang back and said: ›Babaji told me that if you don't eat you will die.« As they were both Babaji devotees, my friend became very concerned. Here were two people who he loved and respected – one, a living Reiki master, and the other an etheric master – who were telling him he had to eat or he would soon die. He sat and asked his DOW and was told: »It's alright, you will be fine – trust.«

He rang me and asked me to tune in, and I realized that he was undergoing an initiation about learning to trust his Inner One. So I asked him to choose between listening to an external master/friend or listening to his DOW. He decided to trust his inner guidance and has been fine.

The amount of people that I meet who choose to trust another's opinion even though their inner voice is telling them it's OK is most interesting. Self-mastery demands being able to trust and act on our inner guidance, regardless what others may say. People constantly project their fears onto each other – more than ever regarding the issue of living without the need of food.

Some readers may say: »Well, so what if he went back to eating, what is the big deal?« The point is that he was at a crossroad, as we all are in these moments of life-changing choices. Had he listened to his friend and begun to eat again, certain doorways that can only be accessed by a set vibration would have been closed to him. By trusting his inner voice, he was able to move into a new field of reality, and experience many different things as a consequence of this lifestyle choice.

We have always assumed that any intelligent and discerning individual would automatically dismiss the idea of personally electing to go without food and water for seven days as being too extreme unless it was part of their blueprint to do this. These ones, having understood the process in the full context of what is involved, may intuitively choose to have this experience and in this case we would expect that they undertake the necessary training that is required to do it successfully.

As the Light Ambassadors all know, it is impossible to extol the virtues of something verbally and do it justice. To gain a full understanding we must experience it ourselves.

I also recommend a study of the Pranamaya Kosha and the five pranas which is an important subject in Ayurvedic medicine as well as in yogic thought. The website http://www.sit.wisc.edu/~fmorale1-/prana.htm covers this in more detail in an article called »The Secret of Prana«.

Enjoy the journey....

NINE

The 21 Day Process continued...

I include the following synopsis from Light Ambassador Christopher Schneider, from the M.A.P.S. Akademie in Germany. Chris has been facilitating the journey of many who have gone through the 21 day process and shares some of his experiences here.
He writes:

»For me the essence of the process is freedom. That´s all it is about. Beyond not having to eat, there is a wide field that opens up through the process. And that is true for those who have done the process as well as those just in the resonance field of the process.

The 21 day process opens us, making it possible to realize all that is going on in and around us, the way we choose and the way we grow, the way we can ignite the flame of the heart and experience the Divine One Within, which is our true and deepest nature. And to make it clear: Choosing can also mean, that you decide not to choose to develop your entire potential and freedom.

For me that is the real meaning of freedom – the way we can experience it on planet earth. And growth doesn't necessarily mean bigger, more beautiful, faster or better. Growth means to be able to be with oneself and others in honesty and truth, to be in love, to acknowledge, to be in silence, besides eating or non-eating.

The question of eating is only a side effect – the process gives us the experience, that we (can) live on prana. It is not about someone replacing the necessity of having to eat by the necessity of not wanting or not being allowed to eat by some external force or belief.

Everyone who has done this process (with Christopher) experienced the moments of clarity and knowledge, the moments where s/he is nourished and sustained by light or prana. This is one of the greatest experiences we make during the process on a semi-physical level. Afterwards there may be doubts coming up representing our emotional state.

Truthfully this is what I call the test phase: We can ask for clarity, for manifestation, for clear signs – physically, emotionally mental and on any other level. And the greatness and gratefulness of the Divine allows us to experience more and to receive proof that comes to everyone in his/her own way. And believe me it is important to allow doubts too. Making them go away is suppressing our personality and we want to accept us before going into higher dimensions are.

Loving ourselves with or without doubts brings us back to ourselves, back to our heart, back to our harmony resonating with God, the DOW. Being clear and honest about our intentions and giving all our energetic bodies clear instructions makes this journey before, in and after the process a fast, efficient and interesting one, that can be smooth, easy and joyful.

The process has a very high potential of revealing and healing, nevertheless there are some mainly physical restrictions that I make for taking people through the process in groups.

My medical background does not allow me to take people with serious health issues; there are physical limitations we have to accept. To point this out is my duty as a caretaker. People come to do the process with me because they want my experience and the medical background. They want a clear guidance that is not limiting but supportive. To accept this together with the support of the Divine makes the process easy, joyful, pleasant, relaxing and challenging if somebody is ready for it. Pebbles or rocks lying in the way placed by oneself are quite natural and just part of this journey.

For me there is no doubt we can live without food or liquid. Also we have to pay respect to the existence of food and nourishment. We may want to master them, then we can choose to let go and this is where the process comes in. My role is some kind of intermediary or ferryman for people wanting to go through the process. I go back and forth. Together with people who eat, I join them and have something. Being on my own as a being with loving the pleasure of taste, I have little pieces of something here and there.

In respect of traditional medicine this is very unhealthy and the combinations and changes very striking. Food is just there for joy and pleasure, it does not feed us. When we are in need, one can eat as much as he wants, there will be no fulfillment and nourishment by food. So for myself, sometimes I eat nothing and drinking reduces itself for several days, and then sometimes I eat for pleasure. And for me, being able to switch any moment was another proof for pranic nourishment.

But this is just peanuts compared to the initiation that the 21 day process can be.

My intention in being a M.A.P.S. Ambassador of Light is bringing people in contact with the topic of prana. As a »Heilpraktiker« (non-university practitioner) this means doing consultations, weekend seminars related to resonance topics, spiritual and non-spiritual healing work. I do preparation seminars, as well as encouraging people in becoming clear in order to know: ›Yes, I am to do the process, that is the next step for me‹.

Yet the caretaking before, in and after the process is another interesting part of my life. For some people there are a lot of questions involved as so many things are taking place on all levels – physically, emotionally, mentally and spiritually. I feel my destiny in supporting and catalyzing these processes of clarification and transformation, and I am happy to assist ›them‹

In the retreats we meet about 1-3 hours 2 times a day. The things we do are meant to be supportive. It is not a »program« or seminar schedule. Everybody is free to participate. Towards the end of the first week, the interest for ›doing‹ something is not very high. During the phase of convalescence (second week) the interest for other things increases slightly besides all this ›free healing‹ taking place in a nice an easy way and during the third week (phase of reconstruction and integration) we usually have many topics, including further living on prana and the practical handling of the new energy and the new strength.

Much more important I think are the phases in between. Being with oneself, experiencing the levels of energy, the transitions, the transformation, the healing ... The hours at ›Schöne Aussicht‹ (beautiful view) give us ideal conditions for going through the process. It is a beautiful and quiet place in a marvellous landscape of southern Bavaria, about 0,5 hour drive from Salzburg, Austria. Each participant has his own room with a nice view, a bathroom with a bathtub, a nice, well-equipped place, just perfect conditions for the process, for the journey to oneself.

To be more practical, this is what I recommend to do before the process and what I cover in my preparation seminars: Open yourself to the possibility to live on prana. You can do meditations, programming, affirmations or whatever suits you best. At the same time it is important to look at the structures of thoughts and patterns. There is nothing you have to do about them. Just accept them and let them go if you want to.

Next set your intentions regarding the date you want to do the process, the money, your family and all the other physical and mind things to be taken care of. For people doing the process with me I have a questionnaire covering wide areas of preparation (on many levels) as well as for finding out the energies involved.

For going through the process nicely, smoothly and easily I advise physical and mental cleansing. Physical includes fasting, colon hydrotherapy and other naturopathic methods of detoxification. One should not do them just before starting the process because some of them can weaken the body, and I don't recommend to start this wonderful journey with a weakened body. The mental and emotional cleansing can be initiated by your intention as well as by meditation, clear mind and thought, going for honesty and truth, and actually you already know what is best for you.«

With love – Chris
»Relax and have fun and
Go for the essence, go for the cream!«

Christopher Schneider: the M.A.P.S. Akademy, Ph/Fax: +49 8860-922022, Fax: +49-8860-9211, Mobile +49 170 432 4288; email govind@gmx.de

Jaxon Wu – Post Process Adjustments

I am guided to include here a few insights from Jaxon Wu on his experience with learning to live on light, as I feel it has great post- process adjustment information. Taken from the Living on Light Forum, I have eliminated any non-relevant details. Jaxon writes:

»Last fall, during my last days at Findhorn, I was sitting at lunch with a friend, Mark, talking about food. In previous conversations, I had told him about my whole raw foods‹ journey over the previous couple of years and somehow the conversation led to what is commonly called »breatharianism«, which I prefer to call ›Living on Light›. Simply put, Living on Light is a state of mind and being by which a person, through Self-Mastery and intimate trust in the Divine Source, allows him or herself to be fully nourished and maintained from that Source without the need for food, water or other sustenance from the physical plane...

I had heard of such people before, in books like Yogananda's ›Autobiography Of A Yogi‹, but never before had I considered such a reality possible or desirable for me. But somehow in that moment, something clicked inside of me, so deep, that I knew this was the next step on my spiritual path. And I mean the NEXT step – my heart was beating fast and my soul was speaking volumes – ›Find the book, Go through the Process, ASAP, No time to waste!!!‹ I had been eating pretty much exclusively whole raw plants and fruits for about two years prior and felt I had reached the pinnacle of joy, pleasure, connectedness and fun in the world of food. I had already been asking the Universe, ›What's next?‹ And as always the Universe responded by throwing the answer right in my lap, clear as day.«

Jaxon found and read my book, underwent the procedure and now continues.....

»The Process was an amazing experience full of insights and miracles, and though it is ostensibly 21 days long, I feel it is only the beginning of an ongoing process of transition on all levels – physical, emotional, mental and spiritual. To describe the period after the 21-Day Process and until one has stabilized and balanced in the new intention, I have coined the term Post-Process.

From what I have heard, this period for some can take no time at all, or as long as 6 months to a couple of years. I myself am at the tail end of my Post-Process, coming to a place of equilibrium and stabilization, which has so far been about 6 months long....

The 21–Day Process went very easily and gracefully. The Post-Process has been more the challenge and test, in which I got to really look at my emotional and other issues / beliefs around eating and food while leading a full and active life. .... At some point in my Post-Process I felt guided to begin eating again, sometimes as much as or even more than I used to before the Process. Another interesting fact was that besides eating raw foods, I was also drawn to eat foods that I was not at all attracted to during the two years prior when I ate only raw whole plants and fruits – cooked food, bread, butter, cookies, chocolate. It was funny, sometimes scary, to watch myself – for someone who had been so disciplined and healthy in his diet for years, I was eating like a junk food junkie (this is relatively speaking of course, because for me, in my way of thinking prior to the Process, anything other than whole raw vegetarian foods was ›junk‹ food...).

Through it all, I kept affirming my intention to Live on Light, asking God to remove the obstacles to the realization of this, and listening to and trusting my inner guidance even though on the surface it was taking me in the opposite direction. On the deepest level it all made sense, and I knew I was still moving forward. I had learned a lot from my raw foods transition which helped me here. It took me many months to make the transition to whole raw foods. Above all during that time, I gave myself full permission to eat whatever I wanted, so as not to be in denial. I had allowed myself to enjoy whatever I wanted – bread, pizza, Thai food and whatever else I had a desire for.

Eventually the desires for these foods just fell away, and I found myself eating an exclusively whole raw vegetarian diet without any sense of lack or denial. I sensed I was going through a similar process of letting go here with Living on Light. The difference was, whereas before the question was what to eat – whole, raw or not, now the question was to eat or not to eat – different parameters, same process.

By March, my inner teacher was moving me back into going without food for longer and longer periods. First a few days at a time, then a week here and there....

At some point an insight came for which I thank Giri Bala, the yogini who lived on light and is described in Yogananda's autobiography. For those of you unfamiliar with her story, as a young girl recently married she was deeply ridiculed by her mother-in-law for her overzealous eating habits. At some point she became so desperate that she cried to God to free her from her need to eat. Her prayer was answered and an angel came to her and showed her a Kriya-yoga technique by which she would no longer need to intake food.

When Yogananda met her she had already gone many decades without food, witnessed by all her family and friends. What he quoted her as saying in their meeting touched me very deeply. She said something like, ›I do not eat because God does not give me the desire to eat. If He gave me the desire to eat, I would eat.‹

What I got from this is insight for the programming and prayers that have brought me through the final stages of my transition:

- I ask for all my nourishment on all levels to be fully met from Divine Light.
- I ask that my desires for food be removed in Divine Perfect Timing in accord with the Divine Plan.
- I ask that whatever desires do come be for my Highest Good, in joy, ease, grace and fun.
- Therefore, I honor whatever desires that come as God's plan for me in this moment.

With this mind-body programming, I released altogether my intention to Live on Light and I stopped trying. What I mean by this is that I found at some point that I was ›trying‹ to go without food, but was in fact denying that I had desire for food – a vicious circle that was putting me out of touch with myself and creating trouble in my immediate relationships.

I realized that I had to give up trying to make it happen and just let the Divine One take the wheel, communicating with me through my desires. If that meant I was to continue eating the rest of my life, so be it – it must be Divine Will for me.

Well, I am learning again, when you really let something go, you set it free to come back to you. Since that time, the Post-Process has become even more graceful (if that is possible). I eat even less fre-

quently but more importantly with no sense of struggle. My last doubts are being finally dissolved and I am resting more and more in the Truth that Living on Light is not only possible, but for me it is Real.«
Love, Magic and Miracles, Jax. Jaxon Wu: Jaxon@divineliving.org
Foundation for Divine Living www.divineliving.org
(Jaxon has done a beautiful CD that some say helps tune them to the process, his theme song »Living on Light« plays regularly on our website.)

Common post-process challenges can be:

* Hair loss – this is short-term and usually settles down after a month or so.
* Change in body temperature – while I have the hottest showers, I still often get cold hands and feet. Most Ambassadors of Light choose to treat the change in body temperature as a challenge to learn body temperature control. I usually just ask my DOW to adjust my body temperature so that I am always comfortable.
* Dealing with our emotional body's addiction to the pleasure of taste, spending months or even years, on a vegetarian, then vegan, then raw food, then liquid diet, beforehand helps to lessen this.
* Weight stabilization – see chapter 10.
* Social adjustments – see family and friends – chapter 11.

TEN

Weight Stabilization – Post Process

»The mind once expanded to the dimensions of a
larger idea never returns to its original size.«
Oliver Wendell Holmes, US writer and physician

As those who have read our first book are aware, the body's
weight will stabilize when we are no longer eating, if we program it to
and are well-connected to DOW Power. This can take effect immediately for some and longer for others and is impeded by deep belief
systems to the contrary.

Consequently, one of the most consistent concerns of people
who lighten up their diets is about weight stabilization. Going from a
cooked food diet to raw food, then to fruit, liquids and prana, each step
along the way can often cause profound weight loss as the body gets
lighter and lighter.

I often say that somewhere in the future, doctors will have two
weight charts – one for the ›light eaters‹ and one for those with more
›regular‹ diets. The ›light eaters‹ will always generally weigh less. Still,
continued weight loss can be a challenge for many whose bodies are
already lean from their normal lifestyle choice.

Aware of this recurring problem, we have been developing new
programs and approaches to the weight loss problem and having success. The people we have used this with have had some good results.
Here is what we have found and now recommend for those of you in
post-process who have weight stabilization problems.

Firstly, stop weighing yourself – do it once a month only. Every
time you step on the scales and you have lost weight, you reinforce
the belief system that »it's not working, perhaps I can't live on prana
after all.« For some reason it does take men longer than women to have
their bodies totally accept they can be nourished this way.

Next, if you choose to eat again to gain weight and then decide
to try just prana again, know that you do not need to undergo the
process again unless your DOW strongly advises you to! That is when

84

your heart sings at the very thought of it. Instead of re-doing the process, just gradually stop eating everything but raw food, then take only fruit and then liquids. If you are fit as previously discussed and expect to be fed by prana, and you will be.

Our body can live easily off prana without doing any 21 day process. The process is a placebo to get us to believe we can do something we'd forgotten we could do. It is also an initiation where the DOW gives each initiate a gift. Remember the 21 day process is only about merging with our DOW.

For one friend of mine, doing the 21 day process gave him the gift of shifting his focus and mental energy from thinking about sex 8 hours a day to thinking about his business – with great results. For another, he remained a vegetarian and would no longer touch meat. (He ate meat shortly before the process). Remember the process is not about eating and not eating, however, if you desire to be free from the need to eat, then this is a procedure you may wish to adopt.

- Pre-process – Program your body to stabilize at the perfect weight for you. Then just adopt an attitude of »of course it will« and forget it! Mind power again. Say:
  »I now ask my body to stabilize my weight at the perfect level to fully manifest my DOW.«
- Pre-process – Stop eating everything but raw food for some months prior to the process. Eat as much as you like but keep it raw and eat a few small meals a day. Train yourself to eat only until you are no longer hungry and never until you feel really full.
- If you follow the pre-process preparation of being a vegetarian, then vegan, then going only on raw foods, then fruit, you will automatically detox and will also quite likely lose weight. So practice mind mastery and use the above program.
- Pre-process – Set yourself a goal to be living purely from prana by ____ (your date) and then ask the Divine One Within you to support your transition into this with ease and grace.
- Pre-process, begin or continue an exercise program and also a lifestyle program to get fit on all levels as per our »Get Fit for Prana« guidelines.
- Ask your DOW for any other guidance that you need, and tell it to give you this guidance in a way that you REALLY GET IT.

- Pre-process – Ask the DOW if this lifestyle is really part of your blueprint right now and tell it that if it is, it is to clear any blockages in your fields that may be stopping you from embracing this lifestyle completely without effort.

- Pre-process – When your weight stabilizes with just smoothies and raw food, go to only smoothies and fruit. Do this for as long as it makes you happy – expect your weight to be stable.

- Next stop eating fruit – just take liquids, smoothies, tea, water etc. Also expect to be healthy, that your weight is stable etc.

- When you can tell that your weight has stabilized and you feel great about living on such a simple diet, try eliminating the banana from the smoothie and then the smoothie itself. And so forth. There's no need to rush and there's no such thing as failure.

- Post-process – If you are losing weight on just tea and water, add a daily soya milk smoothie with either 1 or 2 bananas in it, and flavor to taste. Do this until you gain the weight you wish.

- Post-process – weigh yourself monthly to see when your weight has stabilized. If it hasn't, just relax and trust that your program will work. Expect to be healthy, strong and nourished regardless!

- Pre and post-process – Build up muscle bulk where possible – you can use visualization techniques to help you with this. Strong muscle mass supports a higher radiation of your DOW through your physical body. Weight lifting will add tone, muscle and weight and improve your strength.

- The ability to be sustained by prana after the process is directly related to your fitness levels. The fitter you are on all levels, the more powerfully the One who feeds you, can radiate through you and nourish you as It projects Itself through you. Fitness pumps up the volume that you can cope with. If you're getting tired, sick, losing lots of weight, you are not radiating enough of your DOW. Focus on increasing your DOW Power first and foremost!

- Pre and post-process – do Pranayama breathwork – breathe in rhythmically and command with each breath:
  »I breathe in prana and liquid light. It fills my cells and being. It nourishes me and supports me in total health and wellness on all levels of my being« or whatever you feel guided to say. Visualize simultaneously that you are absorbing prana through all the pores of your skin.

- Experiment and work with your DOW on this as after all the process is about tuning yourself in a way to fully radiate your DOW and only IT has all the answers for you.

Regarding the issue of weight loss, last year in Salzburg in Austria, I met a Light Ambassador from Hungary. Annoyed at losing so much weight during the process after the initiation was complete, one night he sat down in meditation and demanded that his body immediately put on weight. In 15 minutes he put on 5 kilos. Apparently he did this with friends as witnesses and was weighed before and after. Sounds miraculous or is it just another example of mind power?

This brings me to the point that many spend billions of dollars on dietary aids and on cosmetic surgery. If you follow the recommendations in this book, you will improve both the quality and quantity of your life and the need for this can be made invalid. Being free from the game of diets is extremely liberating. I never think about vitamins, minerals or food supplements. I never think about ›going on a diet‹ and use exercise, reprogramming and even acupuncture instead of cosmetic surgery to defy the normal problems associated with aging.

Often people say that if they return to eating after the process when they know they are being pranically fed, that they put on lots of weight. This is because their metabolic rate has changed, and secondly if they are being pranically nourished, then any food they consume will be unnecessary and may just go to fat. Sometimes it sits in the stomach and sends out heat and makes the person itch from the inner burning. Some say that when they eat they feel like a ›fuzzy person – like a werewolf‹ as the food sits there undigested for ages. To me it feels like there are problems with the electromagnetic energy fields of my body, and yet I have found that eating ginger and drinking it in tea is most helpful with this overacidity in the body and itching.

If you want to return to a more regular food consumption and know you are being pranically nourished, you will have to reprogram your body to transmute all that you eat instantaneously into ›calorie free‹ light OR else you will put on weight. You may also need to re-command: »I now stabilize my weight at the perfect level to fully manifest my DOW.«

I also recommend that you regularly tune into your body to feel how it is doing with both systems running. Then think and act fit, toned and healthy. Do daily exercise such as dancing and yoga which will also help burn up any calories while you learn to transmute the food.

If you continue to put on weight you may have to:

a) Stop nibbling and just let prana feed you.

b) Command: »I now ask my body elemental to receive all its nourishment from food.« This will switch you off the prana system, as we all put on weight when we run both systems. Alternatively, you may also ask the body elemental to receive only 50% of its nourishment from prana and just eat a little less. Each person needs to experiment with this to their own satisfaction.

c) Experiment with the amount you are tasting to see what is the perfect level for you. Because so many of the Ambassadors of Light – when free from the need to eat – then choose high kilo-jule taste hits like chocolate or ice-cream, they tend to put weight on quickly.

d) You can maintain both systems and exercise much more to burn off the extra calories.

The fact is that once you are connected into pranic nourishment, if you then go back to food you will probably put on more weight than ever before.

ELEVEN

Family and Friends

»Integrity, hard work, patience, and a willingness to understand another person's perspective are key ingredients in anything we do in life; overlaying that with a sense of fun and enjoyment.«
Stephen de Kanter, Disney Consumer Products

One of the biggest tests for the Ambassadors of Light is dealing with the process of social adaptation as a non-eater. When any person makes a drastic change in lifestyle, it can be very unsettling for family and friends. Going from being a sociable family member sharing over regular meals to someone choosing not to eat can create many problems unless the situation is attended to well beforehand. In some cultures it is highly insulting to refuse the hospitality of food and the love with which it is offered.

As an Italian Light Ambassador told me recently, he was fine with not eating for over five months until he attended a Moslem wedding where refusing to eat was highly insulting. Once he had tasted a little bit of food, he decided he missed it and wanted more so he ate for a while, satisfied this ›missing‹ then went back to liquids. Sometimes the Light Ambassadors take food at social gatherings and push it around their plates as they do not feel it is appropriate to draw attention to themselves. I have done this myself.

When I first underwent the 21 day conversion process, I was living in a household of two adults – Michael and myself – my two teenagers and a cat. On weekends the ranks would swell to include Michael's girlfriend, his two young children, plus extra teenage visitors. All in all it could be quite bohemian and bedlamic and food was always on the agenda as someone was invariably always hungry. Michael and his girlfriend Anna had also undergone the 21 day process and the others were horrified at the idea that we may even think they would like to stop eating. Obviously the choice we made was a highly personal one and, being based on a spiritual premise, was not one we were interested in enforcing upon others.

This brings me to the first point: Never try to convince family or friends to stop eating. It may not be part of their blueprint to do this at this time, and unless the idea of being pranically fed makes their heart sing, then leave them alone. Actions speak far louder than words, and by being a silent example, interesting things happen.

For instance, when people are in the presence of someone who no longer stops for meal breaks or thinks about food, they naturally tend to do the same. Over the years my now adult daughters have become very relaxed about food. If it is there they eat, but they no longer feel they have to eat three meals per day or get concerned if they don't feel like eating for short periods of time. They expect to be healthy and they are. This is the power of mind.

Enforcing any personal lifestyle choice onto another is unacceptable. People must want to do something and are far more influenced by seeing you enjoy the benefits of your lifestyle rather than having you try to convince them ›your way‹ is right. However, at the same time, learning to adjust emotionally without food can be an interesting journey and it is helpful to have family and friends support you as you make this transition. This support can be gained through good communication which is based on the desire for you all to have a mutually pleasurable and mutually empowering relationship.

Hence we recommend that before you undertake the 21 day process, you:

- Discuss with your loved ones what you want to do, why you wish to do it, and what you hope to attain.
- Ask them to read any research material on this that you have read so that they can be better informed. Remember ignorance breeds fear and education liberates.
- Discuss the impact on your lives that this new lifestyle choice may bring.
- Look at ways you can work together so that harmony may be kept in the home.

For example, some women may find it difficult to continue to cook for their family as they make the transition to a food-free life, and on one level it is unreasonable to expect them to. Prior to the process, both partners and teenagers can be trained to cook for themselves and other family members still eating.

Also sometimes family are unconvinced that you can live without food and therefore set up subtle or non-subtle sabotage situations so that you ›come to your senses‹ and eat again. Reading all our research on the matter will help them enormously.

In time, once you have proved to yourself that you can live a food-free life, then you may wish to share one family meal a week for the bonding and pleasure. I met a woman in Rome a few years ago whose husband was horrified she no longer wished to eat. He insisted she keep cooking for him and over time she found she went back to eating again. The constant smells, boredom from lack of flavor and always being around food became too much, yet in her heart she would really long to return to a food-free diet. In the end they compromised and she cooked and ate only at weekends.

Other women I talk to don't mind cooking at all and never find it a temptation to eat regardless of how much time they may spend preparing meals for their families. The point is to reach a compromise where all parties are happy without feeling as though they can't be free to do what inspires them.

In my own life, my husband still loves to eat. A vegan for the past 25 years, and a person with disciplined exercise and meditation habits he still loves to have one meal a day. Before we began to live together, I had one year in a food-free household which I thoroughly enjoyed. My daughters had grown up and left home and my fridge was empty except for cat food and milk for tea. To be honest it truly was a simple life.

Living with people who choose to eat when you do not, is very interesting and can be challenging if you do not have good communication. New habits and routines need to be formed. For example, I exercise when he cooks and eats. It's important to remember that the process is not about discord within or without. It is about harmony on all levels – in our inner world and our outer world. So the better you prepare yourself and your loved ones, the easier life will be before, during and after the process. To live in society as an Ambassador of Light you need to have courage, strength and be committed to your lifestyle and chosen reality.

TWELVE

Facts and Faith – Prove it to Me!

»Doubt is a pain too lonely to know that faith is his twin brother.«
Kahil Gibran, Lebanese poet and novelist.

a) Prove it to me!

As I began to elaborate on this issue of the »prove it to me‹ game, it soon became obvious to me that we needed a separate chapter, yet before we begin this discussion, I would like to say that this is the one issue that completely divides the opinions of the Ambassadors of Light.

I like the following quote by Brian L. Weiss, an M.D. and author of »Many Lives, Many Masters« as it reminds me to be more patient, and allow Divine Time to support the »prove it to me« issue. He writes: »Patience and timing – everything comes when it must come. A life cannot be rushed, cannot be worked on a schedule as so many people want it to be. We must accept what comes to us at a given time, and not ask for more. But life is endless, so we were never really born. We just pass through different phases. There is no end. Humans have many dimensions. But time is not as we see time, but rather in lessons we have learned.« Thanks for the reminder Brian.

I think sometimes in my desire to satisfactorily answer the ›prove it to me‹ questions, I forget that real perspective here. Firstly many of the Ambassadors of Light like myself, feel completely blessed at even being able to discover and enjoy the fruits of DOW Power. Why it has come to us in this way is anybody's guess. It just has. Is it our divine mission, our role? Some think so. The point I forget is that divine revelations and experiences have occurred to many over millennia, and every time someone has tried to prove the existence of the Divine, they have usually found themselves unable to satisfy the skeptical.

As we have often said, skepticism is healthy, ignorance born out of fear is not. Skepticism about DOW Power comes from lack of experience of DOW Power, a situation that can easily be rectified.   The Ambassadors of Light know that we are fed by the light of the Divine, and also that when science has finally proved the existence of DOW

Power, our whole mass reality will be effected. Not because ›ordinary‹ people need to be convinced but because science can then move into new directions. Millions of people have experienced some type of divine or extra sensory awareness or revelation, and thankfully they are no longer reliant on science to say that this is either valid, real or okay.

Times do change, particularly as we learn to let go, trust in the Divine, and open up to higher possibilities which then can become our day to day reality. In his book »Dying for Enlightenment«, Bhagwan Shree Rajneesh said »Don't try and force anything. See God opening millions of flowers everyday without forcing anything.« I think that this is the basic philosophy of many of the Light Ambassadors – just to let the Divine prove Its own power in Its own time. As Daniel Webster said: »There is nothing so powerful as the truth, and often nothing so strange.«

Still, having spent many years involved in the often challenging field of personal research, I am as fascinated as anyone as to ›how‹ this all works on a scientific level and how living on light effects the physical organism long-term.

b) The Three Step Program:

So I would like to share a little more on my personal journey concerning the media question: »but you've been doing this now for years so where is the scientific/medical proof? (with the implied ›apart from your own making of this claim')«.

To this we respond, the first requirement of any »experiment« is to have the test subjects or »guinea pigs« successfully apply the procedure that has been recommended and then also be able to maintain the results of the procedure. To achieve this we followed a three step procedure:

Step 1: Find initial research subjects to test the procedure.

Step 2: Share research findings.

Step 3: Apply research findings en mass with those interested.

STEP 1: Attracting people with the right background, training, discipline and interest was step number 1 in a three part ›marketing project‹ that the Light Ambassadors decided would need instigating. To gain credibility for this alternative source of nutrition, we wanted not just ›short-term miracles‹ but long-term results which of course take time.

Those familiar with the extreme nature of the 21 day process as outlined in the »Living on Light« book can also surmise that having the right people ›self-select‹ themselves to be part of this, could be seen as a daunting task. Nonetheless when working within divinely intended games, this is actually never a problem, and soon the word was spread.

I count myself as being one of the early »guinea pigs« in co-pioneering this particular process work in the west. Like many »spiritual miracles«, pranic nourishment has long been acceptable among the yogis in the East. My personal challenge was that as a naturally private person I have had no interest in being in the limelight with either this or any other matter. Still, I was the one that seemed to ›pick up the gauntlet‹ so to speak.

Many of my colleagues from our early research days soon returned to a more ›normal‹ lifestyle as they felt that the social pressures around not eating were too great. Others could not remain healthy as their DOW connection wasn't strong enough. Others like myself have been confronted with issues like boredom from lack of flavor and dietary variety.

Like with any experiment, this is something that needed to be understood and addressed, particularly as many individuals did not take their journey with this beyond a year or two. Still, surviving for a year or two without eating food is, by normal medical accounts, in itself a feat worthy of acknowledgement.

By our diligent global re-education programs about the benefits of »self-mastery« we have now been able to have social comments change from »impossible« to »yes, I hear people can do this«, which has made this lifestyle choice easier for others who are drawn to this today.

STEP 2: So step 2 has been about re-education and also about finding alternative processes to achieve the same result in a less extreme manner. This has been found, and has been and is being taught, however the time taken to get the same results will be much longer. This is the technique of reprogramming the body elemental to receive all its vitamins and nourishment from prana, which it then does. Proof that this works is the weight gain that everyone soon experiences if they don't then cut back their food consumption.

One interesting discovery is that our reprogramming techniques are definitely working. In Australia before we began our re-education about the power of reprogramming, most people doing this lost between 4 to 20 kgs depending on the individual. Our research project shows that with programming done by the European Light Ambassadors, 35% lost less than 2 kilos. Losing less than 2 kilos over a 21 day fast that then continues into months and years is amazing. Watching people then gain weight while only taking water is also amazing.

With the infant mortality rate as high as it is in third world countries, our research around the historical phenomena of not needing food to live, is continuing »post haste«. Regardless of how many buttons of disbelief this work pushes, pranic nourishment via DOW Power, is a wonderful source of nutrition for the new millennium. Twenty-five years ago it was very socially unacceptable in the west to be a vegetarian and yet today, as research has caught up with people's intuitive instruction, it is even medically acceptable.

STEP 3: Next the Masters needed for many people to make this lifestyle choice, as they knew that if it was left to just a few, our achievements would be labeled as »saint-like«, rather than being seen to be the by-product of a very simple lifestyle choice that requires regular daily discipline. Hence I was invited to the Babaji ashrams in Europe to talk about this, as this was where people with suitable interest and training lived.

c) Going public:
People cannot hide the fact that they don't need to eat from their family and friends. Over time, living on light has become a »grass roots« phenomena practised by individuals for their own personal reasons which have not included being »public« about it to the media. Understandably enough, very few Ambassadors of Light are interested in fame or the lack of privacy that can come from media exposure regarding this lifestyle choice – myself included. Hence it is also impossible to keep track of how many are now doing this on a global level or why they do it, or for how long they do it.

Personally, it has taken nearly 6 years for me to work through my own issues and learning about living on light and to be comfortable with how it aligned with the rest of my service work. It took years for me to agree to become an »international figurehead« as my other work in metaphysical teachings has always predominated. Out of the nine previous books I have had published, only one shares our living on light experience in detail.

In Italy in 1998 I officially accepted the role of global co-ordinator for this field of research. Although I was aware of what needed to be done with this phenomena, until then I thought that this was ›someone else's role‹ as I was much too busy with our other projects. I still feel like this, as to me personally the ability to live on light is very inconsequential and so to have others treat it as a central point of focus in my service work is very strange.

I say this because the power of the Divine is so awesome, and experiencing it brings so many other benefits, that to focus on the living on light aspect, is like paying homage to our God's toenail rather than looking around to see the rest of God's body. To me we are all just molecules in the Divine One's body, and what is happening on planet earth is like a needle in a haystack compared to what is occurring on the cosmic stage. Living on Light has never been my number one focus – dancing with the Divine is.

Yes, it is true that I spent the first two years of my living purely from light journey in private research convincing myself that it worked. This was done by living it, by taking no vitamins, no food except for the odd taste of non-nourishing substances like chocolate for flavor. By personally experiencing benefits like excellent health, increased strength and energy reserves and heightened intuitive abilities – finally in 1997 I could also begin to see the logical global benefits regarding world health and world hunger issues.

As the Ascended Masters say to me: »You don't need to have all the answers to every challenge in the world. Every human being has all the knowledge and details of their life purpose held within them (like a software program in a computer which is your body), and once you have learnt to tune in and listen, you will then be guided how to create your own personal paradise in a way that enhances your planet as a whole«.

Global paradise comes from personal paradise, and one of my roles is to inspire people to find their answers on how to create this from deep within themselves. The greatest teacher each person has is what we call the Divine One Within (the DOW), It has all the answers to both personal and global challenges. All the work of the Self Empowerment Academy is dedicated to inspiring people to learn to connect with their DOW. I personally choose to demonstrate the power of the DOW – or God – by allowing It to feed and nourish me.

d) What I have been doing with my time:

Keeping in mind that my main assignment over the last 7 years has been as a ›cosmic secretary / scribe‹ for the Ascended Masters, since deciding to officially co-ordinate the Living on Light Ambassadry in late last year, we have achieved a great deal:

- We have rewritten and expanded the old website to be 6 times larger and more effective, and have added many new articles, plus 5 networking forums. Calling it the C.I.A., it is our way of keeping tuned to the world and getting feedback.
- We have completed 2 new books on the Ascended Masters‹ teachings – »Streams of Consciousness« – Volumes 2 and 3.
- We have completed this new book »Ambassadors of Light – Living on Light« that covers more of our new research.
- We have formulated and then sent out a detailed questionnaire to all our contacts and networkers regarding the living on light process so we can officially gather data for our work.
- We have officially launched the M.A.P.S. Ambassadry internationally.
- We have officially launched – and begun in-depth research for – the Light Ambassadry's World Health / World Hunger Project.
- We have begun liaisons with the right global research centres that have the necessary equipment required to monitor the bodies of those converting their systems to both receive and produce pranic nourishment.
- We have secured the services of well-known documentary makers to film our experiments with this.
- We have launched our first official M.A.P.S. International Training Retreat.
- More recently in January 1999 we completed the first book in the autobiographical Camelot Trilogy called »The Game of Divine Alchemy«. Book 2 »Our Camelot – Our Progeny« is soon due to be published and »The Wizard's Tool Box« by end 2000.

All our writings are focused on positive personal and planetary progression.
- We have filmed a number of short documentaries in Europe, England and Australia on the living on light phenomena.

All my work before this has always focused on self-mastery, not living on light – even though this has been a major fascination of people. But unless one has attained a degree of discipline in their lifestyle choice, living on light is impossible. For people with a history of choosing quality thinking, quality feeding and quality feeling, living on light may often intuitively feel like their next step.

We have always shared our research with living on light freely in the world and have achieved many wonderful things with this over the last few years since Saint Germain asked me to become public with this.

e) The 21 day process research retreat:
At the end of 1998 while on tour in Europe, I was guided to announce that the Light Ambassadry would like to hold a research retreat in Europe with the intention to scientifically and medically monitor and assess what occurred with people pre-process, during the process and after the process. The response from our audiences was literally overwhelming and nearly four hundred said that they wished to be human guinea pigs.

In organizing our research and this retreat, we have noted many different reactions regarding our bid to prove our ability to be pranically nourished. After the fantastic response from our potential »guinea pigs«, the next step was to continue discussions with appropriate research institutes that were interested in monitoring the participants at the retreat. This was most enlightening and we'll discuss more on this later. Suffice to say that the bottom line appears to be that most research institutes are severely under-funded and figures of some hundreds of thousands of Duetchmarks began to be bandied about with the expectation that the Light Ambassadors would be the ones providing the funding.

Discussions with my colleagues found this to be totally unacceptable considering that we ourselves require no proof as we live it every day. Hence there was nothing to prove, except to a skeptical world, who we knew in time would begin also to realize human potential, as they themselves began to incorporate more healthy and holistic lifestyle choices. From this we collectively decided two things.

Firstly, that offering ourselves to the world as guinea pigs was enough and that if the scientific and medical communities are sincerely interested then surely they can fund their own participation into this field of research – considering the potential global kudos involved in proving this to be fact.

Secondly, we decided to begin the push for what we call retrospective studies on individuals who have been living on prana for some time. This is now being done as each individual is guided, in their own country using the relevant researchers and practitioners that each Light Ambassador could manifest as part of their own Divine Blueprint and role in this research.

Since announcing our intention to hold this research retreat I realized that my desire to do this was splitting the Light Ambassadors into separate camps. Many feel like Chris Schneider in Germany who has closely worked with hundreds of Ambassadors as they have made the transition to live on light. The following is an excerpt of an email he recently sent me: »It is not necessary to prove anything, it does work and we know it. Of course it is a nice game to play, proving it by means of the unbelievers, just like this was played many times before with Galileo, Newton, Keppler, Einstein, Maxwell, Reich, Tesla, and millions of others. Do we really want to go on in this limiting tradition?

If there is a need, we haven't learnt anything .... what are the measurements of proof, trust and reality? To prove this in a scientific way is limiting it to agreed laws or rules – and we are operating outside of these.«

Chris' statements reflect the feelings of many of the Light Ambassadors, including my own, and as the months have gone by I have had to assess my own reasons for wishing to do the research projects. I realized that it came about in response to:

- The continual media question of ›prove it‹ and I'll believe you, and
- My own sincere desire to find out more about what actually happens to our bodily functions from living on light, apart from the obvious.

I have since decided that if it is Divine Will that we continue with these projects of ›proof‹ via research, then it all must unfold in joy and ease and grace. Everything else I am involved in just flows as if held in some divine river of grace yet as we try to arrange these research retreats the energy gets stuck. As I have also since discovered the ›bigu‹ phenomena amongst the qigong masters, I have begun to question the validity of spending time and resources to prove something that has already been researched and documented by other groups.

Also I have come to think that perhaps it is not in the interests of many organizations that the ability we have to live without food is proven, particularly in light of our next story.

f) Being monitored daily:
To me the best proof is to live it and be monitored and followed around daily for long periods. Having done this myself for briefer periods of time, I was fully aware of the total invasion of privacy that having someone follow you every moment brings (I did this with a television film crew in 1997). I was also aware how distracting this can be for others with whom we may live.

Still, I had been telepathically told by the Masters that someone would soon step forward to do this, and in November 1998 I arrived in England and met with a man named Jeffrey Sharp, a London-based Sai Baba devotee. Prior to our meeting he had received ›inner plane‹ guidance that by the end of 1999 he would live completely from Divine Light although at that time he had not heard of our work. Divine ›co-incidence‹ arranged that we would meet and both Jeffrey, myself and Jaxon Wu began participation in a series of London based press conferences.

Jaxon had long been a meditator, was extremely active in many sports and was a raw foodist for some years – he had heard about the prana process while in Glastonbury. Divine coincidence again allowed him to find both the Living on Light book which was still not in the book stores in England, and also make contact with myself personally.

Jeffrey Sharp had completed the prana process and had been later guided to do his bit for the ›prove it to me‹ game. Here is a little of what he and his team had to share with us for the Living on Light Forum of our website...

»Jeffrey Sharp made a promise to himself that he would overcome the need for physical food by the end of 1998. Ten months later, he received information about somebody called Jasmuheen who has already undergone the process and has even written a book to aid and advise others who wish to attain ›Living on Light‹. He immediately ordered the book and on receipt read the details and quickly went into the process. He began the conversion of his being on 4th October 1998 and had never felt better.

In preparation, Jeffrey had undergone periods of raw foods and fruit during the previous two years. He had fasted for a period of six weeks before, taking only one small meal a day and had felt an upliftment and an increase in visionary and psychic experiences. Before the 21 day process, he made physical preparations for his body through the use of colonic irrigation. Here is Jeffrey's story:

After the conversion, I continued to eat intermittently, as was my original plan, yet was later guided to go for a lengthy period without any food or water whilst remaining physically active, and in the public eye. I made myself available for public and scientific scrutiny for a period of six weeks commencing 20th November 1998 and finishing at midnight New Year's Eve.

The offer was publicized through means of a press conference with Jasmuheen in London and repeated calls to local doctors and hospitals. It seemed however, that with the exception of two independent TV crews and a Dutch TV channel, nobody would even take the offer seriously. I was physically followed and monitored, 24 hours a day for the first nine days, in which time I took no food or water. After this I was followed and monitored for approximately 16 hours a day whilst I took no food or sustenance. (For the remaining 8 hours a day, I allowed myself to be locked in a room which had been pre-inspected by an ex-drug-squad officer to ensure no nutritional sources were in the room).

With Christmas looming and no significant interest from professionally qualified people, I decided to commence intermittent eating once again. It seemed this time however, that my vibration dropped each time that I ate.... People seem to have difficulty accepting that I can survive without food, though increasing amounts of my friends and close associates seem to be making the move.«

Jeffrey can be contacted via his e-mail address: Info@ancientwisdom.co.uk – Thanks Jeffrey.

It's interesting to note that even though various Ambassadors of Light have made themselves available to be monitored, the lack of commitment to this seems to come from the skeptics seeking proof. Jeffrey had even contacted the Guinness Book of Records who declined his invitation to follow him around saying that it was too dangerous.

Personally I know that just as vegetarianism is now a well-accepted option in Western society for health and resource sustainability reasons, in time so will pranic nourishment be seen as a valid and quite ›normal‹ lifestyle choice. Convinced of this, many of my Light Ambassador colleagues are not at all interested in playing the proof game.

g) In summary:

As global reporter for the Light Ambassadry, I am well aware of the need for scientific and medical studies in order to have this work taken credibly as a solution to our claim that this lifestyle choice can aid in the elimination of world health and world hunger related challenges.

Beyond all this, the Ambassadors of Light know that everything happens in divine time because we are not solo players, we are team players working together for the betterment of society. However we are not interested in struggle, or doing things in disharmony or playing ›yes we can – no you can't‹ games; and we all know that in the normal course of time, this phenomena will prove itself as many more embrace this lifestyle for its obvious benefits.

So in summary, our ›prove it to me!‹ project is three-fold:

1.) Firstly, the only one you need to prove this to is you. Do this by living without nourishment from food for as long as it takes to convince you that it is possible. Do it long enough to stabilize your weight, release your emotional body's attachment to food and adapt socially. We recommend at least 6 months, however you need to monitor yourself at all times and also be responsible – if you have problems see an alternative therapist or a holistic doctor who understands this journey.

2.) We ask all those who are living on light to do personal research with your pre-process and post-process journey, with holistic practitioners in your own area and record your findings. You may wish to send these to us at S.E.A. or post them in the Living on Light Forum on our website or keep them and write your own book at some stage if this is in your blueprint.

3.)   Yes, I would still like to hold a positive research retreat with switched on and supportive analysts and test subjects and then share our findings with the world. This will happen if it is divinely intended to and can be done in joy and ease and grace as I know that if it is part of the Divine Blueprint for us to do this then the way will be made clear.

4.)   At the moment we have a few detailed documentaries with people being studied in the final stages of completion. Frieder Mayrhofer, a well-known German film maker is seeking a test subject to study over a few months in a controlled environment and I am sure that the right people will step forward to be involved with this. His fax number is + 49 8933 6913.

To be honest, the majority of the Light Ambassadors that I liaise with are so busy with their service work that to stop to prove something they already have proved to themselves, is not an attractive personal proposition. Also many of us have come to a point where it feels like so much fuss is made over such a small aspect of DOW Power that we continually find ourselves trying to redirect attention away from the not eating phenomena and into the DOW Power phenomena instead. In light of what our DOW really can do for us in life generally, the fact that It can feed us is so inconsequential in the bigger scheme of things.

Remember that we are not suggesting that people just stop eating to solve world health and hunger problems. Instead we recommend a complete revamp of an individual's lifestyle to include a raw food or vegetarian diet, daily exercise, daily meditation (contemplation time with your DOW) and the practice of mind mastery. In our experience both this and the mutual commitment to a few common visions, will radically alter the realities of all in our world – regardless of race, creed, gender and religion.

Update on 60 Minutes – October 1999
Recently I agreed to deal with the Australian 60 Minutes team. I did this in the hope that they would do some solid investigative jour-

nalism, to clear the media misinformation on the deaths over the last three years of three people associated with the 21 day process. If I say that it is sad when our loved ones die, people respond with: »Why are you attached to life when death does not exist as the spirit is immortal. Don't you know that the time of our birth and death is between you and your God?« If I say, should we blame a car manufacturer every time someone dies in a car accident, others say: »But three people died and someone should be held responsible«.

On the highest level who is really responsible for life and death on this planet? Yes, learning to drive safely helps, yes, following all the driving guidelines helps, yes, driving sensibly helps but as many now know, sometimes it is just our time to die. Treating our body as a temple, acting impeccably and responsibly in every moment is part of the journey of self-mastery, and if we all do that, then for any of us to take responsibility over the death of another is like pretending we are God rather than ones made in the image of God. It is now the belief of many that each one of us has a time contract each life to be here, and when this is complete we leave either via accident, disease or, like the lamas, we sit in meditation and exit our bodies which then die.

In a recent study done by the Centre for Disease Control and Prevention, it said that sedentary lifestyles and fast food diets are resulting in one in five Americans today being labeled as obese and that this is killing 280,000 people in the USA each year. Are the fast food manufacturers responsible for this?

Surely it is time that we acted as responsible adults and took control over our lives and stopped looking to blame each other when our own choices create problems such as dis-ease and even death. For any of us to take responsibility for another choice is to undermine the very message of our work in the field of self-mastery. Self- responsibility is the key to true inner and outer peace in this world.

Some may say that blame perpetuates victim consciousness. Others may say that people die every day, and yes it is hard for those of us who loved them and miss them. In our grief we feel anger, denial and blame. In our ignorance we see life as limited and reject the very notion that the Divine One Within really is in charge. And in our arrogance we wish to prove to a non-believing world the existence of something that perhaps they are not yet ready to know.

I say this because it was partly my own arrogance and also my naivety, that led me to accept the challenge put forward by 60 Minutes. For years people have been telling me it is impossible to do something that I have been doing for years, and yes, it gets tiring listening to the same old fear and disbelief that always comes from those who have not yet had the pleasure of experiencing their DOW, and so I allowed myself to play with 60 Minutes, lose my joy and become sincerely humbled.

My learning was invaluable. I must admit it was fascinating to be held in what felt like a POW camp with constantly changing rules, and I gained some wonderful insights! Particularly about the effects of carbon monoxide poisoning on the body when one isn't drinking, as I usually choose to do to combat any negative effects of pollution, particularly when I travel. So much occurred during the 60 Minutes set-up that instead of being a beautiful, blissful time as I had previously experienced, and that I had asked them to support; due to their arrogance, ignorance and complete insensitivity, it was a challenge dangerously doomed from the start. It was the antithesis of everything that the 21 day process represents.

Not eating and not drinking in a polluted environment was something the American founder of breatharianism, Wiley Brooks, had done in-depth research on before, but this was not my field. Wiley had told me that he found it difficult to stabilize his weight when he was not drinking and not eating and he felt it was due to the pollution, and I never realized why, but now I do. Without the fluid to flush out the toxins, our body diverts precious energy to do this as it does when it has to digest food in the normal way. So I learnt personally that what Wiley had found is also true for me. Perhaps when we are more in tune, this will not be the case.

I feel that my recent media experience is something that we can all learn from, and I found that we do not need to prove anything to anyone but ourselves. We all know that when we walk our talk and have a deep and profound experience, no-one can take that away from us. Yes, it is unfortunate that although 60 Minutes were given all my research and findings plus 10 years of scientific research by nuclear physicist Lu Zuyin, none of this was read, and yes, it is true that the interviewer decided to portray me as someone who was dangerously deluded. To this I responded....

»What appears to be delusion to some is simply a preferable reality to another, for without our dreams and visions humanity has no hope. Divine revelations come to those who sincerely ask to have them, this is the nature of the Higher Laws of Science that some call Universal Law. Only when humankind understands and applies these laws may peace, true unity and contentment reign permanently on earth.«

60 Minutes were given a brilliant educational opportunity and decided not to take it, yet I am not interested in denigrating anyone except to say that in all my years of working with the media, I have come to understand that what is reported always reflects the consciousness of the journalist and their editor or producer.

Nonetheless I have met some brilliant, switched on and very enlightened journalists who operate out of complete integrity and honour, and the German film-maker Frieder Mayrhofer is one. Frieder has been following the progress of many people as they have been learning to live on light and has unsuccessfully offered his documentary to various television stations who it turns out have been more interested in sensationalism than fact.

People ask me why I persevere with the media, and to this I always say that it is my divine blueprint as a cosmic reporter to do this, as the media is one of the most powerful tools we have for planetary re-education today – provided it is used with honor and integrity and not for the sake of sensationalism. I think one of the problems of some of the less enlightened media is that they underestimate the intelligence of their audience.

After the 60 Minutes show went to air in Australia, they asked for feedback from their audience via a vote to the question: »Do you believe a person could live for six months on nothing but air and light?«, and 68% of the 1,600 who called in actually said YES. The reason that I tell this story is because something magnificent is occurring on earth right now. People are having what I call divine experiences, and what's more, many are now prepared to stand up and be counted.

So what exactly is all the controversy about my work? It seems that the some of the media in our world is convinced that my claim to be able to tune into the power of the Divine and live by Its light is either fraudulent or crazy and deluded, even though the research has been done to prove that it is possible, provided people live a virtuous and spiritually enriching lifestyle.

To me, a spiritually enriching lifestyle is a holistic lifestyle that allows us to be physically fit as we treat the body like a temple, emotionally fit as we treat ourselves and each other with love, honor and respect, mentally fit by being responsible for all our thoughts, words and actions, and applying and understanding the Universal Laws, and spiritually fit by aligning with, and experiencing the love wisdom and power of the Divine One Within us – our DOW.

In a recent interview in Switzerland, another servant of the Divine, the Lady Master Ching Hai was asked about proving the existence of God to people and she said: »How can I prove it to them? I don't want to. I'm not here to prove that God exists or doesn't exist. I just want to help you know God if you want to.« She goes on to say that it is easy to experience God, if you want to, but for those who don't want to that is fine too and that's how I feel.

For those who are willing to apply a little discipline in their daily lifestyle choice, for those who are willing to spend time in the silence of prayer and contemplation via meditation, for those who are willing to be the master of their body, mind and emotions, for those who are willing to put aside personal agendas and truly serve, for those who are willing to love unconditionally, for those who see their body as the temple for the Divine One Within to exist in the world of form – miracles will happen and Holiness and true divinity will reveal itself. This is the scientific principle of Universal Law. No one can prove the existence of God except us, to us, for us. No- one can us give the sincere desire to know who we truly are – beyond our mind, our emotions or our body. Sincerity must come from deep within us, longing to feel the Oneness of creation must come from deep within us. Only we can find and experience our DOW and only DOW Power can unite and harmonize our inner and outer world.

THIRTEEN

The Return of the Qi Masters
Challenging the Status Quo

»I decided to be happy because it is healthy.«
Francois Voltaire, French philosopher and author

The most exciting news for me recently has been the silent revolution of the Falun Gong movement in China and the unification of the qi masters around the world. It really is a time of standing up and being counted, and having the courage to support our beliefs and desires to create a world that honors all life. Bullying tactics such as burning books and arresting people can no longer be supported in the civilized world as effective tools for change.

Many of us whose work is also challenging the status quo are now under what I have come to call the »Illuminati Deactivation Beam«. Readers familiar with my writings, all know me as someone who chooses not to play the game of good/evil as it is just a movie. However, the Masters said to me recently that it is all very well to focus on the Oneness, for we need that to keep us strong, but we are also here to serve which means doing our bit to create positive change on earth in the manner that we have been pre-programmed to do. This means rolling up our sleeves and getting amongst it – all the movies are out there and they will affect us if we let them as we serve in the world. Our presence as advocates for positive change, makes us a target for anyone who does not support what we have to accomplish – pure and simple.

While it is exciting that our global work is finally being taken seriously enough to threaten to challenge the status quo, not once did a major German magazine – who recently printed an article based on unsubstantiated rumors – bother to ring me personally to confirm their ›facts‹ – one could say that this is very sloppy journalism!

To set the record straight, our organization has never been involved in the death of anyone going through the 21 day process, and furthermore we have acted with care, integrity and responsibility each step of the way with our reporting and the sharing of our research.

The woman who died in Australia did so under the care of someone who was subsequently arrested and charged with negligence. He is still awaiting trial and it will be up to the jury to decide if he was indeed in any way responsible for her death and if he lacked the ability to discern that she was in need of medical care earlier than it was provided. Her choice to go through the 21 day process is not the issue for the courts; the concern is that the ›caregiver‹ did not act soon enough to seek medical care for her.

The next issue is the death of a German man which occurred prior to both the publication of my book and my arrival in Germany. Apparently he had decided to do the process after reading the 21 day guidelines called »Choosing God over Illusion« that Charmaine Harley had written that were already circulating the global scene and that I later included in my book.

One of the main reasons I was guided to write the book initially was to make sure that people received more information than what these few guidelines were providing. Issues like mind mastery, meditation, programming and releasing limited belief systems needed to be addressed.

Gossip, innuendo and the spreading of unsubstantiated rumors must stop if we are to progress as a species as it does more harm than good. Discrediting via the spreading of incorrect information is a standard procedure to remove someone from the scene effectively with the hope that the »movement« will just fade away like countless others. Many are working in such challenging and radical new fields that they are also often loathe to support the work of someone else about whom rumors are flying for fear it will bring unwarranted attention to their own area of service.

Yes it is natural for people to then say, well my work is slowly making inroads (we all know how easy it is for all our good work to be discredited by the ›powers that be‹), so therefore I'd better not support ......'s work just in case there is something in these rumors. Sad but true and easily understood.

So gossip, rumors and ›bad‹ publicity that discredits someone, do their damage it seems. They effectively stop us from supporting each other and unifying, or do they? Surely we can use our own discernment and listen to the voice of the Divine One Within us (our DOW) and move beyond such fears. We don't need to be conspiracy theorists to understand how the media have been manipulated for decades by the powers that be to discredit any work that challenges the status quo and those in power.

Some say there is no such thing as bad publicity and a colleague of mine said »Fantastic! It will really get people thinking.« Yes, there are enough of you out there who realize the games that are played by the ›powers that be‹ and are unflinching in your support for positive progression on this planet, and for this we thank you.

Personally I believe in freedom of speech and am unfazed by what people say about our work. I realized very early on that claiming to live free from the need of food would challenge the medical and scientific communities, and that in time we could re-educate people into the knowledge of DOW Power and how to use it for the good of all. What I do object to is the lack of integrity some apply in journalistic standards and I do expect that rumors be checked and substantiated before things go to press.

I love the power of the media – it is a wonderful vehicle for education and immediate change. When negative press succeeds to slow or even stop the momentum of new ideas taking hold, we all go on in life and eventually someone else will rise again with the message of self-mastery and the game will continue. Divine Will always will triumph for it is where the true power lies.

And what happens to the ones of us who back down when challenged with having our reputations sullied by rumor and fear mongering? Well, we could say that we did »our bit« for a while but when the going got rough we got going... and yes that is our choice. Some would say, »That's cool, we can just all come back another life«, and yes, we can re-sit this same initiation that we walked away from now – for all this is just a test to see if we are committed enough to our service or courageous enough to stand firm in the face of adversity.

While every one of us must make our own decision – we ask you all to recommit your life to service, call in ALL the help you have from the higher realms and INSIST on clear guidance. It is like we are cruise liners in a fog on a set course and our tug boats are either the ›external forces‹ or our DOW. Both have strong influences over us now due to the cosmic alignments taking place.

Many of our current initiations are about having courage, focus, commitment – for those of us already doing what we thought was our service – it's not about doing what makes our heart sing as we are beyond that. We are here to serve through thick and thin and we can choose to do this joyously or in struggle. Know that we are not alone – we have a strong force of light around us that can assist us if we let it. Yes, it is true that the singing heart leads the way to our service, yet once we have found our mission then the game changes and becomes very focused.

As I sat in my office, on the 23 July, I received news that China had banned the members of the Falun Gong organization from their practice of their version of qigong (see more on this later in this book). Since their members were recently involved in peaceful demonstrations similar to the 1989 Tiananmen Democratic Movement, we can only wonder if their reported 100 million strong following is threatening to challenge the status quo of an old system that is in need of refinement.

Of course, the ›powers that be‹ there are feeling threatened since the Communist Party have only 60 million members. When China arrested thousands of proponents of the Falun Gong Movement, people from all over the world stood up in public outcry and said »We are not a cult we are just people intent on a better future. We use meditation, qigong and this lifestyle to keep us healthy and happy. Our desire is to enhance our morals.«

Of course it is time for things to change, for without democracy, freedom of speech, common visions that operate for the good of the whole, our planet cannot enter the new millennium with pride. Hunger, poverty, disease, war, riots, violence and greed are symptoms of inner chaos and dis-ease. Meditation, prayer, breathing and sacred dance and a vegetarian diet aid in the elimination of all inner chaos and inner dis-ease – regardless of our race or culture.

Should the arrests in China of over 40,000 qi practitioners, plus the daily reprogramming of the masses by government propaganda be allowed to continue? Two hours of television every day is spent discrediting the qi practitioners by government media.

To the Chinese Government we say: »Let your people enjoy their times of dance and meditation and your world and ours will be better for it«. It is time to stop tactics of fear and listen to each other. The

Falun Gong demonstration in April was intended to send a gentle message to which the Chinese Government has responded with an unnecessary iron fist. Like the Falun Gong movement, the Light Ambassadry has been considered very controversial, as our research findings do tend to challenge the status quo. No, we are not ›associated‹ with the Falun Gong movement but we do support the practice of peaceful and holistic lifestyles.

All over the planet there is now a movement of people committed to peace and prosperity for all. Their individual desire to serve under a common vision is literally creating unity, and unity means service. It means coming together to address the modern-day challenges and doing something pragmatic.

Everywhere I travel I hear of governments cracking down on ›insurgence‹ or what we would term people challenging the status quo. Even herbs and alternative therapies that have been successfully used for thousands of years are now being made so difficult to obtain due to new legislation or they are being made illegal to use altogether. The English-based »Kindred Spirit« magazine did a wonderful unbiased and well researched article on our work in their Summer issue no 47. In the same issue they also reported on the fact that complimentary medicine in the UK is now under threat due to proposed changes in the current legislation that will make the use of herbs and alternative medicines subject to such stringent guidelines – as usually applied to new drugs and pharmaceuticals – that it may make it impossible to use them in treatments legally.

Last year people spent 179 billion dollars on pharmaceuticals according to a March 1999 British report. The idea that we can self-heal or prevent all dis-ease by holistic lifestyles is obviously threatening the ›powers that be‹ who are often more attached to the monetary gain in these fields. Being healthy and happy can happen without any cost to anyone and therefore can obviously not be encouraged. Why? Because the ›powers that be‹ lose too much money if we never get sick, or can self-heal, or decide not to eat, or drive cars that run on alternative energy sources and even water....or....

I hope this helps those of you whose work is set to bring change that others may wish to resist due to their own personal agendas. Regardless of all this it is good to also remember that we are well-supported on all levels and to trust that we have been well- prepared for these roles we now find ourselves playing as we challenge the status quo.

Enough research has been done now to prove the power of qi or prana. The book »Scientific Qigong Exploration« by Nuclear Physicist Lu Zuyin (died 1992) shares his and others, years of detailed research experiments into how qi emissions can heal and affect the body. X-rays of bone fractures that when sent qi, immediately healed – proved by immediate post treatment x-rays. (Further details on this are at the end of section 3)

Anyone working with chi, qi, ki, light or energy is involved in qi mastery. This includes many of the M.A.P.S. Ambassadors, the Ambassadors of Light, the Buddhists, the qigong practitioners and many more. The qi masters from around the world are now uniting to promote healthy and happy living amongst all races and religions and we invite you to join us.

Quotes by Choa Kok Sui
»An intelligent person is not close minded. He does not behave like an ostrich burying his head in the ground trying to avoid new ideas and developments. An intelligent person is not gullible. He does not accept ideas blindly. He studies and digests them thoroughly, then evaluates them against his reason; he tests these new ideas and developments through experiments and his experiences. An intelligent person studies these ideas with a clear objective mind.«

Section 2

Research by Others

1. Dr Karl Graninger
2. Bigu & Qigong
3. Pranic Healing
4. Dr. Barbara Ann Moore
5. Dr. Juergen Buche
6. Prana Power – Pranayama
7. Divine Dance – The Whirling Dervish and Bioenergetics
8. Mitachondria
9. Acupuncture & Addictions.

I have chosen to include the following 9 fields of research here for various reasons. Firstly, because living from prana is not new, and secondly, because there has been a lot of research done with this over many years.

- From 1920 to 1949 Dr. Karl Graninger conducted extensive research on post war victims who survived not eating for long periods of time.
- The Pranic Healing Association headed by the Master Choa Kok Sui has done extensive research in their own field with prana power.
- The qigong ›bigu‹ phenomena.
- Even people who've never heard about living on light – like Charles Mills – have ›stumbled‹ across some interesting ideas through their own separate research.
- Dr. Barbara Ann Moore's journey came to my attention from Dr. Juergen Buche who also writes for us more on what he feels is good pre-process preparation. Juergen is an observer of our work in this field, is currently training his body into pranic nourishment, and as a natural therapist for many years is very interested in the phenomena of fasting and nutrition.
- Prana Power is best known as pranayama and so we explore this and various breath techniques before moving on to

- Divine dancing where we look at ways to boost our energy system a) via the divine dance of the whirling dervishes and b) via the practice of bioenergetics.
- Finally we move on to explore the work of Dr. Michael Smith in New York who has developed a program to deal with breaking our addictions. Dr. Mikio Sankey also provides a few insights on esoteric acupuncture and his suggestions for fitness.

All their research and stories have magically found their way to the Light Ambassadry, and we take this opportunity to say thank you to everyone who has taken the time to be involved with our work and research in this field. We recommend that readers also do their own research into this work if it interests them.

I think it is great to benefit from what others have discovered and so I am guided to guide you to look at the practice of Kriya Yoga as it was through this that Giri Bala was able to exist without food. Kriya Yoga is not something that I have personally studied, and like numerology and astrology, it is a science in itself that you may wish to study further.

The website: http://www.kriyayoga.com provides details on »The Metaphysical Physiology of Kriya Pranayama« – Kriya Yoga is called a scientific method of self-realization. Scientific, because it can be practised by anyone and if properly done, everyone will achieve the exactly same results: God-union and self-realization.

»Devotion to God, Love for God, opens the door to Divine energy, bliss entering through your soul into your spiritual body – even purging into your physical body and providing you with health and strength. But that is just a side-effect of Kriya Yoga never the purpose of it.«

So after we share the details of the above work we will then move on to take a detailed look at our own research by revealing a statistical analysis of the Light Ambassadry's Global Research Project no. 1.

FOURTEEN

The Work of Dr. Karl Graninger

As many familiar with our work are aware, since I began my personal journey with this, I have become fascinated by research. Over the last few years I have discovered so much since I wrote the first book 5 years ago which I would like to share in this next section.

The ability to live without physical nourishment from food is nothing new. As we now know, yogis have done this for millennia but so have many others throughout the world. Although at this point it could hardly be called a common lifestyle choice, everywhere I travel I hear stories about people who survived for long periods of time without taking any nourishment from food.

Because the body is an amazing biocomputer it seems that we can exist on very small quantities of nourishing food even without tapping into prana. Millions of junk food addicts attest to this as obesity reaches epidemic proportions in the Western world. However the quantity and quality of life is definitely affected by lack of proper nourishment unless one is getting it from an alternative source such as prana. Or is it?

When I first toured Germany in 1996, I began to hear amazing stories from people regarding their war experiences. In Frankfurt I met a woman who said that as a post war baby she and her sister had lived for months on just water as there was no food. Their mothers‹ milk lacked the necessary strength to nourish them and while her sister died at 6 months, ›miraculously‹ she survived.

Then I heard a story told by a man who lived close to an orphanage post war. He had rung my organizer and said, »Yes I know what Jasmuheen is saying is true!« When asked how he knew that, he replied that he used to visit the orphanage and they discovered some very interesting facts. Out of the groups of children who were slowly starving to death – as again there were very few rations available – one group stayed healthy. Upon investigation it seems that every morning the woman who looked after this particular group of children, sat with them as they all held hands and prayed to Jesus and

Mother Mary asking to be kept safe and healthy through this time. It seems their prayers were answered and this testifies to the power of our belief and faith.

Can I prove these stories? No? Are they true? I believe they are. Still, let's read on to cases that have been documented and researched more ›credibly‹...

In 1998, a journalist called Stephen Janetzko gave me an article that I believe was published in November 1976, by Germany's Esotera Magazine. It contained an in-depth article called »Sie wurden zu menschlichen Pflanzen« (or »They Changed to Human Plants«) and it appears to have been written by Von Dr. Albert A. Bartel.

Focusing on the work of Dr Karl Graninger, it also reports on Maria Furtner from Frasdorf in Bavaria who lived 52 years drinking only water from the mineral spring near her home. Maria underwent a three week observation period in Munich University Hospital to prove she didn't need to eat. When released from the hospital she walked the 60 km home in three days without problem.

Then there was Resl – Theresa Nuemann, who I mention in my first book. She lived in the Bavarian Forest in Konnersreuth. Her only food each day for 17 years was a consecrated wafer. X-rays showed her bowels to be pencil thin.

Then there was Anna Nassi, who was the child of a farmer from Deutenhofen in Bavaria. Her teacher told the researchers for the article that Anna lived for 6 years on only water.

After the first world war in Europe, Austrian specialist Dr. Karl Graninger noticed that although people had become prisoners of war, not all returned from the war camps unhealthy. For some the fasting, fresh air, meager diets and non-smoking was very beneficial physically.

The idea that some had starved and were quite ill after imprisonment while others were healthier, fascinated him. Consequently from 1920 to 1940 when he died, Dr Graninger conducted research into the phenomena of »inedia paradoxa« – or living without food. Finding 23 cases in the west of Europe, his test subjects were mostly women and children who were observed to live without food for both long and short periods of time. All subjects were found to have character attributes of patience, devotion and godliness.

While Dr Graninger and his colleagues did tests on their own subjects, these were abandoned after 12 days due to weight loss, fevers and weakness. They decided that the success of being able to survive only on water without these problems had a metaphysical link.

They concluded that the ›inedia-problem‹ had to be treated using set points:

- The mental-emotional attitude
- The physical relation
- The religious behavior
- The other cultural circumstances and reasons.

Comparing the experiences of the Ambassadors of Light from our own findings, with the research done by science and medicine, regarding what happens to the body with prolonged periods of fasting, I would definitely agree with the points above.

It is the very attributes of godliness and devotion that allow this phenomena to exist as it does. The key to this is the lifestyles that people follow each day that brings many ›miracles‹ beyond just the ability to go for long periods of time without food.

So before we begin to look in-depth at our findings, let us digress to the research of some others who have also been studying this phenomena. While the path chosen is different, the outcome appears to be the same.

FIFTEEN

Bigu and Qigong

Scientific Studies

In this chapter I would like to elaborate a little on the qigong phenomena of ›bigu‹ which first came to my attention via a transmission that was posted on the Living on Light Forum in the C.I.A. website. It seems that in the U.S., hundreds of people who have attended specific lectures given by a qi master became »breatharians« or »went into bigu« to use Chinese qigong term.

I would like to now include a little research on qigong for those unfamiliar with this practice. It comes from the website http://www.qigong.net/

»A long time ago in ancient China, people gradually realized through their struggle for survival that certain body movements, mental concentration and imagination, along with various ways of breathing, could help them to adjust some body functions. This knowledge and experiences were summarized and refined with time, and passed down through generations... shaping what is known today as the Traditional Qigong.

Qigong was involved in various life aspects of the ancients, harmonizing the relation between man and heaven. The emergence of great masters and various qigong achievements of the ancient times helped to form the basis for the formation of the Chinese culture, including the creation of the written language, the discovery of herbal medicine, and the emergence of various forms of art.

A common characteristic of qigong is the simultaneous training of the body and the mind. The dual cultivation of personality and essence is the main content of traditional qigong. Its style consists of both movements and stillness, and its method is characterized by the combination of the mind (consciousness), qi (bioenergy), the body, and the spirit.

Traditional Qigong is based on the principle of Virtue. Only by emphasizing virtue, being virtuous, and maintaining virtue, and with benign virtuous heart, virtuous character, and virtuous action can we achieve harmony with our surroundings and meet the three required states for practicing qigong: calm, tranquil, and natural. Virtue is the golden key to enter the gate of qigong.«

It seems that the state of ›bigu‹ occurs spontaneously in some qigong practitioners without obvious preparation apart from their daily lifestyle choice – in other words, they have not done any specific process. It is interesting that those who practice qigong are the only group that I have found who have done advanced studies on the state of living without food. Most of the research has been done in Chinese and finding out more has been difficult due to the language problems and also because these qigong practitioners wish to avoid controversy.

The qi masters have said that the present time is not yet appropriate for the widespread ›bigu‹ and that the West overall is not quite ready for this yet, even though lately the situation has improved markedly. They have also said that the reason they do not encourage people to seek the ›bigu‹ experience at this time, is that when one is in the ›bigu‹ state, one becomes very sensitive and, therefore, easily disturbed by the negative thoughts and wishes of the people who have difficulty – to put it mildly – accepting this phenomenon.

While bigu is once again an openly discussed topic in some qigong circles, according to my research source, one man was in bigu for over 3 and a half years, until the controversy started and practitioners were urged to come out of it. As I have said in previous chapters, you cannot hide the fact that you don't need to eat from people.

These qi masters have said not everybody handles this state gracefully; that they know of a few people, »Who became almost psychotic because of the extreme sensitivities on one hand and inappropriate reactions to the various phenomena to which they became exposed, as the result of their bigu state. On the other hand they were especially exasperated by the conflicts at work or with family that focused on their bigu status. On the plus side, they have spoken about incredible lightness and energy and need for very little sleep when in that state. Even now, all those who are officially not in bigu in certain qigong circles now eat very, very little.«

This is totally different to what we have experienced as the Ambassadors of Light are generally people who are focused on self mastery and do the prana program intentionally, while those who come into bigu do so almost accidentally. If unprepared for the power of the DOW, some individuals in the prana program can also become emotionally and mentally unstable, but this only occurs when they have these problems initially as the prana process can exacerbate this.

From my dealings with those who move in the ›bigu‹ circles, I am told that generally »people do not advertise their bigu status. One guy complained that he was in bigu 3 times, each time 3 weeks only and that each time he came out the day after he ›bragged‹ about it. A number of listeners nodded in agreement when he said this. Another person said that the moment he got angry was the end of his bigu experience.«

Apparently the benefits of qigong practice are so varied that the organization involved does not want to attract any more attention regarding the ›bigu‹ phenomena and I know how they feel.

All over the world I hear people saying, »Have you heard about these people who don't need to eat?« I never hear them say, »Have you heard about these people who are so tuned to DOW Power, that they no longer need to eat?« There is a huge difference.

Throughout history there have been many radiant masters on earth who have done, and can do, many amazing things, including qi emissions. The modern day equivalent would be pranic healing as put forward by the Master Choa Kok Sui.

Yes, we can receive energy emissions from wonderful masters or alternatively – with self-responsibility, daily discipline and a very particular lifestyle choice – we can find the master within (our DOW) and allow it to sustain us, teach us and guide us to experience our own highest potential as we are, after all, spiritual beings here to have a human experience.

To discover the Master within, one needs to be in daily silence as per meditation, and treat the body (and our environment) as a temple so that the Divine One Within (DOW) can radiate through us more powerfully. We need to also exercise mind mastery and choose to be aware of our thoughts, words and actions in each moment of every day.

There is no doubt that the living on light journey can be difficult unless one is physically, emotionally, mentally and spiritually fit – for which not everyone has the courage, dedication and discipline or even interest to be. Yet the results are well worth it and allow us to be independent from the need to be in the Presence of both physical and non-physical masters. Many of the M.A.P.S. Ambassadors feel that it is time to exhibit our own mastery on earth – right here, right now.

To many, it is a time of self-mastery and pragmatic living and being an effective force for positive progression in this world. We envisage a world where all are in their mastery, rather than all seeking a taste of the power and benefits of being in the presence of the few known masters in this world.

Finding, then experiencing the Divine One Within (DOW), has always been a challenge, and the living on light journey is just one small initiation to do with trusting our DOW enough to allow it to sustain us on all levels. Like any initiation, it can take years of preparation which often has little appeal to those seeking quick fixes from pills and potions to the challenges in our modern-day world.

Our work is thus focused on preventative medicine by experiencing the radiance from within and allowing our DOW to emit Itself throughout our own lives.

As shared previously, enough research has been done now to prove the power of qi or prana. On page 286 in the book »Scientific Qigong Exploration« by nuclear physicist Lu Zuyin, he shares further about the state of bigu and also about the experiments conducted on people who have not eaten for up to 6 years. »Bigu is a state in which a person maintains a normal life without taking any food. Standard Bigu means very little or no intake of water. Basic Bigu means only drinking water and juice. Non-standard Bigu means ingesting water, juice and occasionally juicy fruits and vegetable soups.«

I have personally experienced all three states of bigu by choice over the last 6 years. As the work of these qi masters is focused on other areas of health, they discourage publicity about bigu as they feel society is not ready to accept the bigu phenomena.

I first found out about bigu and the work of these wonderful qi practitioners via our website, the »Cosmic Internet Academy« which was created for two reasons. One as a library of free information that anyone can access and secondly, as a central place for networking services and information that focuses on positive personal and planetary progression as per the M.A.P.S. agenda. To achieve this we have five forums including the Living on Light Forum which the above information on bigu was originally posted into. It is probably our most active forum as many people are fascinated by human potential.

It seems to me from doing this research about ›research that has been done by others‹, that we are all agreed on a few basic things:

- Firstly, that being able to live free from the need for food requires a good degree of virtuous thoughts, words and actions.
- Secondly, that in order to be fed by ›divine energy‹; we must experience its existence via our prayers, programming or faith and devotions.
- That these DOW emissions can be interfered with by less virtuous external or internal forces – disbelief, anger, ego, etc.
- That without mind mastery and a strong DOW connection, people can become mentally unstable in the ›bigu‹ state as well as in the prana program.
- That whether we cease to need food via bigu or the prana program, all are still sometimes faced with difficult social adjustments.

To me, the practice of the qigong lifestyle and many other spiritual lifestyles, including the Buddhist Four Fold Noble Path, can be likened to the Light Ambassadors practice of DOW matching.

Some of the most powerful work being monitored within the field of prana is that of the Master Choa Kok Sui.

Prana Power and Qi Emission Research

Update 3 October 1999: from the book »Scientific Qigong Exploration« by Prof. Lu Zuyin and Independent Experiential Research by Jasmuheen with the Ambassadors of Light.

While science continues to see spirit and matter as separate they will not be able to fully understand the complexity of the quantum field. Qi is the essence of this field and qi emissions defy normal scientific study which requires the observer to be detached from the experiment. Because of the nature of qi, the observer and the observed are one and the same.

In-depth research has been done on external qi emissions but not enough on internal qi radiation, except we do know that virtuous living, meditation, prayer, programming, diet and exercise directly influence internal qi and its external radiation or emissions. Qi can also be termed prana power or DOW Power.

In my research, qi emissions relate to the field of advanced bioenergetics and the higher light science, which I will cover in greater depth in my new book »The Wizard's Tool Box«.

In the meantime it's great to now know that enough studies have been done to prove that magnetic field measurements coming from internal organs increase greatly when qi is increased through the above lifestyle.

Research has also been done on the effect of qi in improving and regulating the function of the digestive system; how it improves the function of the endocrine system; how it affects our capacity to create changes in the muscular and skeletal systems; how it improves the functions of the respiratory system and the circulatory system; plus how it improves and regulates the functions of the nervous system, as well as the power that qi has in adjusting skin temperature and controlling the body temperature center.

In Eastern philosophy qi is also also called prana and it is known that the body's natural production of prana increases through the raising of the kundalini energy via meditation and a yogic lifestyle. Because qi or prana runs on the neutrino level, it is very difficult to detect as qi is what fills the 99% of space in each atom.

Qigong healing is also not just psychological. It has objective effects independent of the psychological dimension. For example, x-rays of a bone fracture before a qi transmission, then an x-ray of a bone fracture after this transmission, shows how the fracture has been completely healed in a matter of hours or even minutes. Also it is known that qi emissions do not lose their intensity over distance and can be directed by mind, will and intention, hence their effectiveness in distant healing. By moving their inner vision into the magnetic field of a patient, a qi master can provide accurate diagnosis without actually seeing that patient, or being in the presence of that patient.

Traditional qigong theories hold that all things in the universe originate from qi, that everything contains qi, and that it fills the entire universe. This concurs with the Christian idea that God is omnipresent and omnipotent.

A qigong master's qi emanations and power is closely related to his/her own physical, mental and emotional state at the time of the qi transmission. Similarly, the Light Ambassadors‹ ability to be constantly fed by qi or prana depends on the same thing, which is why only those who maintain a high level of physical, emotional, mental and spiritual fitness can live on qi alone for long periods of time.

According to the book ›Qigong Scientific Exploration‹ page 245: »One may question how a person can live without food? First, the gastric and intestinal fluid of Qigong practitioners contain many nutrients. Second, everyone has nutrients stored in the body; yet most people do not how to transform and utilize them. Third, twenty or more days may pass without eating food, yet one can still be energized by absorbing self transformed high energy substances. It is not a question of eating, but rather of absorbing nutrients in a different manner. One can utilize the body's accumulated nutrition and transfer it to gastric and intestinal fluids for high quality nourishment. This also improves the digestive system.

Qigong practitioners do not merely absorb nutrients through their mouths and noses. They can use many other ways to absorb high energy substances for nourishment. Water, for instance, does not have to enter only through the mouth. Light does not have to enter only through our eyes (Like a plant that requires light photo-synthesis, light also has a function in our body.) A Qigong practitioner absorbs high energy substances from the universe that are unavailable to others. In this manner one can eat less, or even not eat for a length of time and still maintain a high energy level. When the absorption of high energy substances is enhanced, one may go without food for a long period of time. That is why Qigong is an ideal way to improve the digestive system of the body.«

Traditional qigong concerns itself with the effect of consciousness on an object and how the observer and the observed are connected, which is something traditional science has not yet accepted. Hence the qigong phenomena raises many questions for science which cannot be answered by current scientific theories. It has become my understanding, from my parallel research to the qigong studies, that until scientists begin to experience their DOW, many answers to the mysteries of life, evolution and creation, will remain hidden from them.

According to the scientists measuring qigong emissions and studies on the bigu state, many people in bigu live on less than 300 calories per day for years without any damage to their physical bodies. In October 1987 Ding Jing, aged 10, went into the bigu state and stayed there for over 6 years with a calorie intake of between 260 and 300 per day. We have found the same amongst the Light Ambassadors, and many continue to live very healthily on calorie intakes that are continuing to defy and challenge modern medical and scientific belief. Personally I have become healthier through bigu and have proved to myself beyond doubt that some other power is nourishing my body.

Dr. Yan Xin is one of the most respected and widely recognized qi masters in China and it is with his co-operation that such in-depth studies have been conducted and shared with the world. Many people have spontaneously entered into the bigu state as a result of being in his presence, and much research has been documented in the Chinese language. In fact over sixty books have been written covering his research into the power and benefits of qi emissions.   Professor Lu Zuyin's book is one of the first to be published in English and was only released in 1997 after a ten year period of research and experimentation. In 1987 I also began to record in my journals my conscious study and research on a) the power of internal qi radiation, b) how our lifestyles can alter the levels of this radiation, and c) how to control our external fields of reality by controlling our qi emissions internally and externally.

The difference between the experience of the Light Ambassadors and those in the bigu state is that we have sought this experience consciously by the practice of meditation and lifestyle choice that promote our becoming fit on all levels.

Like myself, Dr. Yan Xin, who I have not had the pleasure of meeting, has been guided to share this information with the world because of its benefits in the arenas of world health related challenges.

Both of us recognize that major research still needs to be done into the bigu phenomena and trust that as humanity focuses more on DOW Power, that this will naturally come to pass. We present our research to the interested parties in the fields of science and medicine and trust that relevant studies will be done in time and the benefits will then be more widely shared.

After completing the »Ambassadors of Living on Light« book I was given the »Scientific Qigong Exploration« manual, and hence the addition of this as a final comment.

Also, since I completed my research, another person has died from exposure to the elements and slight dehydration while undergoing the 21 day process. Some would say she died as a result of not adhering strictly to the guidelines in my first book on this matter, »Living on Light«. Others would say that her work was complete and she had come to the end of her contract and need to be here. Regardless of the »why's«, I cannot stress enough that we will continue to encourage all beings to take responsibility for their every thought, word and action in dealing with their own lives and others.

Yes, it is part of my blueprint to bring this information to the world. Yes, it is true that I am free from the need to live on food (as we know it) and that my DOW does, has and will feed me. Yes, it is also true that I was led into a field of research, as a result of my experience with my DOW, that may have many wonderful global benefits for health and hunger related issues.

Yes, it is true that whether people believe this or not, there are those who have experienced the power of the Divine enough to know, that when we truly have experienced something we cannot deny it, even though many others may not believe. I have no desire to convince the world of anything, only to share what I feel to be some most interesting research as it is my divine service to do so.

One final note; described as a contemporary sage by former president George Bush, Dr. Yan Xin's focus of research has long been on the benefits of applied qigong into the areas of cancer and AIDS. As a result of attending his lectures, thousands of people have been cured of many major illnesses. Like the Ambassadors of Light, Dr. Yan Xin encourages the respect for the old and care for those in need, while emphasizing the importance of a virtuous lifestyle and the value of love for others.

Compassion, love and selfless service are key factors in the establishment of personal and global paradise as we enter a new millennium on earth, as is the respect and honoring of all life. May we all enjoy our chosen journeys and may these benefit us all.

SIXTEEN

Pranic Healing

»A time will come when science will make tremendous advances, not because of better instruments for discovering and measuring things, but because a few people will have at their command great spiritual powers, which at the present are seldom used. Within a few centuries the art of spiritual healing will be increasingly developed and universally used.«
Gustaf Stromberg, Astronomer

We include the work of Choa Kok Sui here, as the Global Pranic Healing Association has been involved in testing the effects of pranic energy in healing for some time. The following is an excerpt from his book »Miracles through Pranic Healing« which he sent to me last year along with his other wonderful book »The Ancient Science and Art of Crystal Healing«. Both books are well worth reading for anyone interested in the healing power of prana.

PRANA or KI

»Prana or ki is that life energy which keeps the body alive and healthy. In Greek it is called pnuema, in Polynesian mana, and in Hebrew ruah, which means ›breath of life‹...

Basically, there are three major sources of prana: Solar prana, air prana, and ground prana. Solar prana is prana from sunlight. It invigorates the whole body and promotes good health. It can be obtained by sunbathing or exposure to sunlight for about five to ten minutes and by drinking water that has been exposed to sunlight. Prolonged exposure or too much solar prana would harm the whole physical body since it is quite potent.

Prana contained in the air is called air prana or air vitality globule. Air prana is absorbed by the lungs through breathing and is also absorbed directly by the energy centres of the bioplasmic body. These energy centers are called chakras. More air prana can be absorbed by deep slow rhythmic breathing than by short shallow breathing. It can be also absorbed through the pores of the skin by persons who have undergone certain training.

Prana contained in the ground is called ground prana or ground vitality globule. This is absorbed through the soles of the feet. This is done automatically and unconsciously. Walking barefoot increases the amount of ground prana absorbed by the body. One can consciously draw in more ground prana to increase one's vitality, capacity to do more work, and ability to think more clearly.

Water absorbs prana from sunlight, air, and ground that it comes in contact with. Plants and trees absorb prana from sunlight, air, water, and ground. Men and animals obtain prana from sunlight, air, ground, water, and food. Fresh food contains more prana than preserved food.

Prana can also be projected to another person for healing. Persons with a lot of excess prana tend to make other people around them feel better and livelier, however those who are depleted tend to unconsciously absorb prana from other people. You may have encountered persons who tend to make you feel tired or drained from no apparent reason at all.

Certain trees, such as pine trees or old and gigantic healthy trees exude a lot of excess prana. Tired or sick people benefit much by lying down or resting underneath these trees. Better results can be obtained by verbally requesting the being of the tree to help the sick person get well. Anyone can also learn to consciously absorb prana from these trees through the palms, such that the body would tingle and become numb because of the tremendous amount of prana absorbed. This skill can be acquired after only a few sessions of practice.

Certain areas or places tend to have more prana than others. Some of these highly energized areas tend to become healing centres.

During bad weather conditions many people get sick not only because of the changes in temperature but also because of the decrease in solar and air prana (life energy). Thus, a lot of people feel mentally and physically sluggish or become susceptible to infectious diseases. This can be counteracted by consciously absorbing prana or ki from the air and the ground. It has been clairvoyantly observed that there is more prana during daytime than at night. Prana reaches a very low level at about three or four in the morning.«

Exercises to draw energy from air, ground and trees are also covered in this book and he says: »Pranic breathing energizes you to such

an extent that your auras temporarily expand by 100% or more. The inner aura expands to about 8 inches of more, the health aura to about four feet or more, the outer aura to about two metres or more.«
According to Master Choa Kok Sui, pranic breathing is done by:

- Connecting your tongue to your palate
- Doing abdominal breathing (through the nostrils)
- Inhaling slowly and retain for one count
- Exhaling slowly and retain for one count before exhaling which is called »empty retention«.
- You can also inhale for 7 counts and retain for one count then exhale for 7 counts and retain for one count, or do 6 and retain for 3.

»In doing abdominal breathing, you expand your abdomen slightly when inhaling and contract your abdomen slightly when exhaling. Do not over-expand or over-contract your abdomen.«
In later chapters Choa Kok Sui goes on to say:
»Although science is not able to detect and measure life energy or prana, it does not mean that prana does not exist or does not affect the health and well being of the body. In ancient times, people were not aware of the existence of electricity, its properties and practical uses. But this does not mean that electricity does not exist. One's ignorance does not change reality; it simply alters the perception of reality, resulting in misperception and misconception of what is and what is not, what can be done and what cannot be done.«

Note from Jasmuheen: A description of prana as the universal life force energy is in my first book »Living on Light – Nutrition for the New Millennium«.

SEVENTEEN

Dr. Barbara Ann Moore

The fascinating story of Barbara Moore, M.D. of London, a modern-day »breatharian«, is a prime example of a person who has the conviction that breatharianism is a fact and not fiction. Here is the story, as quoted from Viktoras Kulvinskas' hard-to-find 1975 book »Survival into the 21st Century«

A heroic figure is Barbara Moore, M.D. of London. A news release by the London Sunday Chronicle dated 17 June 1951 reads:

»Twenty years ago she ate three normal meals a day. Slowly for 12 years she reduced her eating until she was keeping fit on one meal a day of grass, chickweed, clover, dandelion and an occasional glass of fruit juice. Five years ago she switched entirely to juices and raw tomatoes, oranges, grasses and herbs. Now she drinks nothing but a glass of water flavored with a few drops of lemon juice.«

She says: »There is much more in sunlight and air than can be seen by the naked eye or with scientific instruments. The secret is to find the way to absorb that extra – that cosmic radiation – and turn it into food«.

Each year she goes to Switzerland for the better air and climbs mountains on a diet of water from the streams. »You see«, she explains, »my body cells and blood have changed considerably in composition. I'm impervious to heat or hunger or fatigue.«

She continued: »Winter or Summer, even in Switzerland, I wear only a short sleeved jumper and skirt. In cold weather people stare at me. While they shiver in furs, I am warm. I'm as strong as a man and need only 3 hours sleep for mental relaxation. As my body is free of toxins, I'm never ill. I had to advance slowly from vegetarianism to uncooked fruit and then to liquid. Now I'm working towards Cosmic Food (Air).

I've passed the eating stage and could not eat if I desired as my alimentary canal has changed considerably. It is no longer a filthy tube and is unable to handle any fibre. Instead of thinking my life will end in ten years, I'm growing younger. Anyone can do the same if they try.

The tragedy is that eating is one of the great pleasures of life. To stop eating is to experience discomfort only when the body is adjusting itself to the new course which was the original course. I now find even the odor of food nauseating.«

Viktoras Kulvinskas continues writing in ›...21st Century‹: In 1961, Dr. Morris Krok of Durban South Africa, published ›Conquest of Disease‹, where he reproduced a part of a speech by Dr. Moore, which was written up in: »Life Natural, Ganeshganar, Padukottai, S. Ry, India. Nov. 1960«.

This is an extract:

»By experimenting on myself, I've found that neither energy nor body heat come[s] from food. It's a fact, paradoxical, yet true, that I spent three months in the mountains of Switzerland and Italy eating nothing but snow and drinking only snow water.

I was climbing mountains daily, not just fasting and sitting down and reading a book or gazing at the sky. No, I was hiking daily from my hotel to the mountains, often 15 miles, climbing up to seven or eight thousand feet, then coming down and walking another 15 to 20 miles to my hotel.

During my fasting, I climbed mountains daily; and if I could not on account of bad weather, I'd walk 30 to 40 miles. That proved it to me. Year after year I've done the same thing to find out whether it is true or not. For one year it may work and the next it may not work with the same body. So, I've done it year after year and find that neither energy nor heat of the body comes from physical food.

When I discovered this, I went a step further; I wanted to see whether I could live without food at all; not for two or three months, but for a longer period. I found this also possible, but not quite on an ordinary level, as it were. I can do that in the mountains, but it is more difficult when I come down to an ordinary level [sea level? J.B.]. I find the air is different. I hope in time to live entirely on air... I'm a very busy person and have little time to sleep. I'm never tired or hungry.«

Here is an update to Kulviskas report after Dr. Buche wrote to Dr. Krok to find out more information on Dr. Moore....

»Dear Juergen Buche,

I do not think Barbara Moore is still alive. The article which appears in Kulvinskas‹ book first appeared in late 1950's or early 1960's. The path to a healthy life or breatharianism is first to learn to live on one meal a day – sometime around midday but not later than 4 p.m. But if one is not hungry then this one meal can also be skipped.

In place of the evening meal drink only water so as to ensure that one goes to sleep on a clean, empty stomach. Replace breakfast with more water. The meal that is eaten can include some of the more concentrated foods such as nuts, a little dried fruit and some sprouted grains; fruit can be eaten half an hour before eating the concentrates, some green leafy vegetables and root vegetables such as carrots.

One must experiment with this meal by reducing the number of items eaten; for instance by just having nuts with some grated carrots. But what is eaten is a personal matter as there is no magic in any food. The magic is in the vitality and inherent intelligence of the body and mind which knows how to process and convert what is eaten in its own time and way.

It is my belief that more nonsense is spoken about health and nutrition than religion and the rituals one should follow. When one realizes that persons have attained long lives on a variety of foods, one can only infer from this that food is only a catalyst to stimulate the body's energy which never becomes part of tissue and bone. But too much food can deplete one's energy.«

With regards, Morris Krok
essence@iafrica.com ; P.O. Box 1129 Wandsbeck 3631
South Africa; Phone 31 864521 Fax 31 2670600

Juergen told me recently that he discovered that Barbara had been killed by a car while attempting to walk across the USA and also asked that if you know more about Barbara to contact him – Jasmuheen. The above information came from Dr. Juergen Buche:
e-mail at drbuche@bigfoot.com
http://www.odyssee.net/~expodome/moore.htm

EIGHTEEN

Affirmations and Pranayama –
Dr. Juergen Buche

Dr. Juergen Buche is a physician of natural medicine (Heilpraktiker – N.D.) with 15 years of experience in alternative cancer therapies, fasting and nature cures. Interested in the breatharian journey, he writes for us here on pre-process preparation.

»It is not enough to try to go without food. You must have a pretty good idea concerning the underlying reasons why you want to go without food and live on air. Are you doing this to gain notoriety or fame? Are you doing this because you are ill and want to heal, to regenerate, to rejuvenate? Are you properly prepared to actually draw from the great Universal Source the required sustenance to not only stay alive but to thrive in exquisite health and abundance?

To begin with, I found that daily affirmations are an absolute necessity in order to reinforce the paradigm of self-sufficiency with the SELF being the almighty I AM resident within you. I use the following: ›I AM limitless Love. I am the perfect manifestation of the omnipotent, loving, divine and infinitely benevolent power of the universe which sustains me, nourishes me and heals me on all levels regardless of whether I eat or not. I AM continually renewed on all levels and I AM spiritually, mentally and emotionally balanced. I AM the perfect expression of divine and limitless Love.‹

The above affirmation will sustain you and tune you. Be prepared to be pruned somewhat. Have no fear and dare to be different.

One other important ingredient, in my opinion, is to practice ›Inspirational Pranayama‹ in conjunction with the above affirmations. This is a simple breathing exercise that allows you to consciously tune into the Universal Cosmic Supply and withdraw, at will, all the sustenance you wish. I call it ›square breathing‹. It is extremely powerful to tune into the Universal Substance, prana, and consciously utilize this invisible, all-pervading, life-preserving, rejuvenating, primordial substance.

- Sit comfortably, straighten your back and empty your lungs completely
- Start by inhaling completely to the count of four (seconds)
- Retain your breath to the count of four
- Exhale completely to the count of four
- Keep your lungs empty to the count of four
- Repeat 2-6 ten times once a day or more often if desired.
- Increase the count by one second each week (don't be in a rush even if this appears simple)
- When the going gets rough (maybe at 10 seconds a leg) stay at that level until it is easy
- When taking a breath chant »Sooooo«
- When exhaling, chant »Hummmmmm«.

So, now you are on your way to become an accomplished Breatharian. Good for you! Can you estimate how much time, effort and money is wasted day in and day out – on eating and preparing food? Hardly! Eating is a very bad habit, it seems. People simply eat themselves to death. Experiments with rats have proven beyond a shadow of a doubt that halving their food intake doubles their life span.

The pranayama exercises I explain in my web site, if diligently conducted, can help in a large way to oxidize the catabolic cell refuse that inevitably results from rapid cleansing. The intake of large quantities of water in the morning are necessary to cope with toxic intestinal elimination which, by the way, will go on for months! Why burden the body's eliminative channels when you can accomplish the same in one quick daily ›flush‹? Most people who give up becoming a Light Eater don't do this because they can't handle the Breatharian effort – they give up because of too rapid detoxification and the unpleasantness of the toxic side-effects.

For this reason, I advocate that the aspiring Light Eater work up slowly to the stage where, over a period of several months, he eats less and less cooked and altered food and frugally ingests more and more LIVING foods, not necessarily in terms of quantity but of QUALITY. Even too much LIVING food can be toxic. Read Arnold Ehret's treatise »Rational Fasting« and you will know. The disciplined approach of asking »Is this food still ALIVE?« can progressively cleanse the bloodstream and every cell and tissue in the body. This takes time, more

136

than 21 days I am afraid, but the chances of the aspiring Breatharian staying with the program, having success, suffering less traumatic side effects, are vastly better.

One way, I have found, is a very good way to progressively allow the body to ADAPT to a new set of circumstances such as eating less and less. Withholding food from the body is fine for a short fast but indefinitely – that's another story. Try withholding opium from an opium addict. He will DIE! Therefore, consider this alternative – it leads to the same goal – INEDIA (living on air)...

1) Start by eating every alternate day, i.e. one day on one day off food. Switch to living on raw foods and eat frugally. Do this until you are perfectly comfortable with this regimen and have overcome major cravings.

2) Every three months, add a day of non-eating. Therefore, during month 4, 5 and 6 you will not eat for two days and eat for one. At this stage, stick to fruits on your third day, the eating day. You can mix fruits but not at the same meal. If you eat two days in a row for any reason (oversupply of ripe fruit for instance), then fast for the next three (3) days (not four). Do this for three months or until you are perfectly at ease with this regimen. Overcome all addictions and food cravings. Simplify your life – be in a survival mode.

3) Every three months or so (depending on your success and your body's rate of adaptability) add another non-eating day until you eat only once every seven days. Stick to one kind of fruit only on that eating day and eat frugally. Maintain the affirmations and pranayama. You need not drink much but if cleansing processes are extreme, cut back one fasting day and stay there until you can easily do it. During cleansing reactions you need to drink a lot to help with eliminations.

4) When you can successfully not eat for six days and only eat frugally on the seventh then you are ready to take the plunge into Breatharianism. You are ready to stay on being ›fed by the light‹. Don't think of it as food. Think of this sustenance as LIVING LOVING SUSTENANCE.«

Thank you Juergen.

For readers interested in finding out more, Juergen's website is: http://www.ucinet.com/~knickers/breathar.htm. It is a gold mine of helpful information for cancer patients. Together with Kathy Swan, nutritional counselor, he actively promotes http://seasilver.thread-net.com , a site which has an ideal health solution for those who need fast and complete healing. He altruistically has helped thousands with free naturopathic Internet advice for the past three years, however, he will not diagnose nor prescribe. He can be reached at drbuche@big-foot.com

I would like to add to Juergen's approach of asking »Is this food still alive?« For many, the practice of dieting to lose weight consumes many waking hours for many people. Over the years I have personally found that the saying »if it is not raw don't eat it« to be a very powerful rule and a great way to lose weight and detox the body simultaneously without feeling as though you are going hungry as in normal fasting. The stomach shrinks more slowly and detox is not as extreme. This is a great short-term or long-term ›diet‹ technique.

NINETEEN

Prana Power – Pranayama

»For the rhythm of thy breath is the key of knowledge
which doth reveal the Holy Law.«
The Essene Gospel of Peace – book 1

People often ask me if it is necessary to practice pranayama or Kriya Yoga in order to be nourished by the Divine. I say that as long as we are firmly connected to DOW Power and are free of toxic thinking, then nothing is necessary as it happens automatically. However, as some of the Light Ambassadors seem to go in and out of this zone of power day to day, the stronger our spiritual practices, the easier pranic nourishment is to maintain.

Personally, I love to breathe deeply and consciously every day. I breathe deeply when I am in the shower, or in the car, or in the shopping centres – I breathe deeply everywhere, all day, in one long meditation. I love to sit in the sun in the early morning or late afternoon and breathe, breathe, breathe. When I have been doing bioenergetics and opening up all the lightbody grid lines, sitting in the sun, breathing deeply and visualizing the energy of Lord Helios fill these grid lines with an amazing blast of RA power, it is exhilarating. It's like a cosmic petrol pump to recharge my batteries!

When we squint our eyes we can see prana sparkling in the air. Prana is everywhere, and as we mentioned earlier, some sources say that the majority of our nutritional needs can be fulfilled by the way we breathe. Pranayama involves controlling the breath which in turns controls the effectiveness of many of the functions of the body. Long slow breaths slow the heart, deep breathing warms us; oxygen eliminates pain, slow breathing promotes health and longevity.

In the Encyclopedia Britannica, it is written: »Sanskrit PRANA (›breath‹), in Indian philosophy, the body's vital ›airs‹, or energies. A central conception in early Hindu philosophy, particularly as expressed in the Upanishads, prana was held to be the principle of vitality and

ity and was thought to survive as a person's »last breath« for eternity or until a future life.«

In this chapter I wish to look at ancient practices that boost personal power and increase the radiation of our qi emissions. The first is a more detailed look at pranayama, then we offer a few breath techniques including diaphragmatic breathing with raw foodist David Wolfe. Then finally in the next chapter we look at the techniques of the whirling dervishes and touch on Kriya Yoga.

1. Prana and the Vedas

The following information comes from the website http://www.sit.wisc.edu/~fmorale1/prana.htm, and we include it here as it provides more detail on the subject of prana in yogic tradition.

»All that exists in the three heavens rests in the control of Prana.
As a mother her children, oh Prana, protect us and give us splendor and wisdom.«
Prashna Upanishad II.13

»There is an old Vedic story about Prana that we find in various Upanishads. The five main faculties of our nature – the mind, breath (prana), speech, ear and eye – were arguing with each other as to which one of them was the best and most important. This reflects the ordinary human state in which our faculties are not integrated but fight with each other, competing for their rule over our attention. To resolve this dispute they decided that each would leave the body and see whose absence was most missed.

First speech left the body but the body continued though mute. Next the eye left but the body continued though blind. Next the ear left but the body continued though deaf. Mind left but the body continued though unconscious. Finally the Prana began to leave and the body began to die and all the other faculties began to lose their energy. So they all rushed to Prana and told it to stay, lauding its supremacy. Clearly Prana won the argument. Prana gives energy to all our faculties, without which they cannot function. Without honoring Prana first there is nothing else we can do and no energy with which to do anything. The moral of this story is that to control our faculties the key is the control of Prana.

Prana has many levels of meaning from the breath to the energy of consciousness itself. Prana is not only the basic life-force, it is the master form of all energy working on the level of mind, life and body. Indeed the entire universe is a manifestation of Prana, which is the original creative power. Even Kundalini Shakti, the serpent power or inner power that transforms consciousness, develops from the awakened Prana.

On a cosmic level there are two basic aspects of Prana. The first is the unmanifest aspect of Prana, which is the energy of Pure Consciousness that transcends all creation. The second or manifest Prana is the force of creation itself.

The human being consists of five koshas or sheaths: Annamaya kosha; Pranamaya kosha; Manomaya kosha: Vijnanamaya kosha; Anandamaya kosha.

Pranamaya Kosha:
The Pranamaya Kosha is the sphere of our vital life energies. This sheath mediates between the body on one side and the three sheaths of the mind (outer mind, intelligence and inner mind) on the other and has an action on both levels. It meditates between the five gross elements and the five sensory impressions.«

The best English term for the Pranamaya kosha is probably the ›vital sheath‹ or ›vital body‹, to use a term from Sri Aurobindo's Integral Yoga. Pranamaya kosha consists of our vital urges of survival, reproduction, movement and self-expression, being mainly connected to the five motor organs (excretory, urino-genital, feet, hands, and vocal organ).

The Five Pranas
Pranamaya kosha is composed of the five Pranas. The one primary Prana divides into five types according to its movement and direction. This is an important subject in Ayurvedic medicine as well as Yogic thought. (Prana; Apana; Udana; Samana; Vyana.)

The Vedas say that mortals eat food with Apana, while the Gods eat food with Prana. The mortals are the physical tissues. The immortals are the senses. These take in food via Prana itself. Right food sustains Apana.

While all Pranayama aids in this regard, the most important is alternate nostril breathing, which aids in the balance of the right and left Prana currents. Regular alternate nostril breathing is the most important method for keeping our Pranas or energies in balance... Indeed as the Vedas say we are all under the control of Prana. Prana is said to be the Sun that imparts life and light to all and dwells within the heart as the Self of all creatures. Prana in us makes us live and allows us to act. This is one of the great secrets of Yoga.«

Full details of the Koshas are provided in the website mentioned.

2. Techniques and Effects of Pranayama

From: http://www.lavecchia.com/pranayama2.html

- Note: Pranayama training demands mastery over the asanas and the strength and discipline arising from them.
- Before starting pranayama the bowels should be evacuated and the bladder emptied.
- Preferably pranayama should be practiced on an empty stomach.
- Light food may be taken half an hour after finishing.
- The best time for practicing is in the early morning before sunrise and after sunset. According to the Yoga Pradipika, pranayama should be practiced four times a day, in the early morning, noon, evening and midnight.

Ujjayi Pranayama (victory breath)
- Sit in any comfortable position.
- Keep back erect and equal pressure on the seat bones.
- Stretch the arms out and rest the back of the wrists on the knees.
- Join index finger and tips of the thumbs. (This is known as Jnana Mudra, the symbol of knowledge. The index finger represents the individual soul and the thumb the Universal Soul, union = knowledge)
- Close the eyes and look inwards.
- Exhale completely.
- Take a slow, deep steady breath through both nostrils. The passage of the incoming air is felt on the roof of the palate and makes a sound (saaa). This sound should be heard.

142

- Fill the lungs up, be careful not to bloat the abdomen in the process of inhalation.
- The entire abdominal area from the pelvic wall up to the sternum should be pulled back towards the spine.
- Hold the breath for a second or two.
- Exhale slowly, deeply and steadily, until the lungs are completely empty. Keep the abdomen tight for a few seconds, relax the diaphragm slowly. The outgoing air should brush the upper palate making a (ha).
- Wait a moment before drawing in another breath.
- Repeat the cycles for 5-10 minutes keeping the eyes closed.
- Lie on the floor in Savasana (corps pose).

Effects

This type of Pranayama opens the lungs, removes phlegm, gives endurance, soothes the nerves and tones the system. Ujjayi without the retention of the breath and reclining position of the body is ideal for people with high blood pressure or coronary troubles. Be sure to consult your acting physician.

3. Pranayama – Breath Technique with David Wolfe

From his book »The Sunfood Diet Success System« page 316, David writes, »First and foremost, the breath controls the energy level in the body. We know that everything is energy – matter is just a form of frozen energy. The more oxygen available to your cells, the more energy you have to accomplish your goals and the less food you desire. Many people overeat because they are not breathing properly.

If you feel hungry, sick, tired or worn out, a good way for you to quickly rejuvenate yourself is to go outside and take 30 deep diaphragmatic breaths.... In my opinion, the best pattern for deep diaphragmatic breathing, which I have used daily since age 19, is the following 1:4:2 ratio:

- Breathe in (through the nose), for a multiple of 1 count. The nose simultaneously filters and humidifies the air we breathe. The cribiform plate above the septum in the nose also regulates the temperature of the air entering the lungs.

- Hold that breath for a multiple of 4 counts. This fully oxygenates and stimulates the body.
- Breathe out (through the mouth), for a multiple of 2 counts. The outbreath releases toxins.
- An example of this ratio: Breathe in for 6 seconds; hold that breath for 24 seconds; breathe out for 12 seconds.

Also try this yogic breath technique:
- Breathe in (through the nose), for a multiple of 1 count.
- Hold that breath for a multiple of 1 count.
- Breathe out (through the mouth), for a multiple of 1 count.
- Hold the lungs empty for a multiple of 1 count. this creates a vacuum suction which draws toxins out of the tissues on the following inhalation.
- An example of this ratio: Breathe in for 6 seconds; hold that breath for 6 seconds; breathe out for 6 seconds. Hold lungs empty for 6 seconds.

›Breath power‹ is well known in meditation circles, as I wrote in my book »In Resonance« in the chapter called »The Breath of Life«: »It has been said that if we were to change nothing – not our eating, exercise or thinking patterns and habits – except our breathing pattern, we could radically alter our life span..... if we reduce the number of breaths that we breathe per minute from say 15 to five, we will triple our lifespan...

Apart from aiding in maintaining and restoring health and vitality and increasing longevity, the main benefit of seeking to experience the ›breath of life‹ (the energy that sustains us) is that, due to Its very pure and perfect nature, when we contact and experience It, we are given a range of experiences from deep inner peace, total complete relaxation and better sleep, to the overwhelming feelings of joy and bliss of nirvana or Samadhi.«

As Choa Kok Sui says, »We get most of our ki or life energy from the air we breathe... We constantly drain our life energy or ki by our every thought, every act of will or motion of muscles. In consequence replenishment is necessary, which is possible through breathing and other helpful practices.«

TWENTY

Divine Dance –

The Whirling Dervish and Bioenergetics

In my book »In Resonance« there are more techniques on breathwork, however we recommend that you practise until you find one that suits you. Just know that different breath techniques can be used for different purposes. Deep rhythmic breathing, keeping the inhale connected to the exhale, is always popular. If everyone in the world did deep, slow connected breathing in times of stress there would be a lot less dis-ease. If we all did this daily, and practised mind mastery, there would be no disease.

Once we are able to establish a pattern of deep, fine, connected breathing we gain the key to balance in the dance of the Whirling Dervish. To avoid dizziness you focus on the in breath as drawing up and the exhale as releasing down and out. This up and down focus keeps you centred and balanced.

The Divine Dance of the Whirling Dervish

Discovering the dance of the whirling dervish has been a most exciting revelation for me, and is an amazing way to boost our systems energetically. I had been in training for nearly two years learning about bioenergetics and how to apply it to dance, when my DOW guided me to start spinning.

Intuitively I realized that spinning left to right as in the first technique of the Five Tibetan Rites, would effectively energize my chakra system and also allow me to gain information from Universal Mind. One evening after spinning easily for over an hour without dizziness, I realized that I had been a dervish in another lifetime as it all came so naturally to me, and so I began to do some research.

Some say that the 700 year old dance of the whirling dervishes is one way of »polishing the human heart and allows the soul to be free to commune with the divine«.

The dance of the dervish originated with the poet Mevlana Celaledin Rumi in the 13th century and is said to be an ecstatic dance of surrender that also requires great centred discipline. According to the website: http://www.bdancer.com/med-guide/culture/dervish.html

»Dervish literally means ›doorway‹. When what is communicated moves from presence to presence, darshan occurs, with language inside the seeing. When the gravitational pull gets even stronger, the two become one turning that is molecular and galactic and a spiritual remembering of the presence at the center of the universe. Turning is an image of how the dervish becomes an empty place where human and divine can meet. «

A secret turning in us makes the universe turn. Head unaware of feet, and feet head. Neither cares. They keep turning. Rumi Coleman Barks, translator, *The Essential Rumi*, Harper San Francisco, 1995.

One Spinning technique

»During this solemn religious ceremony it is believed that the power of the Heavens enters into the upward extended right palm and passes through the body and leaves the lower left palm to then enter into the Earth. The dervish does not retain the power nor is he to direct it. He accepts that he is the true instrument of God and therefore he does not question the power that comes and leaves him.

There has been some discussion on which way to spin. My (Thais Banu) research has led me to this simple breakdown:

- Begin slowly and build up and then return slow again.
  Start walking a turn to your right (clockwise) with your arms down at your sides.
- After several complete turn bring your Right palm up (arm is fully extended) and your Left palm down (arm is fully extended).
- Continue turning to the Right several times. (The Sufi I broke this down from preferred 7 complete turns.)
- NOW raise your Left hand half way above your shoulder but not as high as your head. At the same time tilt your head so the Left ear is to the Left shoulder. Continue turning to the Right.
- Drop your head forward so that your chin is close to your chest and your eyes look down at the floor. Arms remain high and you

are still turning to the Right. Slant your head to the Right, your right ear rests close to the right shoulder and you are looking up to the Right hand. Continue turning to the Right.

- Drop your head to the back and look up at the Heavens. Continue turning to the Right.

Always begin the turn to the Right. Only after several full turns do you switch arm positions and reverse the turning to the Left (counterclockwise). One should always end with full turns to the Right. The head swings and circles may move in the opposite direction of the turn. I gladly welcome any comments or additional sharing of knowledge on this fascinating form of Middle Eastern Dance.«

Peace, Thais Banu – Editor and Publisher of »Unveiled Thoughts«

In my personal experience, the dance of the whirling dervish allows for a lot more than has been commented on above. A complete range of mudras and bioenergetic exercises with light rays can also be applied while spinning, and once you are centred via the breath, you can control the spin speed easily at will.

With enough momentum, you actually feel as though you are standing still in the middle of a tornado while the physical body revolves itself in a powerful energy vortex. It feels like your body is a cosmic corkscrew where energy flows through you into the earth. It truly does feel as though you are weightless, defying gravity and as if you are standing in the centre of the universe. Keeping stable and balanced does take discipline and skill but is easily attainable with practice. Adding prayer, programming and bioenergetics makes it more powerful again and of course the purpose of why you wish to do this and what these techniques can be used for needs to be examined.

I recommend that you build up your spin speed and time spent doing this, as if you do this too quickly, you can end up feeling as though your insides are still spinning long after you have stopped. Balance can be controlled also by rocking on each foot side to side and this is a good way to come out of a high speed spin.

I cannot recommend this exercise highly enough as not only does it energize our complete chakra system but it does bring a sense of darshan with the Divine.

Imagining that light is shooting out from all your chakra vortexes and moving into all cells as you spin is also invigorating. Remember that research has shown that the body cannot tell the difference between an event that is ›real‹ and one that is imagined so redefining yourself and boosting your energy fields in this manner can be great fun and excellent exercise.

(More on this Divine Dance can be found in the »Wizard's Tool Box«.)

Bioenergetics

Many know of the term bioenergetics from the work by Wilhelm Reich. Understanding the mind/body connection and seeing us all as spiritual beings here to have a human experience, the way I work with bioenergetic principles takes Reich's and Dr. Alexander Lowen's work to another level.

The website www.bapera.com.br/lowen_i.html comments on this field: »Lowenian work is supported in three points: the first is self-consciousness, to feel one's emotions and feelings; the second is the expression of those feelings, self-expression; and finally the integration of both through self-possession.«

Our work is similar in that, »In the path of Bioenergetic Analysis« two concepts become fundamental: grounding and surrender. »πThe first means rooting, it is the self-sustenance that points to the necessity of a true exchange of energy between the human body and the earth that sustains it. The second concept, surrender, means a profound giving in to oneself, a deep relaxing of the defensive processes ingrained in the organism which maintain the traumatic situation and hinder the vital pulsing of the organism. The road from illness to health goes from an archaic re-action to real action, from surrender to redemption. A third and more recent concept is gracefulness, which to Lowen is related to spirituality.«

Combining bioenergetics with this Divine Dance results in what I have come to call the IMUR Program. Based on Rumi's work and adding a futuristic twist with the Higher Light Science of bioenergy work, we can achieve many things from personal energy field tune-ups, to environmental field control to universal field control.

IMUR stands for Impeccable Mastery of the Universal Realms – it is a program for Kosmic Knights who are committed to service within the Universal Paradigm. More of this program is covered in part 2 of »The Wizard's Tool Box«.

One of the greatest gifts that we can give ourselves is complete mastery over our molecular structure and all of our energy fields. Mastery is about being empowered to exist in a state of pure health, constant regeneration, and freedom from dis-ease on all levels of our being. To be free from dis-ease we need to learn how to tune ourselves. Like taking our car to our mechanic for a tune-up, we can realign/recharge our energy fields and create perfect health within our physical, emotional, mental and spiritual bodies.

Apart from conscious programming, and indulging in quality thinking, quality feeling, and quality feeding (either from pranic nourishment or live food), there are also various practical exercises we can do daily to strengthen our energy fields and create personal and then global paradise. There is no need not to have radiant health in paradise, and bioenergetics is used to take control over body energetically as we learn how to plug more into DOW Power.

Bioenergetics is about environmental field control and is a system of mudras and movements that I choose to set to music for fun. It is part of the Higher Light Science and can be applied via thought, will and intention and action to create some powerful energy dynamics in our world. It allows those living on light to remain uninfluenced by random energies in the world and exist in this sensitive state in a manner that is positive to them and others.

After taking two years in daily training with basic bioenergetic techniques, these have now been added into the dance of the whirling dervish to really bring in some power. In this method, we take the old and new techniques and combine them to make a powerful energy vortex-type ›chamber‹ for healing, telepathic and holographic communication, for re-energizing and more.

A regular bioenergetics routine combined with the Luscious Lifestyles Program, will radically alter our energy fields and enhance and redefine our natural emanation. Full details of this form of field control is covered in part two of »The Wizard's Tool Box.«

TWENTY ONE

Mitachondria – Research by Charles Mills

Dear Jasmuheen,
My name is Charles Mills.

Last year (1998) I completed a Bachelor of Social Science degree with a major in Psychology (7 units out of 18). Also, one third of the units which made up this degree were taken in Philosophy, with others in statistics and sociology. During the course of my studies I formulated a theory regarding cellular energy generation, which I describe as follows:

A: Whilst studying a biology course as part of the Psychology major, I came across two interesting points in a textbook:

That the producers of energy within the human cell are (currently recognized to be) the Mitachondria. That the Mitachondria have different DNA to the cellular DNA (the mitachondrial DNA is passed solely from the mother unlike that of cellular DNA which is a combination of the DNA from both parents), and that therefore Mitachondria are an organism which has been introduced into the cell at some time in the past.

B: From the second point above, it occurred to me that:

1. Mitachondria seem to act much like parasites.
2. That there would appear to have been a time (i.e, before the »parasitic infection« by mitachondria) when human cells (I don't know anything about animal cells) functioned without mitachondria.

C: From points B.1. and B.2. it follows that:

There would appear to have been a time (i.e, before the »parasitic infection« by mitachondria) when human cells produced energy without the use of mitachondria. That there are at least two different ways that cells can acquire energy (one via mitachondria, one without mitachondria).

D: It seems to me that those who might want to take a position regarding the above aspect of cellular energy acquisition might be divided into three camps:

1. Those who simply reject the textbook assertion that cellular energy can be acquired without mitachondria.
2. Those who have no idea how cells acquired energy prior to the introduction of mitachondria.
3. Those who have specific views on how cells acquired energy prior to the introduction of mitachondria.

E: It would seem that those in D.1. would have a healthy portion of the scientific community arguing against them.

F: Those whose views fall into D.3. (e.g. Breatharians who believe that cellular energy can be derived from cosmic energy) would probably have historically experienced scathing criticism from those in D.2. (as seems to be typical of »scientific« criticism of those who operate outside of the physical sciences). However, those who fall into the D.2. camp would appear to have no grounds for disparaging those who fall into the D.3. camp as they both agree on B.1.and B.2.

G: From the above, it seems that Breatharians have as much of a case for their position as anyone else, based on the available scientific evidence and rules of logic and argument.

H: From a new-found Breatharian-friendly point of view I wonder if: Humans originally acquired cellular energy from some form of cosmic energy, and did not eat at all (the »garden of Eden« age). By eating (the metaphorical »apple«), humans ingested the mitachondria »parasite«. The ingestion of the mitachondria parasite caused the cells to change the way energy was acquired by the body (and humans were thereby »cast out of the garden of Eden»).
Each generation receives the curse of the parasite (»original sin») from the previous generation. Individuals can be cleansed of the parasite (»original sin») by specific rites (»baptism»). When scientists attempt to destroy the mitachondria in the cell, the cell also dies. However, I wonder if the Breatharian practices are a way of destroying the mitachondria without fatally harming the cell.

I: It is fascinating how the ideas in H. fit so neatly with the biblical and religious stories regarding the garden of Eden, original sin and baptism.

J. It should be fairly easy to determine if there is any compelling scientific evidence to support this theory: Perhaps a blood sample from a Breatharian could be analyzed by a Pathology Laboratory to see if mitachondria are present within the cells or not.

If a Path Lab is unable to perform such an analysis, I noticed on the Internet that the James Cook University, North Queensland, has a Transmission Electron Microscope (in their Advanced Analytical Centre, I think) which they suggest can be used to investigate mitachondria.

Well, the above is a basic run-through of the theory. I am sure that with more work it could be presented in a more readable and interesting way and with the logic tightened up. There are a number of angles (such as the parallels with religious metaphor) which add additional interest to the basic issues.

I would be very interested to hear what you think of this theory, and whether you are interested in further investigation along these lines.

The point is that there may be ways of causing cells to revert to their earlier method of generating energy. It would be simpler if this involved killing off the »parasitic« mitachondria, as this would be relatively easier to detect. However, the reversion could theoretically only require the »switching off« of the mitachondria energy generation reliance and this would be more difficult to confirm.

With respect to accreditation, reference to my details as follows would be gratefully appreciated:

Charles Mills (B.Soc.Sc.), who can be contacted at: catfish@catfish.com.au

So while Charles recognizes that more research needs to be conducted into this »theory«, perhaps readers interested in this field of research may wish to liaise with Charles directly.

Acupuncture and Addictions

Dr. Michael Smith and Dr. Mikio Sankey

After I had realized that the ability to live free from food is just the result of a specific lifestyle choice, I then realized that if this lifestyle could free us from an addiction to food, then perhaps it could free us from other addictions as well. As ›cosmic co-incidence‹ would have it, I was in the middle of formulating a Heroin Addiction Program for Passionate Youth that I call H.A.P.P.Y.; when further information came to light.

I had been using a formula of:

1. Prayer and commitment;
2. Programming and rescripting;
3. Passion and creativity to stimulate desire
4. Lifestyle choice – friends, foes and different reality movies;
5. Meditation and cosmic connections.

However, once the foundations for these had been laid, I was guided to look at the addict's energy lines, which included their light-body and all their bodies.

With the subject I was working with – a young man I will call Percival – I soon realized that his system was on the verge of total collapse. His light was dimming fast and his system really needed a boost. His DOW had been telling him in his meditations that he needed acupuncture and I had also received the same message.

In working with addictions it is always great to work DOW to DOW as this by-passes the personalities and provides better support for the initiation and our role in service.

Cosmic co-incidence brought us to the St Mary's Church connection. This is a program in Brisbane, Australia, that is funded and voluntarily staffed by a group of dedicated acupuncturists and alternative therapists. Using a five point program of acupuncture needles and a twelve step lifestyle program, they can help anyone who is addicted to anything break their addiction. Based on the work of Dr.

Michael Smith of the ›Lincoln Detox‹ center in the Bronx, New York, USA, this program has been used successfully prior to being brought into Australia and implemented by this group.

I mention this here as those seeking to break their food – or any other – addiction prior to undergoing the prana process may wish to look at using a program like this. Details can be obtained from their program co-ordinator Deirdre Trocas Ph: +61 7 3856 2409. Their clinic, which is open at St. Mary's Church in West End in Brisbane each day, is also seeking support and donations.

Percival is loving the addition of this treatment and his lifestyle is slowly changing. Like all of us, he understands that only his desire to be free from this addiction can make him so. Everything else is a tool to bridge into a new life.

I recommend that you seek to do the acupuncture 5 point program along with their 12 step plan for the treatment of any addiction that you may be wishing to free yourself from.

As my good friend, LA-based doctor Dr. Mikio Sankey, says in his new book »Esoteric Acupuncture – Gateway to Expand Toward Healing«: »A primary focus in esoteric acupuncture is the balancing of qi and the qi flow within the various body systems.«

Dr. Sankey uses acupuncture patterns that establish »a strong and harmonious connection with the higher spiritual realms« and uses Chinese vibrational medicine.

Dr. Sankey's new program of esoteric acupuncture is a result of over 30 years of his personal research and experience of the ancient wisdom. Combining this with Chinese medicine, Mikio also applies his skills as an iridologist, naturopath, reflexologist and acupuncturist. Dr. Sankey promotes mind/body mastery through the practice of yoga, tai chi, qi gong, meditation, pranayama and a healthy vegetarian diet of fresh, organic foods. A diet free from alcohol, sugar, caffeine, and drugs and nicotine is also recommended for optimum health.

Yes, acupuncture, like the 5 point ear system that Percival is currently undergoing, will boost the energy fields of the bodies. But this treatment needs to be supported by what Mikio and countless others recommend, that is, a refinement of our basic lifestyles. Homeopathy and kinesiology will also help with balancing the emotional bodies as we release ourselves from our addictions – including our addiction to food.

The Light Ambassadors recommend that you consult with alternative therapists and those teaching holistic medicine to help you to create your own luscious lifestyle. Look at diet, meditation, exercise and all the things we discuss in the luscious lifestyles chapters. Many Ambassadors have found that while psychotherapy sessions may be beneficial for the treatment of emotional addictions, the practice of luscious lifestyle programs also needs to be done. Healthy diets, regular meditation, daily exercise and creativity all help to change habitual patterns by replacing them with other time- consuming habits that are more positive. Filling moments affectively and beneficially is a learned skill.

Regardless of whether we are addicted to pharmaceutical or recreational drugs, or to sex, love, meaningful work, pleasure or food, alcohol or cigarettes, the only question to ask is: »Do our addictions allow us to be healthy, happy individuals?«

If the answer is no, then take advantage of the wonderful network of talented alternative therapists now serving in the world.

For some, adjusting to life after the prana program can also feel like a junkie releasing an addiction. Ankara, one of the Light Ambassadors from Sweden writes....

»At first I heard a voice every morning saying, ›I'm living without eating‹. I felt special, grateful for being taken care of by the divine, almost afraid to tell others, not wanting to talk about it. Then came a period when I realized that I could drink milk chocolate and taste things that I used to be too sensitive to before. The one that never allowed herself what she was longing for (the good things in life; symbolized by ice-cream, chocolate cookies) woke up. Admitting I DO WANT THIS! And the child that never got enough of the goodies when they once came, joined in: I WANT MORE!

After that one, the disciplined one took over again. STOP IT! NOW! You are not allowed to taste anything for at least a week. Then the divine one came back, saying: Don´t focus on food, focus on what makes your heart sing. AND I LAY BACK IN THE ARMS OF THE DOW and let these voices go on talking, and felt sure that if I had been taken care of so far, it would all work out for my highest good also in the future. LLL – Ankara«

TWENTYTHREE

Research and Statistical Analysis

»The greatest good you can do for another is not just
to share your riches, but to reveal to him his own.«
Benjamin Disraeli, British Statesman and Author

Over the last year or so we have been gathering as much data
as possible about people who have undergone the 21 day process. Using
a specifically designed and very detailed questionnaire – as per the one
in the appendixes at the back of this book – we sought to find out the
following:

Please note we have listed only the yes answers.

1. **Please state your initial reason/s for doing the 21 day process:**
a) 88% did it because it just felt right
b) 75% did it to experience the Divine One Within (DOW) more
    clearly
c) 21% did it for health reasons
d) 11% did it for dietary reasons
e) 3% did it for economic reasons
f) 12% did it out of curiosity

2. **How did you do the process**
a) 45% did it on their own
b) 40% did it with friends
c) 47% had someone overseeing them either daily or weekly

3. **How much weight did you lose during the process?**
a) 35% lost less than 2 kilos
b) 23% lost between 2 and 5 kilos
c) 27% lost between 5 and 10 kilos
d) 22% lost more than 10 kilograms

BEFORE YOU UNDERWENT THE 21 DAY PROCESS

4. **66% said that they programmed their body weight to stabilize before or during the process**
a) 43% said that this worked to their satisfaction
b) 16% of those who said that it didn't, said that they addressed their beliefs around not eating and subsequent weight loss

5. **What other preparation did you choose to undergo prior to the 21 day process?**
a) 58% said they researched all that they could on the subject of living on light
b) 66% said they slowly refined their diet until it was very light and simple
c) 37% exercised their body regularly to make it strong and health
d) 18% said they had a full medical check-up – either a doctor or an alternative practitioner, or both to ensure they were healthy
e) 32% said they had increased their meditation time
f) 66% said they had been doing other spiritual practices
g) 63% said they had been practising mind mastery
h) 53% had learnt to experience the mind/body connection
i) 30% had colonic irrigation therapy
j) 40% underwent other specific detox programs
k) 67% looked at their belief around the idea that ›we must eat to live‹

6. **Before the process I had been living on a**
Vegetarian diet	– 71%
Vegan diet	– 13%
Fruitarian diet	– 18%
Raw food	– 25%
Other – meat diet	– 12%

7. **Before doing the process it was my intention**
a) To never eat again   – 40%
b) To never eat or drink again – 17%
c) To eat again for pleasure only – 41%

d)   To prove to myself that I did not need food to live, having understood the power of the Divine One Within in other areas of my life – 58%

8.   Before undergoing the process
a)   I was very healthy   – 66%
b)   My physical body was fit and strong – 68%
c)   My weight was at a level I was happy with – 58%
d)   I considered myself to be underweight – 8%
e)   I considered myself to be overweight – 28%
f)   I experienced clear inner guidance – 60%
g)   I was well aware that I create my own reality – 83%
h)   I had good relationships with my family – 73%
i)   I had explained to them the dynamics of the 21 day process – 52%, and of these 51% said that...
j)   My family were comfortable with my choice to do the 21 days

AFTER THE 21 DAY PROCESS

9.   Since undergoing the 21 day process
a)   Has your weight stabilized? – 71%
b)   Are you sleeping less? – 33%
c)   Do you find that your energy levels are very high? – 1%
d)   Do you feel as if you are operating mulitdimensionally? – 58%
e)   Do you feel as if you don't fit in when you socialize around food? – 43%
f)   Do you feel mentally clearer within yourself? – 78%
g)   Has your perception of the world changed? – 70%
h)   Do you cope better in life generally? – 70%
i)   Feel lighter, more focussed, yet more at ease? – 75%
j)   Have you become more inspired to be of service to others? – 71%
k)   Have your communication skills improved?
        With others   – 56%
        With the Divine One Within (DOW)? – 52%
l)   Have you been able to manifest any changes more easily in your life? – 52%
m)   Has your service path / life mission become easier to recognize? – 61%

n)   Do you feel stronger and more confident? – 67%

10.   Regarding your inner communication with your DOW
a)   Has it improved as a result of the process? – 75%
b)   Are you maintaining that communication? – 72%
c)   Was improved communication of temporary nature only? –18%
d)   Do you encounter difficulty in communicating? – 23%

11.   Have you continued to stay with a ›liquid only diet‹ – 31%

12.   If yes, do you ever have hunger pains? – 16%
        If yes, have you asked your DOW to feed you – 26%
        Does this work? – 18%

13.   Have you noticed any changes in your emotional state?
a)   Do you feel emotionally stronger, have less tendency to overre-act? – 68%

14.   Have you noticed any changes in your physical body?
a)   Change in shape? – 43%
b)   Change in appearance? – 46%

15.   If you are no longer on a ›liquid only‹ diet, please list your reasons for returning to food
a)   I got very bored from lack of flavor or variety – 26%
b)   I felt socially alienated; was tired of being different or missed participating in the social interaction around food – 17%
c)   Family pressure
        They were concerned for my health – 20%
        They do not believe it is possible to live without eating food – 16%
        I found it too difficult to cook for them and not share meals – 6%
d)   I could not seem to stabilize my weight and felt too thin – 20%

16.   Stress – I often seem to want to ›nibble‹ when I feel stress in life. Those who said yes. – 22%

17. **If at all, how often do you now eat?**   – 21%
    Said they ate either: daily; a few times a week; once a week; every few weeks

18. **Do you get cravings for**
    Sweet flavours? – 67%
    Spicy flavours? – 50%

19. **How do you feel about yourself when you eat?**
a) Do you consider yourself to be a failure? – 11%
b) Do you feel guilty? – 8%
c) Do you feel that in time you will overcome the habit and so there is nothing to worry about? – 25%
d) Do you feel like you achieved what you wanted from the process so no longer think about food and just eat when you feel like the pleasure of the flavor of food? – 23%

20. **If you are still on liquids only do you find yourself thinking a lot about food? – 5%**

21. **Do you feel that your emotional body is still addicted to the pleasure of eating? – 70%**
    Is this a concern for you? – 55%

22. **Do you feel that the 21 day process has affected your sexual energy?**
a) Is it stronger? – 28%
b) Not as strong as it was before? – 20%
c) No change – 52%
d) I was celibate beforehand and will continue to be so – 25%

23. **Your health**
a) During the process I was hoping I may experience some healing – 50%
b) Did this, or any other, healing occur? – 23%
c) Do you feel that your health has improved since doing the process? – 66%

24. Since undergoing the process have you gone for long periods of time without water as well as no food?   – 28%

25. Do you feel that undergoing the 21 day process was beneficial for you? – 91%

26. Information about my lifestyle
a) 85% had been meditating for between 1 & 20+ years
b) 87% had a good understanding of metaphysics
c) 55% said ›My spiritual beliefs that allow me to live a fulfilling and harmonious life‹
d) 31% belong to a meditation group
e) 47% live in or mix in a strong spiritual community
f) 58% network regularly with like-minded people
g) 47% regularly attend their church / temple / synagogue
f) 45% said ›I am more of a spiritual warrior who chooses not to be in groups‹
g) 50% have always been interested in physical immortality
h) 61% said ›I am in full-time service to positive planetary progression‹

Summation: As my colleagues at S.E.A. compiled these statistics, we noticed a few interesting points
a) The Germans were the best prepared
b) Of all, 91% felt that undergoing the process was beneficial
c) 71% were vegetarian pre-process including 25% raw foodists
d) 71% stabilized their weight quickly
e) 66% considered themselves to be fit and strong before they began
f) 85% were meditators and 25% were celibate by choice
g) 87% had a good understanding of metaphysics
h) 61% were in full-time service

Post process
a) 71% still felt emotionally addicted to food
b) 77% felt mentally clearer
c) 74% felt lighter, more focused and at ease in life
d) 72% felt emotionally stronger (less over-reaction)
e) 66% felt their health improved
f) 75% said their DOW connection improved

Demographics

a) 80 research subjects came from: Australia, New Zealand, Germany, Switzerland, France, Austria, Sweden, England, USA

b) 51 % were female; 49% were male

c) Average age was 47 with the youngest being 18 and the oldest being Hildegard in Austria at 93.

Obviously there are many conclusions one could draw as we continue to research the pre and post process preparation and personality types and the individuals‹ lifestyle practices of the Light Ambassadors. No doubt in time more exact physical body testing will be undertaken by medical and scientific research teams.

For those who would like more proof on this, they can research the qigong ›bigu‹ studies. While the 21 day process is a different method and takes personal discipline and training, perhaps the reason that these people spontaneously go into the ›bigu‹ state is due to their levels of devotion, godliness and patience just like those studied by Dr. Karl Graninger with inedia paradoxia post war.

So yes, we support that further studies be done in co-operation with those living on light, to check for both physical and psychological changes. Still, we realize that research departments are underfunded and suggest that these studies can also be done on a more low key level, if required, between the participants and their alternative or traditional medical practitioners in their various countries.

When concluded, we recommend that this information be shared with the relevant educational circles. We know that in time prana will prove itself just as vegetarianism, as even raw food has been accepted in society as a valid choice. In the meantime we will continue conducting our own research as guided and share it freely with the world via our website forums and »The ELRAANIS Voice« newsletter.

So this concludes most of what I want to say about research and how prana affects us personally. Now let's move on to look at how the lifestyles that the Ambassadors of Light choose to live, can influence our current world health and world hunger challenges.

In section 3 we will now look at facts and figures and at our service in redirecting resources.

Section 3

TWENTY FOUR

The Global Position

»The history of the earth has been a history of interaction between living things and their surroundings. To a large extent, the physical form and the habits of the earth's vegetation and its animal life have been melded by the environment. Considering the whole span of earthly time, the opposite effect, in which life actually modifies its surroundings, has been relatively slight. Only within the moment of time represented by the present century has one species – man – acquired significant power to alter the nature of the world.«
Rachel Carson, »The Silent Spring«

The third part of our book »Ambassadors of Light – Living on Light« concerns the global position in relation to issues of health, vegetarianism, genetic engineering, resource sustainability and the effective redirection of resources.

Throughout this section we share research statistics that were compiled by John Robbins for the book »Nature's First Law – the Raw Food Diet« by Arlin – Dini – Wolfe. These statistics provide a wonderful argument for the global adoption of vegetarianism, as a step on the way to achieving the lifestyle of the Ambassadors of Light.

Education about the benefits of this lifestyle may take some time, yet it is a necessary step for all those considering the eventual adoption of the Light Ambassadry's prana program and the global benefits this will eventually bring to all our societies.

Societies must keep evolving, not just for the good of a few but for the good of the whole. Typewriters are being made redundant by computers which offer superior benefits, the horse and buggy was quickly replaced by the motor car and we have come a long way since men rode on horseback as couriers to deliver mail. Now we have electronic mail.

In terms of dietary choices I personally see that the consumption of meat, given what we now know, can be likened to delivering mail via horseback while living on light is equivalent to e-mail – no middle man required, just better technology.

According to Harvey Diamond, the presidents of the National Academy of Sciences, National Academy of Engineering and the Institute of Medicine jointly said: »We believe that global environmental change may well be the most pressing international issue of the next century.«

Harvey Diamond is the author of the best-selling book »Fit for Life« and we take a number of quotes from his next book »Your Heart, Your Planet« as they are very relevant to our next statistical analysis.

So let us look at facts, figures and feedback that affect our global position as a species but first we will begin with current research on how our health and our planet is affected by the consumption of meat. But first some quotes:

- »Nature is an unlimited broadcasting station, through which God speaks to us every hour, if only we will tune in.« George Washington Carver – U.S. chemist and educator.
- »When a man is willing and eager, the gods join in.« Aeschylus – Greek Playwright.
- »Man thinks, God directs.« Alcuin – English theologian.
- »Preaching is to much avail, but practice is far more effective. A godly life is the strongest argument you can offer the skeptic.« Hosea Ballou – U.S. clergyman.

Harmonious Health – Facts and Figures

Statistics by John Robbins of Nature's First Law

»Thousands upon thousands of persons have studied disease. Almost no one has studied health.«
Adelle Davis, U.S. Nutritionist

Medical School Nutritional Training
- Number of U.S. medical schools: 125
- Number of U.S. medical schools with a required course in nutrition: 30
- Training in nutrition received during 4 years of medical school by the average U.S. physician: 2.5 hours

»If this country (America) is to survive, the best-fed-nation myth had better be recognized for what it is: propaganda designed to produce wealth not health.«
Adelle Davis

Heart Attacks
- How frequently a heart attack strikes in the U.S.: Every 25 seconds
- How frequently a heart attack kills in the U.S.: Every 45 seconds
- Most common cause of death in U.S.: Heart attack
- Risk of death from heart attack by average American man: 50%
- Risk of death from heart attack by average American purely vegetarian man: 4%
- Risk of death from heart attack by average American raw-foodist: 0%

- Amount you reduce your risk of heart attack by reducing your consumption of meat, dairy products and eggs by 10% and 9% respectively
- Rise in blood cholesterol from consuming 1 egg per day: 12%
- Rise in heart attack risk from 12% rise in blood cholesterol: 24%

Meat, Dairy, and Egg Industries

- Meat, dairy and egg industries claim there is no reason to be concerned about your blood cholesterol as long as it is: ›normal‹
- Risk of dying of a disease caused by clogged arteries (atherosclerosis) if your blood cholesterol is ›normal': over 50%
- Risk of dying of a disease caused by clogged arteries (atherosclerosis) if you do not consume saturated fat and cholesterol: 5%
- Leading sources of saturated fat and cholesterol in American diets: Meat, dairy products, and eggs
- World populations with high meat intakes who do not have correspondingly high rates of colon cancer: none
- World populations with low meat intakes who do not have correspondingly low rates of colon cancer: none
- Increased risk of breast cancer for women who eat meat daily compared to women who eat meat less than once a week: 4 times higher
- Increased risk of breast cancer for women who eat eggs daily compared to women who eat eggs less than once a week: 3 times higher
- Increased risk of breast cancer for women who eat butter and cheese 3 or more times a week compared to women who eat these foods less than once a week: 3 times higher
- Part of female chicken's body that produces eggs: Ovaries
- Increased risk of fatal ovarian cancer for women who eat eggs 3 or more times a week compared to women who eat eggs less than once a week: 3 times higher
- Increased risk of fatal prostate cancer for men who consume meats, cheese, milk and eggs daily compared to men who eat these foods sparingly or not at all: 3.6 times higher

- Milk is Nature's most perfect food for a baby calf, who has four stomachs, will double its weight in 47 days, and is destined to weigh 300 pounds (136 kg) within a year
- The enzyme necessary for digestion of milk is lactase. 20% of Caucasian children and 80% of black children have no lactase in their intestines (Humanity has gone so far as to create a pill that aids in the digestion of dairy products. This is just as insane as taking a pill before you drink motor oil to help in the digestion of that motor oil. If your body is not designed to naturally digest a certain substance then maybe you should not consume it).
- The diseases which are commonly prevented, consistently improved, and even cured by a vegetarian diet include: Heart disease, strokes, osteoporosis, kidney stones, breast cancer, colon cancer, prostate cancer, pancreatic cancer, ovarian cancer, cervical cancer, stomach cancer, endometrial cancer, diabetes, hypoglycaemia, kidney disease, peptic ulcers, constipation, haemorrhoids, hiatal hernias, diverticulosis, obesity, gallstones, hypertension, asthma, irritable colon syndrome, salmonellosis, trichinosis, etc.

»We live in a crazy time, when people who make food choices that are healthy and compassionate are often considered weird, while people are considered normal whose eating habits promote disease and are dependent on enormous suffering.« *John Robbins*

Pesticides in Livestock

»Many people who attend my health seminars invariably bombard me with fearful questions about what to do with all the pesticides on fruits and vegetables. Never – not once – has anyone raised the question of pesticides in meat, chicken, fish, eggs, or dairy products. Remarkable!

»Animal products have nine times more pesticides and no one seems to be aware of it. Getting stuck on the issue of pesticides in produce while eating animal products is a lot like worrying about getting your shoes wet in a puddle when a monstrous tidal wave is about to obliterate you.« Harvey Diamond.

- Chlorinated hydrocarbon pesticide residues in the U.S. diet: Supplied by meat: 55% ; Supplied by dairy products: 23% ; Supplied by vegetables: 6% ; Supplied by fruits: 4% ; Supplied by grains: 1%
- Percentage of U.S. mothers milk containing significant levels of DDT: 99%
- Percentage of U.S. vegetarian mothers milk containing significant levels of DDT: 8%
- Relative pesticide contamination in breast milk of meat-eating mothers compared to pesticide contamination in breast milk of vegetarian mothers: 35 times as high
- Percentage of male college students sterile in 1950: 5%
- Percentage of male college students sterile in 1978: 25%
- Sperm count of average American male compared to 35 years ago: Down 30%
- Principle reason for sterility and sperm count reduction of U.S. males: Chlorinated hydrocarbon pesticides (including dioxin, DDT, etc.)
- Percentage of hydrocarbon pesticide residues in American diet attributable to meats, dairy products, fish, and eggs: 94%
- A mere ounce (28.4 grams) of dioxin could kill 10 million people.
- Less than 1 out of every 250,000 slaughtered animals is tested for toxic chemical residues.
- The dye used for many years by the USDA to stamp meats »Choice«, »Prime«, or »U.S. No.1 USDA«: Violet Dye No.1
- Current status of Violet Dye No.1: Banned as a proven carcinogen.

»It is our alarming misfortune that so primitive a science has armed itself with the most modern terrible weapons, and that in turning them against the insects it has also turned them against the Earth.« Rachel Carson

Antibiotics in Livestock
- Percentage of total antibiotics used in the U.S. fed routinely to livestock: 55%

- Percentage of staphylococci infections resistant to penicillin in 1960: 13%
- Percentage of staphylococci infections resistant to penicillin in 1988: 91%
- Reason: Breeding of antibiotic resistant bacteria in factory farms due to routine feeding of antibiotics to livestock.
- Effectiveness of all ›wonder-drug‹ antibiotics: Declining rapidly
- Reason: Breeding of antibiotic resistant bacteria in factory farms due to routine feeding of antibiotics to livestock.
- Response by entire European Economic Community to routine feeding of antibiotics to livestock: Ban
- Response by American meat and pharmaceutical industries to routine feeding of antibiotics to livestock: Full and complete support.

For those concerned about maintaining a high level of health and fitness via a vegetarian diet, the following statistics are most interesting.

Vegetarian Athletes
- Only man to win Ironman Triathlon more than twice: Dave Scott (6 time winner) Food choices of Dave Scott: Vegetarian
- World record holder for 1 day triathlon (Swim 4.8 miles (7.7 km), cycle 185 miles (298 km), run 52.5 miles (84.5 km)): Sixto Lenares
- Athlete who most totally dominated Olympic sport in track and field history: Edwin Moses (undefeated in 8 years, 400 meter hurdles)

Raw-foodist athletes
- George Allen (held the world record for walking from Land's End in Cornwall to John O'Groats at northern tip of Scotland; he lives mostly on raw vegetables)
- Barbara Moore (broke George Allen's walking record).
- Fausto Coppi and Luis Ocana (world-renowned cyclists trained on raw-foods by French herbalist Maurice Messegue)

- Dick Gregory (In 1974 he ran 900 miles (1450 kilometers) exclusively on fruit juice; a one-time American comedian, he is now a raw-food nutritionist who often works in the sport of boxing – he has worked with boxers such as heavyweight champion Riddick Bowe.)
- Joe »The Atom« Greenstein (American strongman who enjoyed wide popularity in the 1930s.)

»In sports, raw-foodists will establish new and unprecedented records. The age long dream of athletes is fulfilled by 100% raw-eating.« – Nature's First Law.

Though most of the facts that we have just provided compare a vegetarian diet to an animal-based diet, remember that the differences between the two, however great, are much greater still when one compares the differences between a raw food diet and a vegetarian or vegan diet and a prana diet.

So the above statistics paint a very interesting picture, yet with some basic lifestyle changes, we can literally be free from all dis-ease particularly when we adopt our previous recommendations.

People sometimes ask me if they can do a lot of physical exercise, training schedules and heavy work and still live purely from prana as they have previously believed that they needed a good protein and carbohydrate diet to do this healthily. Of course they can, I often hear reports of people who get fitter and stronger and healthier once they have fully converted to living on light. Again the practice of the Luscious Lifestyle program supports this further.

When I first wrote the »Living on Light – Nutrition for the New Millennium« book, I knew that everyone could live on prana if they wished. What I didn't know then was that maintaining the ability to be free from needing food for long periods of time was completely dependant on our lifestyle choice. I realized over time that those for whom this is natural, meditate regularly, practise mind mastery, have been on very refined and simple diets for many years and have great faith in, trust of and experience of, higher forces.

As we have often stated, the ability to live free from the need from food does take training, and the first step for many is the adoption of a vegetarian lifestyle, so let us look at this in a little more depth.

TWENTYSIX

Vegetarianism

»The greatness of a nation and its moral progress
can be judged by the way its animals are treated.«
Mahatma Gandhi

One of the most interesting things that I have personally found
over the two decades that I practised vegetarianism prior to becoming pranically nourished, was the lack of knowledge that many medical practitioners held in the field of holistic medicine and alternative nutrition diets. Most seemed to be weighed down by the belief that an individual needed protein to survive (true) and that this could only come from meat products (false). In my early research I found that nuts and legumes provide alternative protein to steak.

Over the past few years our work in the field of pranic nourishment has obviously attracted many critics. Not just from the medical fraternity. Medical practitioners have much to learn in their normal training without becoming experts in the field of nutrition as well. According to the previous statistics, relying on your local G.P. for advice on nutrition is perhaps not as wise as doing your own research via alternative therapists who provide a more holistic approach to health and wellbeing matters.

That is not to underestimate the value of our traditional medical practitioners who are very much required in the world as it undergoes its transition into a dis-ease free society. Nonetheless I am sure that all those in the field of health would be most pleased to have individuals be more responsible for their personal health.

Regardless of how well-studied someone is in understanding the human body, evidence that challenges known facts speaks for itself. Although we may not understand it yet, pranic nourishment will come to be seen as an alternative source of nutrition for the new millennium.

In the meantime, one of the most effective things we can all do today is adopt a vegetarian diet. The moral reasons, the health benefits and the long-term planetary resource benefits are undeniable. Yes,

171

people say »what about unemployment that will occur as these industries supporting the slaughter of life shut down?« As Harvey Diamond says, »The production, feeding, growing, slaughtering, and transporting to market 16 million animals every day for consumption is no small feat. The resources necessary to accomplish such a task are astronomical, and the resulting effect on the environment is devastating.«

Consequently, we encourage those who work in industries that support the slaughter of life, to seek alternative employment. Gaining alternative employment is not difficult if you believe in higher purpose and higher powers.

Ask for help to find new employment by using this program: »I now ask my DOW to bring me the perfect job, to reveal to me my true life purpose and to bring me all the people and resources that I need to fulfill this now.«

Then do what is necessary to secure new work on the physical plane. The decision begins with you and the universe will support all those who wish to no longer support the slaughter of life on earth.

Let us move on to look at vegetarianism in a little more detail as per the following research by Jeff.

»The first thing to note about vegetarianism is the caliber of people observing this diet who have gone before us. The following list is very incomplete but indicative that quality minds have followed this dietary view: Pythagorus, Socrates, Plato, Leonardo da Vinci, John Milton, Sir Isaac Newton, Voltaire, Benjamin Franklin, Percy Bysshe Shelley, Thoreau, Ralph Waldo Emerson, Leo Tolstoy, George Bernard Shaw, Mahatma Gandhi, Albert Schweitzer, and Albert Einstein.

Does a vegetarian diet improve health? Since the 1960's scientists have suspected that a meat based diet is related to heart disease. As early as 1961 the journal of the American Medical Association said, »90% of heart disease can be prevented by a vegetarian diet.« Since that time several professional studies have scientifically shown that, after tobacco and alcohol, consuming meat is the greatest cause of mortality in developed western countries.

The reason simply is the excess fat and cholesterol taken on with meat consumption, as opposed to low cholesterol levels provided by vegetable protein. Regarding cancer, of 25 nations eating flesh largely, 19 have a high cancer rate, and of 35 nations eating little or no flesh, none had a high rate.

The reason given for this by biologists and nutritionists is that man's intestinal tract is simply not suited for digesting meat. Flesh eating animals have short intestinal tracts, three times the length of the animal's body, to pass rapidly decaying toxic producing meat out of the body quickly. Since plant food decays more slowly, plant eaters have intestine at least six times the length of the body, which is the case with man. The second problem is the chemicals that are added to the meat in the rearing of the animals. This process starts before death and continues after the death of the animal, even though they are not listed on the packaging, they are definitely present in the meat.

The American Dietetic Association says that most of mankind, for most of human history, has lived on a vegetarian or near vegetarian diet. Much of the world still does, and even in industrialized countries the eating of meat started extensively only a hundred years ago with the invention of the refrigerator.

The fact is the human body is neither designed to – or copes well – with eating meat. The recommended protein dosage of 150 grams, given as an ideal daily intake twenty years ago, has now been reduced to 30 grams. The excess protein in a meat based diet is not only wasteful, but in fact extraordinarily harmful.

The long held view that the eight amino acids not produced in the body could only be had from a balanced meat and dairy product diet is now established to be incorrect, and in fact, a balanced vegetarian diet is quite ideal in that regard.

The difference between a meat eater and a plant eater is quite pronounced, and one of the most obvious differences between humans and carnivores is that the carnivore has stomach acid ten times stronger than humans, to allow the digestion of meat, and of course as previously mentioned, the intestinal tract in humans is twice as long as that found in carnivores, relative to their body size.

Another major point is the fact that the inequity of people starving can be resolved easily, simply by western developed nations foregoing their current meat eating habits. For every sixteen pounds of grain fed to cattle only one pound of meat is returned, according to figures from the United States Department of Agriculture. They also report that 90% of grain produced in America goes to feed livestock – cows, pigs, sheep and chicken – that wind up on dinner tables.

A good illustration is that someone sitting down to eat an eight ounce steak, is the equivalent of fifty people sitting down with a full cup of cooked cereal grains. The fact is that the average European or American meat eater uses five times the food resources of someone from an undeveloped country. Simply bringing down meat production by only 10%, it is estimated that it would release enough grain to feed 60 million people.

Water consumption is also excessive in that one pound of wheat requires only sixty gallons of water, whereas production of one pound of meat requires approximately two and a half thousand gallons of water.

The ethics involved in the breeding and preparation of meat are unacceptable to most thinking people, and if they were required to kill their own animals, then of course, they would have grave second thoughts about persisting with their diet.

Mahatma Gandhi said, ›I do feel that spiritual progress does demand at some stage we should cease to kill our fellow creatures for the satisfaction of our bodily wants.‹

Consumption of meat is a large component of the incorrect distribution of resources, and arable land usage, in that with a change by the current meat consumers, to a vegetarian diet, the excess automatically introduced by their change of lifestyle, would resolve the problems that reduced quantities of arable land and increased population present.«

Facts : Humans and Livestock Statistics
- Human population of the United States: 300 million
- Number of humans that can be fed by the grain and soybeans eaten by U.S. livestock: 1.4 billion
- Percentage of corn grown in the U.S. eaten by livestock: 85%; percentage of corn eaten by humans: 15%
- Percentage of oats grown in U.S. eaten by livestock: 95%
- Percentage of protein wasted by cycling grain through livestock: 90%
- Percentage of carbohydrate wasted by cycling grain through livestock: 99%
- Percentage of dietary fiber wasted by cycling grain through livestock: 100%
- How frequently a child dies of starvation: Every 2 seconds

- Amount of potatoes that can be grown on 1 acre (4,047 square meters) of land: 20,000 lbs. (9,072 kg)
- Amount of beef that can be grown on 1 acre (4,047 square meters) of land: 165 lbs. (75 kg)
- Percentage of U.S. agricultural land used to produce beef: 56%
- Amount of grain and soybeans needed to produce 1 pound (or kilogram) of feedlot beef: 16 lbs. (7.3 kg)
- Amount of protein fed to chickens to produce 1 pound (or kilogram) of protein as chicken flesh: 5 lbs. (2.3 kg)
- Amount of protein fed to hogs to produce 1 pound (or kilogram) of protein as hog flesh: 7.5 lbs. (3.4 kg)
- Number of children who starve to death every day: 40,000
- Number of pure vegetarians who can be fed on the amount of land needed to feed 1 person consuming meat-based diet: 20 (This number could be closer to 150 if you're talking about pure raw-vegetarians.)
- Number of people who will starve to death this year: 60 million
- Number of people who could be adequately fed by the grain saved if Americans reduced their intake of meat by 10%: 60 million.

According to Harvey Diamond, »Twelve million tons of grain will be freed up each year from a vegetarian lifestyle. There are those that say that even if the food was freed up and made available, somehow it would still have to be brought to the people. True. But at least they would have a chance of receiving it. There is no chance if it's all fed to livestock.«

So the Light Ambassadors who choose to live from prana recommend that if you wish to be a lot healthier and even be free from the need to eat food, then you first:
- Become a vegetarian
- Then become a vegan and cease consuming all animal products
- Then move on to raw food, then go to fruits
- Then liquids, then prana.

The more gradually you make this dietary transition, the easier it will be to let go of your emotional body's addiction to the pleasure gained from eating a wide variety of foods.

If all the Light Ambassadry manages to achieve in the next few decades is the elimination of the unnecessary slaughter of animals, we will have done well. For, as discussed in the previous chapters, the ability to live on light will come from the gradual refinement of our thinking, feeling and choice of fuel for the body.

A yoga teacher friend of mine in Belgium was telling me how much resistance some of his new students had to becoming vegetarian until he began to talk about getting so refined that you didn't need to eat. To this they responded, »Not eat – you've got to be joking!« To this he said, »Well, perhaps you can just take on a vegetarian diet instead?« To which they all said, »Great! No problem!« It's all relative.

Research is now also being done in the field of the genetic manipulation of food – some say with the aim of reducing the cost of food production. Others call this ›Frankenstein food‹ and will not touch it. Here are some facts and myths...

Human Evolution

Genetic Engineering and Cloning

We include the following data here, as genetic engineering has become a concern for many who are committed to positive planetary progression. In this chapter we look at two issues – firstly, genetic engineering as it relates to food production, and secondly, genetic engineering as it relates to cloning, as the two issues really go hand in hand.

a) Genetic Engineering: The Myths and Facts
by Stewart Carolan

Myth No. 1 Genetic engineering is a natural development of traditional breeding methods.
»Fact – Genetic engineering involves taking pieces of DNA from one species and inserting it into the DNA of another in order to mimic certain desired characteristics, e.g. from fish to tomato or from human to pig. Where in nature do we find DNA from a fish, a scorpion, a spider, a virus or bacterium, an animal or even HUMAN DNA introducing itself into the DNA of a vegetable? These are all examples of the type of genetically engineered transplants that have already been done.«

Myth No. 2 Genetically modified foods are safe to eat.
»Fact – In 1989 in the US 37 people were killed and 1500 left permanently disabled after eating a genetically engineered food supplement. A soya bean engineered with a gene from a brazil nut was withdrawn after it was discovered that it gave rise to allergic reactions. Current safety regulations are hopelessly inadequate.
And no long term tests have been done on the effects of eating genetically engineered food. What is known is that these effects are unpredictable and potentially FATAL. Most processed food now contains

one or more genetically engineered ingredients. As these ingredients do not have to be labeled, the only sure way to avoid them is to eat organically produced food.«

Myth No.3 Genetic Engineering is a precise science.
»Fact – Right now science only understands the function of about 3% of DNA. The relationships that govern the expression of genes are understood even less. Any change in the DNA at any point brings about changes which scientists cannot predict. The claim by some that they can is both arrogant and untrue.«

Myth No.4 Genetic engineering of crops is done to benefit the environment.
»Fact – The government's own nature watchdogs (English Nature, English Heritage etc.) as well as all the major environmental organizations and a growing body of scientists are calling for an immediate ban on genetically engineered crops until a great deal more research has been done, because of the increasing evidence that they can have a devastating impact on wildlife and the environment.«

Myth No.5 Genetic engineering of crops is being done to use less herbicides and pesticides.
»Fact – Corporations are engineering crops to be resistant to their own brand chemicals. This means that a field can be covered with the herbicides and everything will die except for the resistant crop.
Their seeds and chemicals are sold together as a package which dramatically raises their profits. The British Agrochemical Association predicts that worldwide sales of herbicides will increase as a result of genetic engineering. For example, the market for glufosinate, one of the chemicals being used, is expected to rise by $200 million a year.«

Myth No.6 Genetic engineering benefits the farmer.
»Fact – The inherent instability of genetically engineered crops has already led to widespread crop failure. Monsanto recently had to pay out millions of dollars in compensation for its genetically engineered cotton crop. Calgene's »Flavor Savor« tomato, engineered for improved shelf life, had unexpected problems and was a financial disaster. Herbicide resistance has already spread from genetically engineered crops to weeds.«

Myth No.7 Genetic engineering will feed the developing world.
»Fact – Intensive farming practices are inappropriate in countries where people depend on a wide variety of local crops. The restrictive and expensive contracts that farmers have to sign when using genetically engineered crops will continue to force poor farmers off the land. To suggest that the developing world will benefit as a result of genetic engineering is manipulating the public, and being used to hide the truth that this technology is being developed to line the pockets of multinationals.

With thanks to the Genetic Engineering Network in the UK for this information.
Comments/feedback/contact:sthpc@hotmail.com
With love, light and laughter, Stewart Carolan

Watching a program on this very topic last recently on Sixty Minutes, it seems that Monsanto are spending billions on plant genetics with the desire to harness the power of mother nature and feed a growing population. Research also shows that genetic manipulation in the fields of pharmaceuticals may aid in the elimination of cancers. Again, this is most interesting since so many cancers seem to be diet and lifestyle related in the first place.

Opponents would argue that switching resources to focus on a global vegetarian diet for all will be a lot healthier and address not just population agendas but also the pressing environmental issues that we outlined previously.

Opponents also say that the frightening thing is that people are not advised of the extent of genetic modifications e.g. half of all soy products have been genetically manipulated and as many are aware soy is a meat protein substitute consumed by many vegetarians who would rather have organic food than genetically modified food.

Opponents of genetic engineering are also concerned about how this research is applied and by whom. As not all ›powers that be‹ operate with integrity as divine beings acting impeccably in their service to mankind, and to some this is a real issue of concern. The link between Monsanto and those who set up the original FDA guidelines is also interesting.

Again, we can choose to be aware of what is in the food we eat, or eat raw food only, or even aim for a food-free diet which will eliminate many of these problems.

b.) Evolution and Cloning
Research by Jeff from the Encyclopedia Britannica

»The founder of the modern theory of evolution was Charles Darwin. In 1859 he published »On the Origin of Species by Means of Natural Selection« establishing the theory of evolution, and more importantly the role of natural selection in determining its course. In 1871 he published »The Descent of Man and Selection in Relation to Sex« which extends the theory of natural selection to human evolution. Darwin is seen as possessing an extraordinary mind and he introduced a new era in the cultural history of mankind, following on from the Copernican revolution that had begun in the 16th century.

»The significance of these discoveries was that they led to the conception of the universe as a system of matter in motion governed by the laws of nature.

Briefly, Darwin's theory as summarized in ›The Origin of Species‹ is: As many more individuals are produced than can possibly survive, there must be in every case a struggle for existence, either one individual with another of the same species, or with individuals of a different species, or with the physical conditions of life. The individuals having any advantage however slight, over others, have the best chance of surviving and procreating their kind. On the other hand, any variation in any degree harmful to the continuation of that individual's line is rigidly destroyed. This preservation of natural variations and the rejection of injurious variations is natural selection.

The central argument of Darwin's theory of evolution starts from the existence of hereditary variation. Experience with animal and plant breeding demonstrates that variations can be developed that are useful to man.

Natural selection is defined by a measure called ›Darwinian Fitness‹ or ›Relative Fitness‹. Fitness in this sense is the relative probability that an hereditary characteristic will be reproduced, that is the degree of fitness is the measure of the reproductive efficiency of a characteristic.

Religiously motivated attacks started during Darwin's lifetime, mainly directed by fundamentalist Christians. However, the Pope in 1950, issued written comment, ›Of the Human Race‹, that accepted the theory of evolution as the development of humanity, further enforcing the evidence of God. The Pope's point is that it would be a blunder to mistake the Bible for an elementary book of astronomy, geology and biology. The argument was clearly directed against the Christian fundamentalists who see in Genesis a literal description of how the world was created by God.

Even though Biblical fundamentalists make up a small minority of Christians, they have occasionally gained political influence in the United States. Four American States prohibited the teaching of evolution in their public schools.

The most recent event of consequence in the evolutionary process has been the development of cloning, using genetic engineering. In this sense, a clone can be defined as an individual organism that was grown from a single body cell of its parent, and that is genetically identical to it.

Cloning has been commonplace in horticulture since ancient times. Many variations of plants are cloned by obtaining cuttings of the leaves, stems and roots and replanting them. A vast variety of fruit and nut trees represent clones.

The body cells of adult animals and humans can be cloned in a laboratory. Adult cells of various tissues, such as muscle cells that are removed from a donor animal and maintained, while receiving nutrients, manage not only to survive, but to go on dividing, producing colonies of identical descendants.

By the 1950's scientists were able to clone frogs, producing identical individuals that carry the genetic characteristics of only a single parent. The technique used in the cloning of frogs consists of transplanting the frog DNA contained in the nucleus of a body cell into an egg cell whose own genetic material has been removed. A few cells then begin to grow and divide just like a normal fertilized egg to form an embryo.

Mice were first successfully cloned in the 1980's. The embryo is artificially implanted into the uterus of a mouse that brings it to term. Cloning a new animal from the cells of an adult as opposed to an embryo is considerably more difficult. Almost all of an animal cells containing the genetic information needed to reproduce a copy of the organism, but as cells differentiate into the various organs of the developing animal they express only that genetic information needed to produce their own cell type.

The first success in cloning an adult mammal was achieved by a team of British Researchers in Scotland in 1996. They were able to produce a lamb using DNA from an adult sheep.

The physical applications of cloning are economically promising but philosophically unsettling. The cloning of human beings is fraught with ethical and moral dangers. If cloning can ensure the infinite replication of specific genetic traits the judgement is then, which genetic traits, and who makes that decision.«

I think my most interesting discovery in the field of metaphysics is that we as humans, are clones of our God, and as such, have amazing power – when we use love and wisdom – to create anything our hearts desire. The only stipulation that is now upon us, is that we create in a manner that benefits the whole human race and not just the few. Creating a world free of hunger and disease seems a worthwhile adventure and utilization of our creative skills.

Religious unification via a focus on a common vision seems a logical step for any compassionate and intelligent person – particularly at this point in time. Separatism via the focus on the differences of our ideologies promotes war, fear and chaos. Joining forces to address issues like poverty, hunger and famine and the redirection of resources is far more beneficial for us all than the promotion of belief systems that create chaos.

Combining people resources and financial resources to address common problems is now imperative, and this can only be done by choosing to put aside our differences and focusing on things that affect us all, regardless of our race or religion.

Poverty and Hunger

Famine and Malnutrition

»God grant me the serenity to accept the things
I cannot change, the courage to change the things I can,
and the wisdom to know the difference.«
Reinhold Niebuhr, American religious and social thinker

Poverty, hunger, malnutrition and famine from warfare are very real issues that threaten the survival of many as we enter a new millennium. They are also symptoms of social dis-ease. Greed, lack of compassion, selfishness, apathy and hatred are all underlying factors that determine the way resources are distributed on our planet and also our social harmony.

Of the current 5.7 billion people living on the planet, an estimated 1.3 billion live in poverty. Poverty effects individuals and families throughout the world, although most of the poorest people live in the developing world, where they represent one-third of the population.

About half of the severely impoverished people live in South Asia. Another 25% of the total are in South East Asia. Extreme poverty is concentrated in Africa, particularly the countries south of the Sahara Desert. Africa has about 16% of the world's total poor. But fully half of all Africans are poor. Generally, it is fair to say that poverty is a rural matter with 80% of the world's poor living in rural areas. The rural poor are either landless, or with farms too small to yield adequate income.

However, the distribution of the poor is changing swiftly. Lured by jobs and quality of life in the cities, an increasing number of poor gravitate to towns and cities. Most of the migrants are men, leaving women behind to manage the families. Some 300 million urban dwellers in developing countries currently live in poverty, without sufficient income to meet basic food and shelter requirements. This is also, of course, having a negative effect on the urban environment.

Approximately 600 million people in urban areas of developing countries live in poor health and under life-threatening conditions. In some cities more than half of the population live in slums and squatter settlements. According to the New York Times over 20% of the population of the greater New York metropolitan area live below the poverty line. More than a quarter million of the city's population have stayed in homeless shelters over the past five years. London has around 400,000 registered homeless, and the situation is even worse in cities of developing countries.

Poverty, of course, is a general pre-condition for hunger. Famine is the most dramatic example of hunger, and while famines have been historically a result of inclement weather, rains not falling and so forth, warfare has been the most common cause of famine. In addition to destroying crops and food, warfare also distributes the distribution of food. While famine is still prevalent throughout the world, the capacity now of the modern distribution system makes this an inequitable situation, which is totally unacceptable. We both have the capacity and the ability to make sure all now are fed. It only takes political responsibility to ensure this occurs.

Feeding the poor is never politically popular, particularly feeding foreign poor, but as the consciousness of the planet unifies and as national boundaries tend to evaporate as currently being demonstrated in Europe, this is something that must be addressed. The Assistant District Director General of the United Nations Organization for food and agriculture said recently, »Globally there is enough food to feed the world, but it is not equally distributed and many people do not have the means to buy it.«

Living on Light – A Solution to times of Famine

Apart from better global food distribution services and re-education regarding nourishment, what those of us in service can do is to seriously consider the benefits of pranic nourishment on a global level. Now that literally thousands have proven to themselves that nutrition can come from an alternative source to food i.e. prana; then the quicker this information becomes part of the global stage by each of us »walking our talk«, then the sooner the hunger-related problems can be positively addressed.

Yes, some members of both the UN Council and UNICEF are aware of our work but at this stage perhaps they may not see it as a viable solution. The success of pranic nourishment in combating global hunger is dependant on a massive re-education program into self-responsibility and self-refinement that honors all our bodies from the physical to the spiritual.

The Ascended Ones say that our media exposure has now reached more than 500 million people, and while our ability to be pranically nourished is often disbelieved, as Saint Germain has shared with me so often, »seeds are being planted«. The idea that there are people who are free from the need of food has now been anchored in the grids and is now a part of human awareness.

How long until eating for pleasure rather than need becomes an everyday possibility is up to each Ambassador of Light. The more of us who allow the Divine Force within us to sustain us – if we are joyously guided to do so – and the more of us who talk about the possibility, the sooner the idea of not needing to eat food will move from the miraculous into the everyday.

A journalist once said to me that young children die each minute from starvation and malnutrition and that changing our beliefs and mind-set about nutritional requirements of food would not save them. When we understand the dynamics of energy, we understand that children are linked to their parents' energy fields, particularly that of the mother until they are 18 months to two years old. They then begin the process of separation which some schools of thought say is completed between 14 and 21, depending on the individual. Change the lifestyles and beliefs of the parent and the community and the child will change.

This change is necessary as the facts are that malnutrition contributes to nearly seven million child deaths every year – more than any infectious disease, war or natural disaster, according to the 1998 State of the World's Children Report released by UNICEF, the United Nations Children's Fund.

No less than half of all children under the age of five in South Asia and one-third of those in sub-Saharan Africa, as well as millions of children in industrialized countries, are malnourished.

Three-quarters of the children who die worldwide of causes related to malnutrition are what nutritionists describe as »mildly to

185

moderately malnourished« and show no outward signs of problems.

When adults are exposed to the reality of many individuals worldwide being able to live on light, they will lose their fear and change their mind-set. This will lead to a modification in the frequency and quality of the energy they emit, and their children will respond accordingly. Everything is interconnected. The secret is in the understanding of the power of the mind over our molecular structure. Those who have not felt the power of their DOW may not understand the experience of feeling interconnected to everything.

It is also important to keep our focus clear. The pranic nourishment solution is a bridge to freedom only because it is one way to unlock the majestic power of our DOW. It is not about whether we eat or don't eat, but whether we need to. It is about being free from the erroneous fear that says, »if we don't eat food we will die«, and it is also a wonderful skill to have in times of famine from war or earth changes. As guru Maharaji once said, the less we depend on things external to ourselves for our own happiness, the sooner we realize that true happiness lies within.

It is the lifestyle of the Ambassadors of Light, that if adopted by more, will bring dramatic change. When this lifestyle is applied in the West many people will naturally become more service-minded and more active in compassionately addressing the problems of others. So much can be taught freely to change what is happening in these situations. For example:

We know that prana comes in on our breath. In fact some say that we receive 70% of our nourishment independent of food via breathing. Prana is an invisible forcefield that permeates every atom and we can manufacture more of it throughout our body at will. Meditation raises the kundalini energy and increases the flow and potency of prana through our cells. We can practise deep breathing exercises and imagine that with every breath we are filling our lungs and cells with a powerful dosage of vitamins and minerals that are contained within the invisible prana.

As all people can breathe and breathing is free, this is the first tool to teach people regardless of where they now live. To do pranayama, means to do particular breathing exercises that feed and nourish the energy fields of all the human bodies.

As part of the redistribution of resources program that we discuss later, pranayama breathing exercises and even qigong can easily be taught throughout societies – to all, including young and old and improve their health and vitality levels. Coupled with programming and mind power techniques, radical transformations can be made regardless of our circumstances. Use the breath techniques in section 2 daily and feel the difference.

More can also be immediately taught about the amazing capabilities of the human bio-fields including the mind/body connection, and how to effectively reprogram ourself to be free from limiting beliefs. The human body will die from lack of nourishment but not from lack of food as we know it. Prana via DOW Power truly is light nutrition for the new millennium and is a viable alternative source of future nourishment for our evolving species; and it is available now and for free.

People die from starvation because they have not yet been taught about this alternative nutrition source, nor about mind mastery and the power of their focused thought to create a different reality. Many have not yet discovered the true power of the Divine Force within and how breath techniques can nourish them on all levels. Being able to live without food from the physical realms becomes quite simple when we understand how.

To the »disadvantaged«, breathing is free and breath techniques can be taught to gain increased nourishment and health and longevity. Thinking is free, so mind mastery programming techniques can also be taught immediately. The power of prayer and healing through song can be taught as well as a basic understanding of universal law.

In esoteric circles, it is well understood that people choose in each embodiment the culture, their parents, their race and the locality of their embodiment. Yes, many are aware that people have entered into environments of poverty and suffering to complete karmic ties, connections and chapters that have been unfinished from other lives. Regardless of this, the M.A.P.S. Ambassadry is very aware of the apathy that can come when one looks at the game of karma. It is easier to dismiss and be inactive rather than active by saying »It's their choosing – it is nothing to do with us«. Apathy separates, compassion unifies.

Warfare, however, has been the most common human cause of famine. In addition to destroying crops and food supplies, warfare also

187

disrupts the distribution of food through the use of siege and blockade tactics.

The Light Ambassadry's proposal for global disarmament will eliminate this problem of warfare and many of us are now in service fulfilling our divine contracts to pragmatically create change for global civility. With pranic nourishment we do not need to grow crops, so famine from drought will not be a problem. With pranic nourishment we do not need to slaughter animals or even eat a ›balanced diet‹ and we will not get malnutrition, as all that our body needs comes from prana.

Yes, there are various Light Ambassadors, who are beginning to spread out across the globe into third world countries and teach the ability of living on light by being an example in the midst of those who have so little. While individuals in third world countries may not have much on a material level, they have all the power they need within them – DOW Power – to completely change their experience of their life.

To the Ambassadors of Light, everything is interconnected, and while Gandhi said: »It is unwise to be too sure of one's own wisdom. It is healthy to be reminded that the strongest might weaken and the wisest might err«; to those who have experienced the power of their DOW, the words of Aeschylus the Greek playwright will always ring true: »God loves to help him who strives to help himself«, and »Conscience is the perfect interpreter of life.« – Karl Barth, Swiss theologian.

TWENTY NINE

Population, Land Scarcity and Sustainable Development

»Ignorance is not innocence, it is the root of corruption.«
Carrie Nation

Another issue of concern for many is land scarcity and sustainable development. When Isaac Assimov was asked by Bill Moyers on a news interview what he considered to be the most urgent problems addressed by society, he said, »Population and the rainforest.«

At this time, world population is growing 8 times as fast as the increase in cultivated land area, and even though the fertility rate has halved since the 1950's and stable world population is now anticipated, nevertheless the wellbeing of hundreds of millions of people is threatened due to anticipated land scarcity. In the early 1960's only 4 countries had insufficient arable land to feed their population without intensive agriculture. But they were wealthy enough to import what they needed.

By 2025, 29 countries are projected to be land scarce. An international benchmark of less than one-seventh of the size of an American football field has been set for the amount of land required per capita. Below that level of arable land per head, intensive and generally expensive agricultural methods, using inorganic nitrogen fertilizer for example, are required.

In the next century there will be a requirement to grow enough food for an additional 3 billion people. The projections are at 2025, when approximately 8 billion people are estimated to be living. China will have a projected population at that time of 1.5 billion and will represent more than half of those who would be affected by arable land scarcity, in 2025.

The problem of scarce arable land is that the scarcity invariably has the greatest effect where the farmers are unable to afford fertilizers and other means to boost agricultural production. For example in

Africa, one in three Africans is malnourished, and although African farmers have been increasing their annual production, it has not been enough to keep up with the continent's current population growth.

An additional problem is that in 2025, 12 of the 29 countries projected as being lacking in arable land will also be classified as water scarce, with less than 1000 cubic metres of renewable fresh water per head available for agricultural, industrial, or domestic purposes each year.

The resulting shortage of food can be indicated by the availability of emergency grain reserves, which is the international food security measurement. The reserves peaked in 1986 when there was enough grain for 14 weeks‹ world consumption. In 1994 there was sufficient reserves for less than 9 weeks. On a per capita basis grain production has been declining since 1984.

In 1990, 1.4 billion hectares of land was under cultivation throughout the world, which represented an increase five fold in utilized land for arable purposes since 1700. The rate of expansion of arable land currently is less than .2% per annum, and is declining.

Each year, 25 billion metric tones of nutrient enriched topsoil is dislodged by wind and rain, most of it finding its way into waterways. And the soil that is left is less able to hold water and eventually becomes too dense with salinisation. The build up of salts and other minerals in the soil is a problem for a sixth of the world's crop land that is irrigated, and which produces more than a third of all crops and a half of all cereal grains.

Modern agricultural methods have been responsible for dramatic increases in food production in the last few decades. However, they require man-made fertilizers and pesticides that have unfortunate environmental effects. Agriculture also absorbs large quantities of water, roughly two-thirds of fresh water used world-wide, is for agricultural purposes. So we have the problem of while in the future the currently increasing population stabilizes, diminished agricultural land is available, and consequently reduced food is produced relative to current population growth.

The immediate answer to the problem is simply for northern countries, that is developed countries, to consume less. It is essentially the consumption of the northern hemisphere developed economies that creates the problem, in the sense that their consumption per head is a huge multiple of residents of undeveloped countries.

It takes little imagination to see the benefits of a relatively austere, compared to an excessively consumptive, lifestyle, particularly for those with substantial income and credit, where it is obvious that undeveloped countries are unable to compete on the basis of the capacity to pay. So the problem of scarcity of land and the sustainability of development and resources is really an esoteric discussion. The fact is that there is plenty for all, right now and it's only a matter of political will, which is controlled by the demonstration of the popular electoral muscle, to bring a more balanced and fair arrangement into effect.

»Look upon success and failure with any equal eye.«
Bhagavad-Gita

Statistics
As discussed already, one of the greatest concerns by many regarding our planet's future, is overpopulation and how to feed the growing number of people that are considered to be living below the poverty line globally. Still, the following population statistics are quite encouraging.

Population Statistics
Current status: 6 billion with 1.3% growth per annum = annual addition 78 million. Projection: By 2050 will be between 7 and 11 billion – averaging 9 billion.
Factors affecting population growth
1. **Fertility   1950's – 5 births/woman**
   1999 – 2.7 births/woman
   Birth-rate has declined in all regions, for example:
a) 6.5 to 5 in Africa
b) 5 to 2.5 in Asia
c) 5 to 2.5 in Latin America and the Caribbean

2. **Aids and our population**
Facts: In Botswana 25% adults are infected by HIV
Figures: Life expectancy now: 1990-5   60 years
                                 2000-5   40 years
          By 2025 22% less than today due to HIV

3. Age and our population
Facts: People are living longer
Figures: 1998 – 66 million were over 80 = 1% of population
        2050 – 370 million will be over 80
        1998 – 135,000 were more than 100 years old
        2050 – 2.2 million will be over 100

4. Gender make-up in our population.
Fact: Women outlive men.
Figures: 1988
190 females to 100 men who are over 80
287 females to 100 men who are over 90
396 females to 100 men who are over 100

5. Longevity locations (based on total numbers)
1. China; 2. America; 3. India; 4. Japan; 5. Germany; 6. Russia.

6. Downturn in population growth
Economic development – At a certain stage of development the imperative to have a large number of children to support their parents in their old age is eliminated, and as the internationalization and globalization of economies goes on, the universal standard of the smaller family size seems to lock in. The development of an effective oral female contraceptive has altered the role model of women, with smaller families allowing for other outlets, such as a career. The downturn of population means sustainability of life will be easier and at the same time quality of life and longevity will be higher. The standard of morality and behavior of individuals has been given a template with the Human Rights Declaration and against which we hope all will eventually measure well.

Feedback on the issue of over population
Many people have held concerns for some time about the effects that an ever increasing population growth may have on earth's future and yet the above facts and figures quoted from the United Nations website, find that we really have little cause for concern. Provided that we learn how to effectively redistribute the resources on our planet, take personal responsibility for our lifestyles by working on an holistic level, over population should not be a factor of major concern.

Now let us move on and look at statistics regarding food production and the cost to our resources and environment.

Soil
- Historic cause of demise of many great civilizations: Topsoil depletion
- Percentage of original U.S. topsoil lost to date: 75%
- Amount of U.S. cropland lost each year to soil erosion: 4 million acres (16,187 square kilometers) (size of Connecticut)
- Percentage of U.S. topsoil loss directly associated with livestock raising: 85%

According to Harvey Diamond a vegetarian lifestyle will save seven hundred million tons of top soil each year and »one hundred and twenty million acres of land, choice land, could be made available for more prudent use.«

Trees
- Amount of U.S forest which has been cleared to create cropland to produce a meat-centered diet: 260 million acres (1.05 million square kilometers)
- How often an acre (4,047 square meters) of U.S. trees disappears: Every 8 seconds
- Amount of trees spared per year by each individual who switches to a pure vegetarian diet: 1 acre (4,047 square meters)

Rainforests
- A driving force behind the destruction of the tropical rainforests: American meat habit
- Current rate of species extinction due to destruction of tropical rainforests and related habitats: 1000 per year.

»The tropical rainforests of the world are probably Earth's most precious resource, offering refuge to three quarters of all living things on the planet. This lush green belt of forest that circles the equator is frequently referred to as Earth's lungs.«

Water

- User of more than half of all water used for all purposes in the United States: Livestock production
- The quantity of water used in the production of the average cow: sufficient to float a destroyer
- Water needed to produce 1 pound (.45 kg) of wheat: 25 gallons (95 liters)
- Water needed to produce 1 pound (.45 kg) of meat: 2,500 gallons (9,465 liters)
- Cost of common hamburger meat if water used by meat industry was not subsidized by U.S. taxpayers: $35 per pound ($77 per kg)
- Current cost for 1 pound (.45 kg) of protein from wheat: $1.50
- Current cost for 1 pound (.45 kg) of protein from beefsteak: $15.40
- Cost for 1 pound (.45 kg) of protein from beefsteak if U.S taxpayers ceased subsidizing meat industry's use of water: $89 (Harvey Diamond says the cost is US$35 a pound and that »in California alone the cost of subsidizing the meat industry is US$24 billion per annum!«)

Petroleum and Energy

- Length of time world's petroleum reserves would last (with current technologies) if all human beings ate meat-centered diet: 13 years
- Length of time world's petroleum reserves would last (with current technologies) if all human beings ate vegetarian diet: 260 years
- Principal reason for U.S. intervention in Persian Gulf: Dependence on foreign oil
- Barrels of oil imported daily by U.S.: 6.8 million
- Percentage of energy return (as food energy per fossil energy expended) of most energy efficient farming of meat: 34.5%
- Percentage of energy return (as food energy per fossil energy expended) of least energy efficient plant food: 328%
- Amount of soy beans produced by the amount of fossil fuel needed to produce 1 pound (.45 kg) of feedlot beef: 40 lbs. (18.1 kg)

194

- Percentage of raw materials consumed in U.S. for all purposes presently consumed to produce current meat-centered diet: 33%
- Percentage of raw materials consumed in U.S. for all purposes needed to produce pure vegetarian diet: 2%

Sewage Systems
- Production of excrement by total U.S. population: 12,000 lbs. (5443 kg) per second
- Production of excrement by U.S. livestock: 250,000 lbs. (113,400 kg) per second
- Sewage systems in U.S. cities: Common
- Sewage systems in U.S. feedlots: Nil
- Amount of waste produced annually by U.S. livestock in confinement operations which is not recycled: 1 billion tons (907 billion kg)
- Relative concentration of feedlot wastes compared to raw domestic sewage: Ten to several hundred times more highly concentrated
- Where feedlot waste typically ends up: Human water supply

Obviously by the above statistics, anyone can see the radical and positive impact that living on light will have on our planet in the long term. No need for sewerage systems, no more animal slaughter, no need for such comprehensive systems of waste elimination, no need for such huge oil reserves, no need for deforestation... the list goes on.

THIRTY

Our Planet – Our Progeny

Redirecting Resources

»We have not inherited this earth from our parents;
we're borrowing it from our children.«
Author unknown

In a recent speech on human rights and peace, the Dalai Lama said: »If we are serious in our commitment to the fundamental principles of equality which, I believe, lie at the heart of the concept of human rights, today's economic disparity can no longer be ignored. It is not enough to merely state that all human beings must enjoy equal dignity. This concept must be translated into action. We have a responsibility to find ways to achieve a more equitable distribution of the world's resources.

We are witnessing a tremendous popular movement for the advancement of human rights and democratic freedom in the world. This movement must become an even more powerful moral force, so that even the most obstructive governments and armies cannot suppress it.

It is natural and just for nations, peoples and individuals to demand respect for their rights and freedoms and to struggle to end repression, racism, economic exploitation, military occupation, and various forms of colonialism and alien domination. Governments should actively support such demands instead of merely paying lip-service to them.

As we approach the end of the 20th century, we find that the world is becoming one community. We are being drawn together by the grave problems of overpopulation, dwindling natural resources, and an environmental crisis that threaten the very foundation of our existence on this planet. Human rights, environmental protection, greater social and economic equality and peace, are now all interrelated. If we are to meet the challenges of our times, human beings will have to develop a greater sense of universal responsibility.

We must all learn to work not just for ourselves, our own family or own nation, but for the benefit of all humankind. Universal responsibility is the key to human survival and the best guarantee for human rights and for world peace.«

Many of us are focused on creating positive personal and planetary progression, not just for ourselves, but also for our offspring. The idea that we can live in harmony and unity as healthy people who respect and honour each other is not just a pipe dream. Yet in order to have healthy, happy and productive adults in society we need to have healthy, happy and productive children.

This is achieved in three ways – home education, school education and life education. Before we address the issue of education let us take a look at where we stand today.

Our Planet – Facts, Positives & Other Views

As the caretakers of tomorrow's world, it is a time for creating a sustainable future, by acting with wisdom today.

FACTS: According to the new updated version of »The Gaia Atlas of Planet Management«, it has been a decade of records – of successes as well as disasters.

- The highest world temperatures ever measured on global warming.
- Levels of ozone in the upper atmosphere fell to record lows.
- Famine and drought have struck many regions of the developing world.
- Our wanton destruction of species and habitats has escalated to record highs – from tropical forest decimation to African elephants killed for their ivory.
- The worst news is that the twin pressures of human numbers and over consumption of the Earth's resources are still increasing. Our numbers are now predicted to rise not to 8 billion, but to 11 billion by 2050.
- The gap between the »haves« and »have-nots«, between the resource-intensive North and low-income South, is still increasing.

197

- Damage to the land, pollution, and destruction of species and habitats are proving intractable under this relentless pressure. But many nations are now making major efforts to conserve forests and land, improve human health and access to birth control, and conserve and recycle resources.
- Our economic troubles have led to world recession, poverty, debt, and hunger all of which are affecting more people than ever before.

But these very problems are sparking new economic, educational, environmental and political approaches.

POSITIVES

- The environment movement has grown worldwide, with individuals and governments recognizing the concept of sustainability. Seeing the vision of Gaia as a living planet, many are awakening with a new level of respect and love for our earthly home.
- There has been an enormous rise in activity and concern by individual citizens, as consumers, as voters, as campaigners, as caretakers of the earth.
- New political parties are being formed with a focus on unity and sustainability.
- We are making huge improvements in using energy more efficiently, and the family of nations have got together to ban CFCs in an unparalleled show of global co-operation.
- Unprecedented relief efforts have been accompanied by the raising of world consciousness as to the underlying causes of hunger.
- In many countries individuals are now pioneering the radical (to Western culture) idea of living on light, and being sustained by prana, which has global ramifications as a viable solution to world hunger.
- Global efforts to provide clean drinking water for all have helped hundreds of millions of people in the developing world.
- We have made a landmark agreement to conserve the pristine environment of Antarctica from exploitation, and negotiated international treaties to begin to conserve bio-diversity.

- The best news has been the end of the Cold War, sudden and inspiring, and the rise of global concerns for democracy, internationalism, and peace.
- Global military expenditure reached a record high of $1,000 billion a year, but the peak is passed and we now live in a world less fearful of nuclear conflict, and with a record number of countries enjoying liberal democracies. This show of unity was demonstrated against the French nuclear testing in the Pacific, more recent peaceful demonstrations in China, the Kosovo aid given – all these changes have shown that a startling revolution in human perception is possible and unfolding currently!

Hence it appears that we have a great need for continued re-education on the planet so that resources can be shared more equitably. Chaos upon our planet is not from a lack of goods or services or even the equal distribution of such. Chaos among humanity comes from a lack of common purpose to unite the diversity of all cultures and societies prevalent today. The chaos we witness on a planetary level comes simply from the:

- Lack of honor and tolerance among races and cultures
- Lack of clarity on personal and global levels
- Lack of vision that we are one people sharing one planet
- Lack of purpose and drive in our personal existence
- Lack of awareness of why we are truly here and what we can achieve as a species, and
- Lack of knowledge of the higher nature of our being and of universal law which governs the forces of creation.

One cannot create permanent global change for the good of the whole until one looks dispassionately and logically at the individual as a whole. Beings in wholeness are the forerunners in a changing global power. As Aldous Huxley the English Author once said: »Experience is not what happens to a man. It is what a man does with what happens to him.«

The following information focuses on what we see as the most powerful forces available to mankind today – the human resource factor. Now more than ever in this age of technology, RE-EDUCATION can be both potent and also the most effective tool that we have in creating and supporting global transformation – especially when coupled with the redirection of our resources.

We realize that eliminating global health and hunger challenges won't happen overnight, but it will happen as the Luscious Lifestyles and DOW Matching Programs inspire us to become fit on all levels.

The Ambassadors of Light also wish to inspire people to create personal paradise – including excellent health – which will then flow into global paradise. Yes, this is a huge re-education program that we are currently inviting humanity to undertake, yet it will bring results but it must begin with each one of us personally.

To many of the Ambassadors, there is no need for people to live in poverty, starvation, and without decent shelter or a good holistic education. All societies can be disease-free and all peoples can know physical, emotional, mental and spiritual health.

To achieve this, we encourage people to take advantage of the plethora of information supplied by the medical fraternity and also alternative practitioners, holistic educators and spiritual masters on earth. These are people willing to help individuals experience complete wellness in many aspects of their life.

The Ambassadors of M.A.P.S. do not seek to reinvent the wheel. What we seek is to encourage people to take responsibility for their life. The individual who seeks to enhance their own lives and the lives of all on the planet will need to exercise common sense and discipline in their daily lifestyle choice, and yet the rewards from doing this are beyond words.

Each of us through our daily lifestyle choice has the power to redirect resources around this planet by unifying with a common vision and a clear agenda.

While we recognize the need for the refinement of many systems on earth, in this section we wish to address the following:

- The human resource factor
- Education in the new millennium
- Tithing and aid organizations
- The benefits of the dissolution of prohibition
- The benefits of global disarmament
- The forgiveness of third world debt
- Raising money for social welfare programs.

Yes, we represent the voice of Gaia in our environmental concerns. The Ambassadors of Light also represent the voice of the indigenous and our forefathers of wisdom. In their image we may rise together along with the Star Trek generation and and our future space cadets. All are hooked into the cosmic, or religious, channels in their way. Personal reality is just a movie after all, and we are suggesting that we put aside all practices that create separation and finally look at the benefits of being unified in a common vision.

a) The Human Resource factor

Before we can effectively discuss the redistribution of resources, we need to assess the type of resources available to us – human and non-human. The most precious are our human resources. Without good companionship and camaraderie, life as we know it can be quite meaningless. In this we include our relationship with ourselves and honoring ourselves enough to experience who we really are – beyond our mind, body and emotions.

From the moment the Light Ambassadors came onto the global stage, we have spoken of the power of the DOW. It is all powerful, all knowing, and lives in everything, including us. When we focus upon It, magic happens in our lives – our fears dissolve, our lives feel purposeful and health and happiness arrive if we listen to Its guidance. Our world mirrors our beliefs about who we are and many have now risen to challenge these beliefs.

Yes, the Light Ambassadors encourage people to experience DOW Power, and move beyond limited thinking. It is well-known that the human resource factor is more powerful when individuals unify. As U.S. author Edward Abbey said: »In social institutions, the whole is always less than the sum of its parts. There will never be a state as good as its people, or a church worthy of its congregation, or a university equal to its faculty and students.«

We know that through open communication and intelligent discussion, resources can be effectively redistributed and systems can be refined so that all prosper in unity on earth. Yet before we can create and experience global unity, we must have personal unity, which means issues about our health, wealth, lifestyles, love life, friends, family, hobbies, passion and purpose in life need to be satisfactorily addressed.

This can only be done effectively when we understand that we are more than just our mind, body and emotions. Consequently the Ambassadors of Light feel that the key to positive human evolution lies in holistic education.

b) Education in the new millennium
»Our school education ignores, in a thousand ways,
the rules of healthy development.«
Elizabeth Blackwell, U.S. physician and author

»If you think education is expensive, try ignorance.«
Derek Bok

Many of the Ambassadors of Light have experienced the power of a cosmic force that is undeniable in Its wisdom. It has given us some basic intelligent alternatives while reminding us that, we don't have to have all the answers – we just need to know our bit. If we do our bit with honor and respect for all life, big change will come and education will provide the blueprint for this change to continue without chaos.

To define what we mean by education we include the following extract from ›Education in the New Age‹ by the Tibetan Master and Alice A. Bailey:

»Education has three major objectives, from the angle of human development:

FIRST, as has been grasped by many, it must make a man an intelligent citizen, a wise parent, and a controlled personality; it must enable him to play his part in the work of the world and fit him for living peaceably and helpfully and in harmony with his neighbors.

SECOND, it must enable him to bridge the gap between the various aspects of his own mental nature, and herein lies the major emphasis of the instructions which I am now proposing to give you.

In the esoteric philosophy we are taught, as well you know, that on the mental plane there are three aspects of the mind, or of that mental creature we call man. These three aspects constitute the most important part of his nature:

- His lower concrete mind, the reasoning principle. It is with this aspect of the man that our educational processes profess to deal.
- That son of mind, which we call the Ego or Soul. This is the intelligence principle, and is called by many names in the esoteric literature, such as the Solar Angel, the Agnishvattas, the Christ principle etc. With this, religion in the past has professed to deal.
- The higher abstract mind, the custodian of ideas, and that which is the conveyor of illumination to the lower mind, once that lower mind is in rapport with the soul. With this world of ideas philosophy has professed to deal.

»We might call these three aspects:
- The receptive mind, the mind as dealt with by the psychologists.
- The individualized mind, the son of mind.
- The illuminating mind, the higher mind.

THIRD, the gap between the lower mind and the soul has to be bridged, and curiously enough humanity has always realized this and has talked therefore in terms of ›achieving unity‹ or ›making the at-one-ment‹ or ›attaining alignment‹. These are all attempts to express this intuitively realized truth.«

Having made the commitment to self-responsibility and established communication with the »Illuminating Mind« of the DOW, one then begins to receive very specific information about their true life purpose. Many Ambassadors are now actively involved in holistic global re-education programs.

U.S. journalist Susan L. Taylor said: »Everything hinges on education. Without it, you can't advocate for proper health care, for housing, for a civil rights bill that ensures your rights.«

Education in the new millennium must be holistic, it must address all issues that concern us as spiritual beings here to have a human experience. We all know that healthy and happy adults tend to also breed healthy and happy children.

To achieve, this the M.A.P.S. Ambassadors of Light recommend a few tips such as:
- Children be educated in the personal and long-term environmental and global benefits of a vegetarian diet.
- That all children be encouraged to be involved in regular, if possible daily, non-competitive exercise that they do just for fun – dance, yoga, swimming, stretching, athletics etc.

- That all children are taught creative visualization techniques to learn to self-heal their bodies if the need arises.
- That all children are given regular daily doses of love and affection and taught the value of self-love.
- That all children are educated in the power of the mind/body connection in the creation of dis-ease.
- That all children are encouraged to spend daily time in silence talking to God (or whatever higher power they or their parents understand to be the Force behind Creation).
- That all children be encouraged to get to know and interact with the angelic realms. ›Angels or (spirit beings) are real‹ is their motto.
- That all children be encouraged to express their creativity in a manner that makes their heart sing.
- That all children be encouraged to develop other amusements in life apart from television. That television viewing be restricted to programs that have a positive influence on developing minds.
- That all children be encouraged to revere their whole being as a temple for the Divine to always radiate through.
- That all PARENTS voluntarily undergo specific parenting training before they can qualify to become parents. We all train for our driver's license and also attend educational institutions for our careers. Many M.A.P.S. Ambassadors consider parenthood to be one of the most important careers on the planet. We recommend that »parenthood training« and the above attributes and holistic education become a continuing presence in all school curriculums.

Holistic education must begin at home, be continued at school and encouraged as a lifestyle by society. The sooner we take responsibility for the fact that we are all part of a whole that affects and is affected by the whole, the sooner we can co-create constructive systems to address our world health and world hunger challenges. This is the very core of quantum physics today in that the whole can be affected just by our observation of it. This is also very Tao.

M.A.P.S. is not a movement of anarchy, it is about refining our existing systems so that they work for all. This can be achieved by adding a metaphysical approach to our modern-day challenges. Fear of change comes from lack of education.

Next to disarmament, holistic education is vital to our progression as a species. Science and religion are just two different spokes on the same wheel – as are traditional and alternative medicine – and do not need to be in conflict as both have valid roles. People need to be taught in schools, in their homes and in their communities about the power of:

- Universal Laws – what they are and how they operate and how we all benefit by using them.
- How to tune ourselves as a system of energy and obtain purposeful and healthy and happy lives via something like the Luscious Lifestyles Program.

As societies are made up of individuals – strong, fit, happy people make strong and happy societies. One of the goals in our ›World Hunger, World Health Project‹ is the eventual elimination of the requirement of hospitals – apart from emergency care – and other health care facilities, as we eventually move into a society of individuals who are disease-free and can self-heal when appropriate.

The Ambassadors of Light step forward at a time when the systems on our planet need to be honestly assessed, then refined as new programs are adopted to suit a changing world. We often tithe our time and/or our money and serve just because we can.

c) Tithing & Aid Organizations
»Good actions are the invisible hinges on the doors of heaven.«
Victor Hugo, French Poet and novelist

The adoption of a vegetarian lifestyle, particularly in industrialized countries, will immediately free up resources. Another way to aid in the redistribution of resources is through tithing. There are many ways to tithe. We can tithe our time and energy to support good projects and see our dreams collectively fulfilled. We can tithe a proportion of our income to a worthy cause knowing that as we open the door to give, we also attract and receive in kind.

Governments, communities and individuals can all promote good health via the promotion of a vegetarian diet along with the idea that this is also very beneficial to resource sustainability and our environment. We don't have to be too smart to imagine the impact that eventually living purely from prana will have on our planet environmentally.

And yes, it's true even though people laugh when I say, we can donate the money we save by being on a lighter diet and from not needing health care, to charity and aid in social welfare. Tithing is a wonderful gesture on many levels and many recommend that in the West this be 10% of our income.

From the money we can all save by eating less and not needing to pay for health care, we can:

- Support a child or two from the World Vision programs
- Donate to the Save the Children Fund
- Give it away to the homeless in your neighbourhood
- Give it to any other charity you are strongly drawn to
- Give to a friend or family member in need.

The important thing here is the giving without expectation of reward.

If Australians can spend 11 billion dollars on gambling in 1998, surely we can afford to tithe just a little. We can also tithe our time, money and goods to the existing aid organizations that are currently dealing with world hunger issues. Accessing information from the American News Service on U.S. Hunger Programs, Paul Bush from New York states: »Charitable feeding programs across the nation are facing an increasingly tough time getting enough food to serve the roughly 26 million poor people who rely on food banks.« Apparently over the last four years this has become more difficult as food banks have taught big chains (their usual source of left-over food) to be more efficient. Their new precision ordering, inventory control, and damage prevention programs have meant that these usually big donors to the hunger programs, now give fewer donations.

Although famine is still prevalent throughout the world, the ability of countries to import food and the efforts of international relief organizations have lessened the effects of modern famine. European nations, the United States, and other developed countries have not reported any instances of famine during the 20th century. Other countries, such as the Soviet Union, avoided high rates of mortality by their ability to import food and to distribute it quickly and efficiently. Famine continues to be a problem in parts of Latin America, Central Africa, and Southeast Asia.

Resource redistribution via existing aid organizations also needs support and refining. There are a multitude of stories of supplies never reaching their target destinations due to bureaucratic bungling, corrupt systems and simple inefficiency. The aid organizations are fully aware of these problems and are doing what they can to rectify the situation. Tithing is a wonderful way to support these organizations as they serve the third world peoples. In the meantime, we will continue our research and share our findings as an additional solution to these challenges.

The best way we can all help as individuals, is to get fit by eating lesser and lighter food, exercise, meditate, learn to get in purpose and in passion in life and clean up our own emotional baggage by changing our attitudes in life.

Once people have found the never-ending well of true happiness that is independent of wealth and cultural influences, then these individuals become naturally more altruistic, service-orientated, and can set about redistributing the resources on our planet so that all humankind have their basic needs met.

Sai Baba says people serve, simply because they can. We in the West are in a position to take care of people who have less than ourselves. Yet it is not the mind-set of our mainstream society to share wealth and resources; in fact social influence encourages the opposite.

The Ambassadors of Light recommend that people change their lifestyles, no longer needing to spend huge amounts of money on food, or alcohol, or the things that they chase to receive the levels of happiness that they can achieve from meditation and more spiritual practices – we recommend that this money be tithed to charities so that we can not just take from this planet, but we can also give. The more we open ourselves up via the process of tithing and giving, universal law dictates the more we shall receive.

We would now like to list information on organizations that you can contact for reduction of hunger in this world. The data comes from the website http://www.thehungersite.com/hungerresources.html

The Hunger Site

Like the food banks, the hunger site has been set up to aid in the distribution of food throughout the world. You may ask... How does food that is donated via the hunger site get distributed?

»The donated food is distributed through large international relief organizations. The hunger site has no political, religious, or other

affiliations, and we select these organizations on the basis of how efficiently they distribute food to the people who need it most...

The hunger site has placed in operation a very simple way of
distributing food. It also lists the many organizations that we can contact to give our support. They go on to say:

- »About 24,000 people die every day from hunger or hunger-related
  causes. This is down from 35,000 ten years ago, and 41,000 twenty
  years ago. Three-fourths of the deaths are children under the age
  of five.
- Today 10% of children in developing countries die before the age
  of five. This is down from 28% fifty years ago.
- Famine and wars cause just 10% of hunger deaths, although these
  tend to be the ones you hear about most often. The majority of
  hunger deaths are caused by chronic malnutrition. Families simply
  cannot get enough to eat. This in turn is caused by extreme poverty.
- Besides death, chronic malnutrition also causes impaired vision, list-
  lessness, stunted growth, and greatly increased susceptibility to dis-
  ease. Severely malnourished people are unable to function at even
  a basic level.
- It is estimated that some 800 million people in the world suffer from
  hunger and malnutrition, about 100 times as many as those who
  actually die from it each year.
- Often it takes just a few simple resources for impoverished people
  to be able to grow enough food to become self-sufficient. These
  resources include quality seeds, appropriate tools, and access to
  water. Small improvements in farming techniques and food stor-
  age methods are also helpful.
- Many hunger experts believe that ultimately the best way to reduce
  hunger is through education. Educated people are best able to break
  out of the cycle of poverty that causes hunger.«

So thank you »the hunger site«; we recommend that you famil-
iarize yourself with the work of the organizations listed in the appendixes at the back of this book; support them where possible, and then
also look at giving yourself real freedom of choice by getting to know
how the Divine One Within can feed you.

Another way to effectively raise money for social welfare programs and our »World Health World Hunger Project« is by the dissolution of prohibition.

d) Prohibition

The following is an excerpt from the third book in the Camelot Trilogy called »Our Progeny – the X-re-Generation«. In it we look at suicide among youth, drug use and prohibition, passion and purpose, vegetarianism, the Vedas and more. The research we have found on the effects of prohibition is as follows, and it is from the chapter dealing with addictions called »The Mistress of Nirvana – Drug Lords and War Lords«

»Prohibition gave rise to Drug Lords and War Lords as the search for ecstasy and enlightenment continued. Creating a billion dollar business that many fought hard to keep alive, to them the rewards were too great to consider the damage. In truth deaths from mind expanding drugs was hardly a statistic of crises – yet to those who love the kids on the street any death was unnecessary.

According to the United Nations, as earth completed the old millennium, the annual drug global production was 5,000 tones of opium, 500 tones of heroin when refined. Cocaine production added 500 tones more, to stimulate searching minds into altered states of reality.

Those calling for the abolition of prohibition argued that past prohibition only increased the wealth of the alcohol suppliers. Now drugs on the street were the same. Drug lords were war lords hell-bent on protecting their billion dollar industry, and without conscience, ignored the destruction of families.

In underdeveloped nations, forty per cent of street kids were sniffing glue with disastrous effects. Still these figures seemed so inconsequential when millions more died each year from tobacco and alcohol consumption. As income increased, so did the amounts spent on recreational drugs and pharmaceuticals.

Among the five million injecting drug abusers worldwide, 200,000 died each year. Add HIV and AIDS from drug-related deaths and addictions were expensive. Re-education was imperative, yet while prohibition persisted, the funding required to fight crime, escalated out of control. Drug cartels experienced prohibition just like a day at Disneyland.

The offspring of OH-OM in Europe and America were spending 120 billion dollars per annum. To the reformists, prohibition was ineffective and the problem continued to grow. Profits from illicit drug sales went untaxed, while addicts struggled to seek alternate realities and passions that would expand their minds and not destroy their bodies.

As E (one of the the main characters in the book – Jasmuheen) prepared to launch the Alliance, she realized she was soon going into a Europe in war. Drug lords or war lords – there seemed so little difference, the existence of both just propagated death.

Watching David Suzuki on television in ›The Nature of Things‹, she saw how effective reforms were being made. The death rate of intravenous drug users from AIDS in Amsterdam was half that of New York. Prohibition ruled America and statistics cried out how useless this road had become, in comparison to nations where drug use was treated as a disease and not a crime. In New York city eighty per cent of the intravenous users were HIV positive compared to less than one per cent in Holland where needle exchange programs were supported.

The evidence was obvious and to so many who took these findings on board, the laws were archaic and draconian. The USA had the highest drug use per capita, while other nations like the UK established harm reduction programs that saw those addicted to the Mistress of Nirvana gain control of their lives. Instead of working to score they were working to live.

Nations were turning their backs on both war and prohibition in a desperate bid to find civility in lifestyles and peace. In the world in transition, new chemical solutions produced drugs with less side effects and the ability to cancel the experience of the opiate high. Until they could find a new passion, this held promise for those already in the grip of their addiction.«

e) Global Disarmament

The issue of global disarmament is a complex one that has many aspects that need addressing. As with prohibition, there are many shades of grey in this argument which keep us from making decisions and taking a stand. However, the underlying fact is that the only reason we spend money on »national security« issues is fear; and the threat of war and also even prohibition keeps the arms dealers involved in a business that is worth billions of dollars in revenue. Many intelligent people are now asking: »Who is benefiting the most financially from the production of weaponry«, and »Why is it allowed to continue?« Creating an enemy is a wonderful way to perpetuate the life of an industry that for financial reasons many wish to keep alive. Fear of aliens, fear of despots, fear of drug lords and war lords.

By choosing to have no enemy and by allowing our DOW to dissolve our fears, we can finally disarm ourselves against each other. One glimpse of the Divine is enough to dissolve many fears. Fear comes from feeling disconnected to the Divine, it comes from not knowing who we truly are. Fear comes from feeling separate to each other and from lack of faith in the existence of true Holiness.

Many of the Ambassadors of Light now believe that global disarmament is vital for our prosperous progression into a new millennium. Why? Obviously because it is not necessary to live our lives in fear, and it is a waste of precious human and financial resources to be at war – look at Kosovo. Bomb them then rebuild them. Our governments spend 868 billion dollars per annum on arms which could be reallocated into social welfare programs. As John F Kennedy once said: »The greatest prayer is not for victory but for peace. There's no such thing as a winnable war.«

Yes, it is true that our governments are addressing the issue of how much is spent on arms, and also exactly what our need for security entails. The following research by Jeff fills us in on this picture.

US President, Harry Truman is quoted having said, regarding national security, »Talk quietly and carry a big stick«. There's obviously wisdom in this in that countries of ongoing effective neutrality, such as Switzerland, nevertheless have a substantial standing army. In other words you have to be prepared to defend yourself to be able to be left alone.

Since the Cold War has ended, the spending proposed in 1999 by the U.S. is 232 billion dollars – a reduction of only 7% from the average peace time cold war levels. The US Government's plan is to continue reductions so that ongoing cuts occur. The problem is, in any restructuring of an existing arrangement, individual congressmen in the US who have to approve reductions have vested interests to defend, such as bases and manufacturing plants in their districts.

The other major discussion is the cost of procurement of more hi-tech weapons e.g. the current F22 fighters cost 134 million dollars – the F16s which are being replaced cost 17 million dollars. Defense procurement costs for the Federal US Government, despite reductions, still account for nearly 70% of all Federal Government procurement.

While the free world certainly appreciates the duty of policing that the US morally fills, nevertheless the capital spending and recurring costs of the military in the US are a major slice of government spending. The consequent effects are felt throughout the world in third world countries, by the level of funds that are absorbed in this regard.

The question is what level of defense is adequate? It would not be unreasonable at this time to say that the level of defense capacity held by the US is excessive and certainly could be reduced substantially, with no loss of security for either the US or the world. Of course achieving this is a matter of political skill. However, people power, with the capacity of writing to congressmen and members of parliament, e-mailing, faxing and phoning, should never be underestimated. Remember of course, the politicians respond incredibly quickly to large numbers of aggrieved voters.«

Yes, disarmament is continuing worldwide, even if the trend is slowing down. On the other hand, a negative side effect of disarmament is becoming more apparent: surplus weapons. About 165,000 conventional heavy weapons, 5,000 nuclear delivery vehicles and 18,000 nuclear warheads as well as thousands of tons of chemical weapons have become surplus as a result of disarmament. Many governments have been taken by surprise by the enormous amounts of these »waste products« and they do not seem to be able to cope with the political, security and practical aspects of disarmament management.« Conversion Survey 1997: Global Disarmament and Disposal of Surplus Weapons, BICC (Bonn International Center for Conversion).

According to the above report there is a contradictory trend: Disarmament and armament are now standing side by side as eighty-six of the 156 countries studied reduced their military expenditures in 1995, and on the other hand, in 60 countries the military sectors expanded. This report also combines data on military expenditures, weapon holdings, armed forces personnel and employment in arms production and shows that there was a three per cent disarmament last year and that the military sector was reduced worldwide by an average of 21 percent.

In another study called »Disarmament and Development – A Global Perspective«, that has been prepared under the auspices of the

Center for International Development, University of Maryland, College Park, and the World Academy of Development and Cooperation, Washington, D.C.: »The escalating arms race and increasing pressure for Third World development have created an intensifying competition for scarce resources. The escalation of the arms race has resulted in slower and more uneven economic growth and development. The disappointing history of disarmament efforts and the unsatisfactory results in establishing a new international economic order underlie the reluctance to perceive a viable relationship between development and disarmament.«

While it would be naive to suggest that global disarmament can occur immediately due to the above facts, it is a program that needs to be expedited and internationally supported on all levels. Yet until we each disarm ourselves, we cannot disarm our nations. Disarming ourselves from fear is the greatest challenge facing humankind today, and the only force strong enough to free us from our deepest fears is DOW Power.

f) Third World Debt

One of the things many of the Ambassadors of Light are now supporting is the forgiveness of all third world debt. It is to be our planet's peoples first global act of compassion.

The Light Ambassadors have come to realize that due to the very act of this forgiveness of debt, the universal forces will step in and support this action on all levels because of the spirit in which it is being done. The »wealthy west« will not miss these repayments.

In an article called »Release from Unpayable Debt«, UNICEF estimates that 500,000 children die each week because of the third world debt crisis. Jubilee 2000 says that canceling the debt is the best way forward. »Let's wipe the slate clean and let poorer countries start again.« It is a radical view, though it has some powerful advocates including Archbishop Desmond Tutu of South Africa.

»We were shocked to discover that for every pound these countries receive in aid, they pay three pounds in interest payments. How can they ever get out of their financial crisis?« asks a member of St Michael's church, Paul Gruzalski.

One answer is the Jubilee 2000 organization, which is campaigning to mark the millennium by canceling the debts of poor nations. On May 16th 2000, politicians from the seven most powerful economic nations will meet in Birmingham to discuss this debt crisis. Jubilee 2000 hopes that 100,000 people will join a demonstration outside the talks to add pressure to the campaign.

According to an article dated Sunday, 27 September 1998, on the website http://www.igs.net/~tonyc/3rddebt.html:

Experts estimate Third World countries have already paid twice as much to industrialized countries as the original $1.5 trillion they borrowed, and say that many of the debtor countries are effectively bankrupt.

»Since the debts were first contracted in the 1960s and 1970s, the economies of many Third World countries have been devastated by a dramatic drop in the prices paid for their commodities and the soaring price of oil. The campaign to cancel the debts of about 45 countries is now worldwide, and includes not only churches but relief organizations such as Oxfam.« This campaign is being proposed by Canada's Churches and Ottawa's Anglican Bishop John Baycroft said canceling the debts would make it possible to save the lives of millions of children in third world countries.

Britain seems to be one of the most innovative countries in relation to dealing with issues like prohibition, and third world debt proposals. While global campaigns to cancel third world debt have not yet succeeded, on March 3, 1999, London British Chancellor of the Exchequer Gordon Brown unveiled proposals to reduce third world debt by $50 billion by 2000 via reform of World Bank and International Monetary Fund debt relief schemes.

According to this news item, Brown also said that the IMF should sell a billion dollars worth of its gold reserves as part of the drive to ease the crippling debt burden of the poorest countries.

»This will require a mobilization of the world community, international organizations, governments in the developed and developing world, charitable organizations and individuals«, Brown said as he unveiled his blueprint for easing the debt burden.

The plans include calls for developed countries to increase their aid programs to $60 billion dollars. This money should be spent largely on health and education initiatives, said Brown.

»The UK will go into the millennium with targets to increase debt relief, international development assistance and charitable giving to the world's poorest countries,« said Brown after unveiling his plans to British religious leaders.

The chancellor said that he would offer charities tax advantages as part of a drive to achieve a sharp increase in aid payments from charities to the developing world. He hoped that charity relief would reach one billion dollars by the end of 2000.

The forgiveness of third world debt requires a unified act of compassion.

»Compassion can be roughly defined in terms of a state of mind that is non-violent, nonharming, and nonaggressive. It is a mental attitude based on the wish for others to be free of their suffering and is associated with a sense of commitment, responsibility, and respect towards others.« *Dalai Lama*

g) Raising Money for Social Welfare

Even with the eventual forgiveness of all third world debt, many acknowledge that the human spirit needs more than just decent food and shelter to survive healthily and happily. As Chancellor Brown said, health and education and social welfare programs need also to be addressed.

In third world countries, the social welfare systems are either virtually non-existent, overworked, or overloaded and severely underfunded. As our statistics have shown, poverty is rising not just in third world countries but social welfare programs in many countries need immediate refining.

Once third world countries have been released from their debts, they will be able to focus on education and welfare programs more effectively. Many cannot disagree with the ethical and social argument for doing this, however there is one concern that when released from debt, the money saved may not go back into local social welfare programs.

Yet it is easy enough to put a stipulation on this in exchange for the releasing of this debt. Interest and repayments from third world countries is crippling their economies and is keeping them stuck in poverty. Please read the statistics on poverty, hunger, famine and malnutrition to see that resources really need to be redirected into these areas.

Many of the Ambassadors of Light feel that the forgiveness of third world debt must go hand in hand with the following commitments in order to be truly effective:

1. Global disarmament as people move from fear and into love through DOW matching. In the past we have spent nearly a trillion dollars annually because we choose to live in fear – to me this seems both illogical and poor resource management.

2. Dissolution of prohibition which takes the profit from drug cartels and puts it into the hands of government via taxes, to be used for better causes. Recreational drugs are not like alcohol and cigarettes. They kill less, yet the lifestyle and illicit nature of the supply and demand channels, need assessing and redirecting. Money in the hands of drug lords or governments is the issue, not the usage. Usage goes on regardless whether the moral factions of our communities like this or not. Holistic education when young will help prevent the problem as recreational drugs are used by a wide variety of people and for many reasons.

3. The sponsorship of holistic education which includes individual health programs that teach people how to be dis-ease free. This will also free up billions of dollars we spend annually on pharmaceuticals, health care programs, and dietary aids as we get fitter and healthier. Drugs treat symptoms and not the cause. Vegetarian diet, meditation, exercise, breath techniques and mind mastery will eliminate disease. Get sick and take pills, or don't get sick in the first place. Preventative medicine must be encouraged.

4. The global implementation of a vegetarian diet which frees up long term resources usage, decreases illnesses such as heart disease and cancer which has obvious flow on effects financially, and also creates a stronger moral backbone in society as we eliminate the slaughter of all life on earth.

5. Religious unification and tithing.

Conclusion

As groups currently exist who can work with our governments and those whose service is in this field, to arrange the above, we see no point in getting into a long philosophical discussion about the above ideas which are already well-supported globally. A search of the world wide web will find more than enough institutions who are well advanced in these fields of research and implementation.

Yes, it is true that the forgiveness of third world debt will be an expensive exercise for Western countries. However we need to measure the human cost against the monetary cost of the current situation and provided points 1 to 5 are adhered to, problems should be minimized.

Imagine what we could do for social welfare, unemployment, hunger and health challenges if we successfully redirected these resources. Billions from global disarmament, billions saved on pharmaceuticals as people no longer get sick, billions saved from fighting drug wars with prohibition. From just these three areas alone enough financial resources could be redirected to wipe out the debts of all third world countries and set up very effective social welfare programs.

So we recommend that each country design a program redirecting the resources from the above after they have agreed to introduce the various programs mentioned in this book. The resources redirected and saved can then be channeled into their own social welfare programs. We also recommend that holistic education must be implemented in all countries through all learning institutions. Part of the Light Ambassadors' focus is the application, via re-education, of sensible lifestyle choices as preventative medicine and to treat the cause of dis-ease in society, not just the symptoms. It is no longer a time to blame our governments, or our parents, or our cultures for the limitations we personally experience in our life. We have the potential to know great things because of them. People can rise out of adversity, be stronger and better for it, and our attitude determines the quality of existence here – nothing else. Blame seems to only keep people trapped in victim consciousness.

Millions are now unifying – Buddhists, Christians and Jews; plus Moslems, musicians, magicians and masters of all kinds. All are people committed to environmental issues, or to issues like drug wars and prohibition, or to basic human rights and things like healthy food, proper shelter, clean water, no child labor plus a decent holistic education for all. They are everyday people who feel like, »Surely we can all get it together since we all want love, we all want health, we all want abundance and friendship and more?« They also know that the best teachers are those who teach by example.

To implement these programs effectively will take people committed to service, civility and action who are united under one common vision, the basis of which is peace and prosperity for all.

Dancing with Democracy

The Declaration of Inter-Dependence

»If there were angels, no government would be necessary.
If angels were to govern men, neither external nor internal
controls on government would be necessary.«
James Madison, 4th U.S. President and political theorist
»Federalist Papers, no. 47 – 1788

As someone who works consciously with the angelics nearly every day, I really enjoy the above quote. Without contact with – and experience of – the higher forces, the divine nature in man seems to shrivel and die or is overcome by issues of our lower nature – ego, greed, mistrust, fear, insecurity and more.

This lack of experience of our divine or angelic nature is evident in so many ways on earth. For example, over this last century millions of lives have been lost due to war – fought for greed, fought for freedom from oppression, or fought for religious or ›ethnic cleansing‹; millions have suffered and lost so much. To many of the Ambassadors of Light, war is the most powerful example of the travesty of human rights.

Democracy has three basic meanings in its contemporary use. One, a form of government in which the right to make political decisions is exercised directly by the whole body of citizens under the procedure of majority rule. Two, a form of government in which the citizens exercise the same right, not in person, but through representatives chosen by them, and three, a form of government that is a representative democracy in which the powers of a majority are exercised to guarantee all citizens a certain enjoyment of individual rights.

Social systems have been changed over the millennia to reflect the consciousness of individuals who are proactive in educational and political arenas. Let us not underestimate the power of vision and action by any one person, nor the power that we all have as individuals to unify under a common vision and promote lifestyles that demonstrate that we are one race called ›human‹ living on one planet called earth – happy and unified.

As the Dalai Lama said in his speech on human rights and peace: »The widespread concern about violation of human rights is very encouraging. Not only does it offer the prospect of relief to many suffering individuals, but it is also an indication of humanity's progress and development.

Internationally, our rich diversity of cultures and religions should help to strengthen fundamental human rights in all communities. Underlying this diversity are basic human principles that bind us all together as members of the same human family.

However, mere maintenance of traditions should never justify the violations of human rights. Thus, discrimination against persons of different races, against women, and against weaker sections of society may be traditional in some places, but if they are inconsistent with universally recognized human rights, these forms of behavior should change. The universal principle of the equality of all human beings must take precedence.

The world is becoming increasingly interdependent and that is why I firmly believe in the need to develop a sense of universal responsibility. We need to think in global terms, because the effects of one nation's actions are felt far beyond its borders. The acceptance of universally binding standards of human rights as laid down in the Universal Declaration of Human Rights and in the International Covenants of Human Rights is essential in today's shrinking world. Respect for fundamental human rights should not remain an ideal to be achieved but a requisite foundation for every human society.«

As we end this millennium, we see how so much power is held in the hands of so few. Some act with compassion and honour, others do not. Many have taken prominence upon the global stage and have been given worth and credit. Some have seen how to make a positive difference, others have seen and are also doing it.

Others have been driven by personal agendas that have created separation and pain. Under them, many have suffered, while others have grown and become stronger for it. Some have led rebellions bringing anarchy or war – such has been the power of our beliefs.

As we enter a new millennium agreements need to be made as

One Peoples living on One Planet and until these agreements are made, unity will continue to elude us. In summary some of the agreements the Ambassadors of Light have made are to serve and support:

- The cessation of slaughter of all life.
- Global disarmament.
- Holistic education programs in all institutions of learning – these will focus on physical, emotional, mental and spiritual fitness and life skills which combine DOW Power and DOW matching tools.
- The cessation of rainforest destruction as the need for deforestation changes because of our new vegetarian lifestyles.
- Religious unification under common visions as »One People One Planet«.
- The redirection of resources.

While the above points support global paradise, for the creation of personal paradise, the Light Ambassadors:

- Invite the people of this earth to immediately begin to adopt a vegetarian lifestyle.
- Invite people to formulate the practice of their own ›Luscious Lifestyles Program‹ based on our recommendations.
- Invite all to be responsible for our own health and happiness.
- Invite all to discover the real purpose to our existence on life which is learning to thrive and not just survive here, and giving and receiving.

We recommend the above as a starting point of an agreement as we enter into this new time together. By making this internal commitment to experience DOW Power, changes will begin to happen in our lives that will bring magic and harmony among all. By making this commitment amongst each other these changes will be expedited. Furthermore, the Ambassadors of Light invite humanity to:

1. Let the past go. Let the past fall behind us, yet let us stand on it also, for without the past we would not be where we are today. As Jesus said, let us all turn the other cheek. In this we call for the immediate forgiveness of all third world debt among all countries.

Let the thoughts, words and actions that originally created separation between the Middle Eastern Arabs and Jews; the Moslems and

Hindus in Pakistan and India; the Catholics and Protestants in Northern Ireland; and the Albanians and Serbs in Kosovo, be forgiven now. Ask your DOW for the learning around these conflicts be complete, ask also for perfect solutions to be found and make the decision to now move on in peace.

2. The Ambassadors of Light ask that:
a) All people lay down their weapons of war in forgiveness;
b) All people disarm their homes and lives now;
c) All countries cease the design, manufacturing, trade or sale of weapons by the time we enter the new millennium;
d) All people honour the commandment that civilized people do not kill and immediately reprogram our minds to no longer see war and slaughter of life as a viable option for future change;
e) In line with this, the Ambassadors of Light recommend that the slaughter of life cease immediately with the adoption of global vegetarianism.

3. The Ambassadors of Light call now for the adoption of the theosophical model of brotherhood. This is our »One People, One Planet Project«. In M.A.P.S. we have re-written this to be the Declaration of Interdependence (see end of chapter). This model is designed to unite us under and into a common vision that we can use as a positive blueprint for change.

4. The Ambassadors of Light call for the global support of the Luscious Lifestyles Program so that all may know happiness and health, and can enter into a new millennium in peace, and in prosperity. The Luscious Lifestyles Program is a flexible enough blueprint that has been tried successfully by millions and can be modified to suit each individual with the stipulation that any program created MUST honor all life.

5. The Ambassadors of Light call for the commitment to personal and planetary paradise for all, by all. Through re-education all are encouraged to honour all models that are beneficial to all. All models creating harm and promoting fear and chaos are to be refined by those who run them. The Luscious Lifestyles Program will change the consciousness of the creators of these models allowing them to be more in line with the Five P Program – Positive, Personal and Planetary Progression and Paradise.

This is our invitation to the world as we enter this new millennium. With a common vision and agreements in place, that come from the heart and the desire to serve, we can begin a new chapter on earth taking pride in who we have become. It is time to learn from our past and move on in the knowledge that we are far more than just our mind, emotions and body.

Religious leader Mary Baker Eddy said »Give up the belief that mind is, even temporarily, compressed within the skull, and you will quickly become more manly or womanly. You will understand yourself and your Maker better than before.«

Learning to tune into the Divine and trust It, aligns us automatically via our resonance, with a world that many would dare to call paradise. This is the essence of the living on light phenomena – DOW Power and the ability It has to guide us into new realities of existence.

The M.A.P.S. Global Declaration of Inter-Dependence
»The greatest gifts you can give your children are the roots of responsibility and the wings of independence.«
Denis Waitley

In accordance to the guidelines of M.A.P.S. – the Movement of an Awakened Positive Society and the Ambassadors for M.A.P.S. – we submit the following Global Declaration of Inter-Dependence which is an amended version of the current Declaration of Independence.

When in the course of human events, it becomes necessary for individuals to revise and refine the existing social, educational, economic, political and spiritual structures which have previously flourished on earth, and to assume among the powers of the earth, the separate and equal station to which the Laws of Nature and of Nature's God entitles them, a decent respect to the opinions of mankind requires that they should openly declare their desire for a new state of being and co-operative lifestyle for humankind on Earth.

We – the individuals of M.A.P.S. – declare this now and hold these truths to be self-evident:

- That all of humankind are, in essence, created equal. That is all hold equal rights to explore their true human potential. This potential is the knowledge and experience of their Creator and of themselves as spiritual beings having a human experience
- That all life on earth is endowed by their Creator with certain unalienable Rights,
- That regardless of race, religion, gender, age or culture, all human beings have an undeniable Right to Life, Liberty, and the pursuit of Happiness.
- As such, their Rights would encompass a decent standard of lifestyle which includes:

    a) adequate shelter, nutritional food, holistic education, freedom of speech, freedom from oppression, freedom of choice for spiritual worship

    b) plus the Right to be fully conversant with Universal Law.

On governing institutions – M.A.P.S. Ambassadors acknowledge:

- That to secure these basic humanitarian Rights, Governing and Educational Facilities are instituted among humankind, deriving their just powers from the consent of the governed. Thus we encourage all individuals to take up their right to actively cast their vote to support the individuals in these areas of Government and education who can best facilitate the manifestation of these Rights.

- That whenever any Governing or Educational Institution becomes negligent, or incapable of achieving these ends, it is the Right of the People to alter or to abolish it, and to create new Institutions, laying its foundation on such principles and organizing its powers in such form, as to them shall seem most likely to effect their Safety and Happiness. Prudence, indeed, will dictate that governments long established should not be changed for light and transient causes.

- In this we expect that the people electing individuals to represent them in Institutions for Service and Care:

    a) be active in service to their immediate community

    b) that prior to serious community involvement, each individual learn how to utilize Universal Law and personally create their own health, wealth and be responsible for their own happiness.

On social matters, M.A.P.S. Ambassadors ascertain that all individuals also have the right to:

- Be given access to information on Universal Law so they can begin to understand the highest power of Divine Alchemy and thus, by the conscious day to day application of these Laws, they may experience their true human potential
- Be encouraged and inspired to create an individual model of reality that allows their heart to sing and also honors ALL life in a way that creates global community co-operation and not separation
- Become an efficient and effective global community, free from overt – or covert – manipulation from media, governments and any inequitable economically driven forces.
  Feel safe enough in their country and living environment to not have to bear arms – M.A.P.S. encourages global disarmament.
- Breathe clean air and drink clean water and as such all patents and devices that promote personal and environmental health are to be recognized and shared freely.

The M.A.P.S. Ambassadry also ascertains that lasting planetary peace and harmony, effective governments, global co-operation and sustainable development will come automatically to all humankind when they understand the power of the Creator who dwells within them. Hence we advocate the active promotion and education of Self Knowledge which is personal experiential knowledge of this Divine One Within that many call God or DOW Power.

~ end of declaration ~

THIRTYTWO

Service, Civility and Action –

Dance to Enhance

»He must be independent and brave, and sure of himself
and of the importance of his work, because if he isn't
he will never survive the scorching blasts of derision
that will probably greet his first efforts.«
Robert E. Sherwood

Service is about compassion. It is about providing a helping hand because it is needed, and because we can. Service is not about reward, it is about being willing to do just the bit we've been asked to do, and to do it impeccably.

Recently when asked, the Dalai Lama said that the best thing someone could do with their time was serve, and if they couldn't do that then the next best thing was to not create harm.

When someone is invited to, or desires to serve, they begin another level of personal change. Their DOW begins to further develop within them the qualities of courage, wisdom, dedication, discipline, unconditional love, strength and vision. These things are needed because often when one begins to serve it means helping to stimulate change. Sometimes this even means challenging the status quo in a way that creates resistance.

Gandhi, Martin Luther King, the Dalai Lama, Mother Theresa and countless others are examples of people who have dared to challenge the status quo by their service to fulfilling higher visions.

- Gandhi challenged morals and racial issues.
- Martin Luther challenged the status quo on the equality of man and segregation issues.
- The Dalai Lama is challenging the right for the preservation of homelands and culture, and change through non-violence.
- Mother Theresa challenged the status quo with her seemingly effortless supply of kindness and compassion.

The list goes on. Throughout centuries there have always been factions who have challenged the status quo, because it is what keeps the game evolving. And now as we enter a new millennium millions have risen up to support the need for change. People who have seen that one person can make a difference, and people who have a strong desire to serve.

The reasons that lead people to their desire to serve are multifaceted. Some do it because they can. Some do it because they are called. Some do it seeking answers and to give their life meaning and purpose.

Many intellectuals and philosophers and people of vision are born to challenge the status quo. German philosopher and author Nietzsche made people think. One could say he offered information based on years of experience of the seeking of the evidence of higher things. When he found it, he spoke of it in terms of »On Blissful Islands«, in his book »Thus Spoke Zarathustra«. I call these »blissful islands« the zone, and I call his »superman« what happens to us when we merge with our DOW.

Nietzsche is talking about the ability man has to create a better world for himself and what we in M.A.P.S. term, the creation of personal paradise. And when we surrender to the idea that we can exist on blissful islands as Nietzsche would say, many decide to serve so that all may enjoy this different world as well.

Yet even if it was written in the script of human destiny that we would endure a new millennia of war and chaos and poverty and destruction and fear, the Ambassadors of Light would still all serve. Service is not about fulfilling our personal agendas. It is about being willing to put these aside in the knowledge that when one serves the Divine Creator in Its Will on earth – Thy Will Be Done – then all life will come into harmony. Thankfully we gather together now to serve in the unfoldment of a plan for paradise.

In our God's cosmic movie, this is what we are currently being cued to do. Serve in the revelation of paradise. Serve so that all may have the experience of paradise. Serve as students and masters and children of the Divine. And yes, if the going gets tough, the tough can get going. It's a free will game after all.

U.S. clergyman and novelist, Frederick Buechner said: »Pay mind to your own life, your own health, and wholeness. A bleeding heart is of no help to anyone if it bleeds to death.« Yet when we connect to DOW Power, we have an unlimited supply of inspiration, energy, and wisdom at our disposal and without this connection many get burned out from the constant demands of choosing a lifestyle of service.

In the process of self-refinement and self-responsibility we become aware of the myriads of choices we all have each day in life. The first step to creating positive and permanent progression on this planet comes from within, the connection to DOW Power and then next is our ability to communicate with each other.

As Denise Breton and Chris Largent, authors of the books »The Paradigm Conspiracy«, »Soul of Economies« and »Love, Soul and Freedom« share: »Dialogue is the real source of order in human societies ... together we investigate who we are, what's going on, and which paradigms we want to shape out social systems. Order isn't imposed from without; it grows from sharing our inner journeys. Dialogue gives us the awareness we need to make social systems support us and our evolution.

Dialogue moves us beyond closed-system patterns. It opens the field and invites open investigation. Nothing is off limits. One of the main tasks of dialogue is to help us identify unconscious limits and sacrosanct patterns, so that we can pull them up for conscious reflection. The automatic, programmed response – the rigid role response – is exactly what dialogue questions. Dialogue challenges fixed roles so we can restructure them.«

So many have now experienced the human body as a complex system of energy that can be tuned or untuned like an instrument. Conscious tuning via reprogramming and lifestyle choices is one of the first decisions we can, as adults, make that will support our desire to be fit to serve freely. It is a time to ask whether our thoughts, words and actions are logical and civilized and whether they make a positive difference to all of our lives here. It is time to put aside all ideas that separate us as One Peoples on One Planet.

Life is so vast and so complex, are there really that many who KNOW what is going on? »On what level?«, a thinker may ask. In industrialized cultures many know where they are going, and they have both personal and global visions and goals. Come their day of death, they may have achieved these goals to their various degrees of satisfaction. Some exit this world with a feeling of »if only«, lamenting with

»if I had my time again« scenarios. Some surpass all their goals and yet approach their exit with fear and trepidation, unaware of what it will entail. Some, like the Buddhists, apply the Bardo and learn to exit gracefully. Personally, I prefer to see physical death as the time the DOW chooses to move on from the confines of its present vehicle. Still it is time to focus on the here and the now.

The understanding that the basis of all life is energy, and that the quality of our life is dependant on which frequency band each of us as a system automatically attracts – randomly or consciously – can be most helpful. Some call the highest frequency that we can attract and radiate, God. Some call it the Divine One, or Allah, Jehovah, Vishnu, Krishna, Christ consciousness, Buddha, Infinite Supreme Intelligence, and other labels that address the Creative Force and give it a more personalized and definitive form.

For those uninterested in theology and religion, ask yourself if there is anything that may be improved in your life physically, emotionally, mentally or even spiritually and if you feel »yes, there is«, then do some experiential research. Work smart and use your discernment as there is a plethora of new age, indigenous, ancient wisdom and religious answers to life's questions.

And when we have tuned ourselves just like we may tune up our car, then we will often find ourselves becoming altruistic. This is expressed by our being more charity-minded, purpose-minded, service-minded, or the altruistic-minded attitude of »I'd like my life here to make a difference«.

When we ask we do receive, and because the answers come, we are freed to be a thinker, a visionary, a co-creator, a marionette, a worshipper and sometimes even one who is worshipped. Worshipped because an energy of such strength and purpose and wisdom has the potential to flow from us to the degree that people fall in love with the ›DOW Power‹ emanations. Going beyond superficial beauty or survival plane intelligence, the Supreme Self, our DOW, reveals Itself to those with eyes to see and hearts to feel.

For those already in the awareness and experience of the obvious benefits of self-refinement and self-responsibility, does it really matter what we call our God? Surely we can all commit to being civilized enough to look for the commonalties that bind us rather than our obsession for differences – a focus which continues to separate us.

As Jeff found in his research for the M.A.P.S. Manifesto and our chapter on the importance of religious unification:

»All faiths evolve from earlier faiths. The current major faiths in the order of emergence are Hindu, then Buddhist, then Christian, then Islam. A theological study will confirm 50 perfect similarities between the Buddhist and Christian faiths, and as a matter of interest, only four substantial differences on matters of consequence.«

Continuing to focus on our differences is a limited habit which is like catching a train to nowhere – a train on a circular track with passengers getting on and off according to their pre-set curriculum and the evolution of their belief systems.

There are many tracks like that in life. The many »politically correct«, or not, tracks that represent symptoms of a society in transition. The point is that we are being invited to carefully examine, ›which track are we wishing to be on both personally and on a global village level?‹

So much that is said and done is either self-defeating – eroding systems that reflect their creator's level of awareness – or self-enhancing and contributing positively in synergy with our parents, our partner, our children, our communities and our countries and our planet.

I have personally spent decades consciously attracting, finding and being given information and experiences that fill in the unspoken blanks that our parental and educational systems are often untrained to address adequately. These are the purpose, passion, pleasure and power agendas. Driven by the desire to rise above mediocrity, I was inspired to have my existence right here and right now make a positive difference. A little altruistic, yes, but also a highly civilized calling; where civilized means treating all life with love, honour and respect.

Now that our work has attained a degree of global recognition, we are exposed to media criticism which is often unjustified. The Brisbane Sunday Mail, upon hearing that we were holding the M.A.P.S. Retreat at Noosa, also couldn't help themselves as they went to press with the headline: »Foodless Cult sees the Light«. While the article was quite informative and good coverage for us they couldn't resist using the words »The controversial Breatharian Cult...« which is so funny considering the caliber of people who make up the Light Ambassadry and the millions of qi practitioners in the world.

The Oxford Dictionary says a cult is a »system of religious worship esp. as expressed in ceremonies; devotion or homage to person or thing.« Qi masters are predominantly focused on living lifestyles that enhance the planet and their own lives. This is not a system of religious worship although religious masters are often honored for their wisdom. Many people today choose to follow the Divine One Within rather than an external master, including the majority of the Ambassadors of Light.

Do spiritual people gain benefit from the teachings of those who have gone before? They would be stupid not to. Science and medicine always builds on the theories and hypotheses of previous ›great minds‹ in these fields.

So the fear seems to be for people who may get ›brainwashed or mesmerized‹ by one charismatic leader in a way that is detrimental to them, their family or society e.g. the Jonestown and Waco massacres. Some may say that the people attracted to these ›charismatic leaders‹ are rebalancing karmic relationships from other times and are undergoing an initiation to develop trust in their own DOW Power and how to use personal discernment. Dealing with issues around disempowerment and the consequences of giving our power away is a very important lesson in life for all spiritual beings having a human experience.

Yes it is sad that these suicides and massacres happen, but does that mean we should treat all people as gullible and easily led? Should the ›powers that be‹ then employ fear tactics and ban information ›for the good of the people‹? Should the ›powers that be‹ be supported in the way that they label anyone who challenges the status quo or who seeks to refine existing systems as a ›cult‹ because their message is not understood? Or do they do this because they understand the message too well and feel that it threatens their own power base?

Should we assume that all people on earth lack discernment and therefore ban and/or discredit all ›charismatic‹ teachers or leaders who dare to challenge the status quo? Or should we encourage the use of logic and basic intelligence and remind people about the importance of using personal discernment so that they can listen to the deeper messages that many are now bringing onto the global stage?

Perhaps we also need to look at who spreads these rumors and what they have to gain from this. In my experience, nearly all fear comes from ignorance, and holistic education is the key to long-term positive progression on our planet.

Service is also about doing specific actions to plug in to our DOW, get our parts, remember our training, play our roles and choose to act in a manner that will make a positive difference. I call this the dance to enhance program. As the Ascended Master Hilarion said in the book »A New Heaven, A New Earth«:

»We stress that there can be no single prescription for success, and that man on earth must not expect other beings to provide some ready-made formula which will ensure that his civilization will never again dissolve into chaos. Man's salvation must be from within, and this means that it is up to humanity as a group to decide its future course. No guide, no angel, no extraterrestrial council wishes to interfere with what will be one of the grandest acts of creation that mankind has ever performed: the genesis of a new society based on the Love of God manifesting in human hearts.«

THIRTYTHREE

Progeny's Pearls & Programs

»People in this world are prone to be selfish and unsympathetic;
they do not know how to love and respect one another.
They argue and quarrel over trifling affairs only to their own harm and
suffering, and life becomes a dreary round of unhappiness.«
The teaching of Buddha

I'd like to think that the above quote is generally not true. I like to think that we are an intelligent and loving species who act with compassion, honor and respect. Yes, we may need a little fine-tuning, and yes, we need to be responsible for our own health and happiness, but point us in the right direction, give us a few good recipes for change and anything can happen! By combining the Luscious Lifestyles Program with re-programming we can step into this new millennium with good skills. As the Indian author A. Parthasarathy once said: »Modern civilized men without self-development are but intelligent savages living in spiritual slums.«

The Power of Thought, Word and Action

Researching neuro-science has established a state called plasticity which is our brain's inherent capacity to change. This is actually mirroring the universal law of change and adaptation. The human brain constantly designs new patterns, new combinations of nerve cells and neurotransmitters in response to new input and stimuli.

Each individual has the potential to rewire the brain's neural map and reconfigure it in a manner more conducive to producing the life they are looking for. So utilize the programs listed throughout this book and remember that when we ask we will receive. This is universal law.

Programming utilizes thoughts, words and prayers and has the ability to create new software for our bodies – the hardware – to run more effectively in life. Here are some interesting thoughts, quotes and programs for all to apply in life to aid in the creation, revelation and experience of personal and global paradise.

We have chosen to begin with love as:

- »Love is a canvas furnished by Nature and embroidered by imagination.« – Voltaire
- »Love is a friendship set to music.« – E. Joseph Cossman
- »Love is a better teacher than duty.« – Albert Einstein
- »Love is a fruit in season at all times, and within reach of every hand.« – Mother Theresa
- »Love is all we have, the only way that we can help each other.« – Euripides

a) Luscious Love

»True love whispers impeccability,
when softly stroking sweet tactility,
with agile gymnast's flexibility,
from doubt and chaos comes stability.« J.C.

- Love comes to us all in many ways – through family, friends and also our lovers, and sometimes even strangers. Love comes to those who welcome it and give it.
- In order to give and receive love, it helps to know and love ourselves.
- If we do not consider ourselves worth loving, can we allow others to truly love us?
- Each morning praise yourself – and those you care about – for the good qualities that imbue you all.
- Give thanks to your DOW for all the good that is in your life, focus on what works in your world and choose to be sincerely grateful.
- Spend five minutes each morning and/or evening filling your mind and heart with things that you have to be grateful for – even if it's just having a friend or a warm bed. The more grateful we are for what we have in life, the more we will be given by our DOW to be grateful about. This is Universal Law.
- Commit to create mutually empowering and mutually pleasurable relationships with all that you meet on earth.

- Forgive all those who you feel have ever hurt, betrayed or angered you, and who you have ever hurt, betrayed or angered. Forgive yourself.

DOW program:
- »I ask my DOW to bring me all those with whom I can have a mutually beneficial relationship.«
  »I ask to complete all learning from karmic ties, in joy and ease and grace, so that I may be free to give and receive and enjoy love, in all areas of my life.«
- »I now accept and give thanks for the abundance of love that is mine.« Visualize yourself , eyes closed, standing in the middle of the universe. Your arms are wide open in receiving position. Imagine all the abundance of love, health and wealth etc flowing into you.
- »I give and receive love easily in my life.«

b) Hot Health

> »Good health's opponent is anxiety,
> and sound habits include sobriety;
> direction enhanced with variety,
> a fit, strong, purposeful society.« J.C.

- Health of our total Self – our body, mind, spirit and heart – comes to all who are prepared to exercise a little personal care and self-nurturing plus a little daily discipline regarding our lifestyle choices.
- Meditation creates a healthy spirit, mind and heart.
- Exercise and a light diet creates a healthy vehicle for us to be high on life.
- Hot health comes from a basic lifestyle choice.
- Experiment – feel the difference!
- For hot health, laugh a lot and do what makes your heart sing!

DOW program:
- »I now command that my physical, emotional, mental and spiri-

tual bodies be perfectly aligned to the beat of my DOW so that I may fully enjoy and express Its presence.«

Health of others and health of our planet – outer pollution is a sign of inner pollution.

»After you're older, two things are possibly more important than any others: health and wealth.« Helen Gurley Brown
»...and passion and purpose...« Jasmuheen

c) Wise Wealth

> »Being frugal creates liquidity,
> but fortune's fate avoids timidity;
> the kitchen's heat provides humidity,
> at first a mist, but then solidity.« J.C.

- Be aware of the abundance of opportunities – when we look for abundance, it comes.
- Open up to receiving abundance from sources ›known and unknown.‹
- Utilize the Cosmic Bank of Abundance – expect to have all your needs taken care of by your DOW.
- Know that OH-OM (your God) is your true employer. Expect to be paid if you choose to serve OH-OM's Will on earth.
- Create your own Kosmic Kredit Kard and place it in your wallet.
- Place there also a small crystal that you have programmed to always keep your purse filled with more than enough money than you need.
- Also do what is practical on the earth plane to pay your bills – be responsible, but also expect that you can manifest and do work that you love and that is also beneficial to Gaia in some way.

DOW program:
- »I now ask to complete all my learning from past, present and future lives regarding abundance. I ask my DOW to remove any blockages within my fields that are stopping me from receiving

236

all the abundance that is mine.«

- »I now command that all resources that I need to thrive on earth and fulfil my purpose and passion, in alignment with Divine Will, be brought to me in Divine Time.«
- Then chill out, and every time you worry about money reprogram with the affirmation: »I accept and give thanks to all the abundance that is mine and welcome it from sources known and unknown.«
- Finally, be aware of your thought patterns around abundance. Reprogram limiting thoughts with limitless ones.

d) Passion and Purpose

> »A mould producing passion viable,
> purpose directed, undeniable;
> achievements that are verifiable,
> a character that is reliable.« J.C.

For many to feel passionate about life, they need to feel as if they have a purpose.

DOW program:
- »I now command that the purpose about which I am passionate be revealed to me clearly.«
- »I am now in purpose and passion in my life and have all the abundance that I need.«

e) Conscious Creation

> »Change to refined from barbarian
> careless eater to dietarian
> no information, to librarian
> Piscean self is now Aquarian« J.C.

- Be aware that your thoughts create your reality. Perceive it then receive it.

- Learn how to tune in to your DOW, then chill out and choose to find joy in each moment.
- Be conscious of how you fill each moment of each day. Quality thoughts, quality feelings and quality feeding creates a quality life.

DOW program
- »I ask my DOW to guide me in each moment of each day so that my life will enhance the planet and so that I will feel enhanced by being here.«
- »I ask my DOW to arrange all circumstance around me so that I may forever be free from doubt.«
- »I ask for my eyes to be kept wide open to the cosmic rhythms and my heart to feel Its love. I ask for my ears to always hear angelic voices including that of my DOW. I ask for the honor of serving in this most majestic game. This life I do give so willingly and free. I dance to enhance from now on!«

»So be it! So be it! So be it!«

f) Sex – Pheromone Fever

> »Between the sheets there's no formality,
> seduction's ally is mentality,
> a canvas of your personality,
> the primal drive of sexuality.« J.C.

- Passion begins in the mind, practise the tantra of the Tao.
- Purpose comes from the heart and mind being in harmony.
- Potency comes from the Tao – learning how to direct your energy.
- Protection is part of life – ›if it's not on – it's not on‹ – think ›safe sex‹.
- Make a list of what you would like in a lover, keep it in a drawer.
- Assign a lover angel – give it the list and say that that is what you would like – or someone better.
- Be aware that all major relationships are karmically connected.
- Understand that your partners often mirror who you are.

238

DOW program:
- »I surrender all my relationships to OH-OM with the intention that my relationships be brought to their perfect level of expression so that we may be free to live our lives to our highest potential.«

g) Addictions and Doorways

> »In bleak landscapes crying destitution,
> the addiction's painful institution,
> or alternately a revolution,
> the light plants mystical contribution.« J.C.

Addictions come from our perceptions and our preconceptions in life. Resolutions pave the way for change which will not come until we really want it to. By getting addicted to our DOW, all our other addictions will automatically be taken care of and put into their right perspective.

DOW program:
- »I ask to complete my learning around my addictions so that I may be free to move on and joyously fulfil my purpose upon this plane.«
- »I ask for clear and easy to understand guidance from my DOW in all areas of my life so that I may live each day in purpose and passion.«

h) Planetary Positives

> »Politically correct is inclusion,
> bigots are denied their self delusion;
> behaviour templates have nil exclusion,
> the planet's bonding is no illusion.« J.C.

The future is as rosy as we wish! Social, educational, economic, environmental, and political agendas affect all:

- Understand people power – vote. Write letters to people with influence.
- Remember DOW Power and that no man is an island. Everything we do and don't do, affects the field.
- Elect politicians that best represent your ideals and visions for a united earth.
- Tithe to those less fortunate – what we give out comes back to us.

DOW program:
- »I ask that the very next piece of my part in the movie of OH-OM (the Divine Blueprint on earth) be clearly revealed to me, I ask that all the people, all the resources that we need to fulfil this role come to me NOW.«

i) Harmony and Humanity

> »Some say the mystic is egotistic,
> idealistic is not realistic,
> however simplistic is artistic,
> ritualistic is illuministic.« J.C.

- Live in synergy and experience Unity.
- Be mentally free from self-imposed borders and boundaries.
- Respect and honour all life.
- Imagine a world in peace and harmony where all have decent food, shelter and holistic education, where all are fit on all levels.
- Remember: First in imagination, then in will, then in reality.
- Employ the angels – they must obey your DOW.

DOW program:
- »I ask that each and every day unfold in complete alignment with Divine Will, that all my sharing in each moment be for the highest good of all.«
- »I ask that every cell of my being, every level of my being, mirror perfectly the Divine perfection of my DOW.«

»So be it! So be it! So be it!«

240

Programs can be politely requested, or commanded and are made either to the Divine One Within you or your God (the One Source – or One Heart, One Mind that I call OH-OM). No one knows you better than your DOW, talk to it, program it, ask for guidance, learn to trust it and enjoy each step of your journey!

On Religious Unification

Just our commitment and desire to find and enjoy the evidence of Holiness will indeed change our world regardless of what we all call our God. The evidence of Holiness comes to us automatically when we use the following program.

- »I now surrender into the experience of the revelation of paradise on a personal and global level. I ask the universe to bring me the evidence of Holiness and Godliness and graciousness and divinity in such a manner that I am permanently moved beyond doubt.«
- »I now choose to forgive all those who have ever harmed me or my ancestors. I ask for forgiveness for all that I have ever done that has created harm.«
- »I now enter the new millennium with the love of my God in my heart, accepting and honoring of all who honor life.«

So be it. So be it. So be it.«

When DOW Power awakens en masse the way it now is, changes automatically happen. Earth is not the first planet to be going through this. Some will cross into a new millennium feeling safe in every way, others will drag themselves in feeling all degrees of pain:

- To the environment we wish to offer no more pollution.
- To the animals we offer compassion and freedom from slaughter.
- To ourselves we invite the experience of the DOW.
- For the evidence of Holiness, we say thank you.
- To the angels we say welcome.
- And to each other we say the same. Welcome to the movement of an awakened and positive society.

So we hope that you have enjoyed the research in this book and the sharing of my personal journey – what more can we say except that our love our light and laughter is with humankind as we all choose to transition graciously into this new millennium.

Yes, I will continue to tour and lecture on this research and new projects. We will also be holding seven day M.A.P.S. Ambassador Retreats globally – for further details just tune in to our website.

I would like to thank everyone who has supported our work in this field over the last few years, I know that for many of the Ambassadors of Light it has been a most fascinating journey, and the idea that we can take positive action today to create a planet we are proud to exist on, to me, is such a gift.

Appendices

Living on Light Global research Project no. 1

As part of our research, we are seeking feedback from those who have actually undergone the 21 day process as outlined in the book »Pranic Nourishment« (also called »Living on Light«). If you are interested in participating, you can obtain this questionnaire from the Cosmic Internet Academy website at:

www.selfempowermentacademy.com.au

where it is available in both English and German.

New Guidelines for the 21 Day Process

By Jasmuheen and the M.A.P.S. Ambassadry – JULY 1998 – can be obtained from the Living on Light Forum in our website.

Light Ambassadors Network

English, European and USA contacts of people who have undergone the 21 day process, and as individuals are happy to talk with others regarding their experiences.

ENGLAND
- Simon Palmer – E-mail address: sipalmer@hotmail.com
- Jeffry Sharp – E-mail address: Info@ancientwisdom.co.uk
- Daniel Jacobi-Braunschweig (Canary Islands) – E-mail address: DanielJ@infocanarias.com

USA
- Moises H. Koube – E-mail address: ag499@rgfn.epcc.edu
- Jalien Shandler – E-mail address: pichuma@earthlink.net
- Steve Torrence E-mail Address: Storrence@perfectscience.com
- Jaxon Wu – E-mail address: jaxon@divineliving.org

AUSTRIA
- EL-AN-REA – Tel: 0676 4063048

GERMANY

The German book »Der Lichtnahrungs-Prozeß Erfahrungs-berichte« goes into great detail of many people's experiences, and also lists people who are happy to talk about their experiences.

• Christopher Schneider: E-mail address: ApfeldorferSeminare@t-online.de. Christopher also regularly looks after groups of people who wish to undergo the process.

• Buszia Wucher, tel: 02226-6121. He is a yoga teacher, aged 70+, strong and I believe still on prana.

SWEDEN

• Curt Jonnson:
E-mail address: ivdqq20d2@ bboard.sixdegrees.com

ITALY

• Paola Cericola (network coordinator)
Scuola Di Respiro Via Carlo Alberto 39 : 00185 Roma
Ph: 06 4462523 Fax 0774 509301

• Michael Hardy
Istituto Europeo Pensiero Positivo
E-mail address: positivo@yacc.it
Michael does pre-process preparation courses

CROATIA

• Damir Modric Tel: 00385 1 318374
E-mail address: anamo@zg.tel.hr

Living on Light in Sweden
by Curt Jonsson

Until some time in 1998 I had never heard the term »breathar-ians«. Supposedly these people lived on air – just as vegetarians live on vegetables. I was told that there was a woman in Australia who had lived on air for five years.

I believed that it was true. However, I thought she must be a rare exception to the rule. I am convinced that some yogis can live without food or drink and that they can even be buried for weeks without dying. Yet I did not think that I could learn to do something similar – not within a reasonable time and not without a lot of training and giving up my normal life.

Then I read Jasmuheen's book ›Living on Light‹. I started to glance through it, and gradually I became more and more interested. Slowly I began to grasp what it was all about. She described a process, that would be possible for me to undergo. It was really not about eating or not eating. Instead it was about gaining access to the unlimited resources of man. And that is something that has always interested me.

To be honest, from the beginning my partner Ankara Nygårds was a lot more enthusiastic than I was. However, as soon as I had digested what it was about, I was completely ›sold‹. We started to discuss if it would not be possible to invite this Jasmuheen to Sweden.

Through the internet we found out that she was touring in Germany right then, so ten days later we arrived in Munich to participate in a weekend seminar, together with over 200 people.

That seminar was a turning point for me personally. Ever since then, nothing has been the same. It is true that Jasmuheen herself has a lot to do with it. She is so radiant and lively, and she speaks about energies, angels, re-programming of your cellular memory and other things so naturally and also with a good deal of sparkling humor.

But that was not all. There was something in this phenomenon that spoke for itself. Being nourished by prana, the universal life force. It was about having all your needs met by the Universe – or God. It was definitely also about being sensitive to guidance from the divine part of yourself and to act in accordance with what made your heart sing. All that was music to my ears. I now know that my process of living from prana actually started then.

As agreed with Jasmuheen, when I got home I translated ›Living on Light‹ into Swedish, and it has since then been published. And quite spontaneously I changed my way of eating. Soon enough I would only have fruit, tea and water. I realized that I would do the 21 day process. I was intrigued by it. I longed for it.

And in January-February 1999 I and my partner both underwent this initiation. It was actually an extraordinary experience, to say the least. Being an author, I have now written a book about my way to the process, my experience of the process, and my life after the process. It has taken the form of a novel, and I hope that people will find it both exciting, entertaining and instructive. It is called ›Light from the Other Side‹.

I am now member of a small group in Sweden, and we have accepted the challenge to spread information about living on prana and in accordance with the ›Divine One Within‹. This also includes making the most of our creative abilities and other latent qualities. To this effect we are planning many interesting activities. One of which is to organize Jasmuheen's seminars in Sweden.

This little group is called ›CuAnElCh‹ and consists of Ankara Nygårds, Elinda Lindberg, Christopher Schneider and myself. You can find more information about us on our web site: http://www.cuanelch.nu

You can also contact us by email: info@cuanelch.nu or qurre@hotmail.com, by phone +46 (0)247 232 86 or by so-called ›snail mail‹:

Cuanelch
Västibygattu 38
S-793 60 Siljansnäs
Sweden.«

Food Resource Distribution Organizations

If you go into the www.thehungersite.com you can click directly onto the following sites which contain general information about world hunger. Additional information can be found at the sites of the hunger and relief organizations listed further down.

Food and Agriculture Organization of the United Nations (FAO) ; United Nations Development Programme ; US Agency for International Development (USAID) ; World Bank ; World Hunger Program at Brown University ; Hunger and Relief Organizations

Listed below are some of the larger hunger and relief organizations. There are numerous other organizations throughout the world that also do invaluable work in the effort to end hunger.

Africare; American Red Cross; AmeriCares Foundation ; Bread For The World; CARE ; Catholic Relief Services; Congressional Hunger Center; Educational Concerns for Hunger Organization; Food First – The

Institute for Food and Development Policy; Food For The Hungry; Freedom From Hunger; Heifer Project International; The Hunger Project; InterAction; International Rescue Committee; International Service Agencies ; Lutheran World Relief; MAZON; Oxfam International; RESULTS; Save the Children Federation; Second Harvest; Share Our Strength; United Nations Children's Fund (UNICEF); United Nations World Food Program (WFP); World Emergency Relief; World Vision.

Other Books on Breatharianism
Can be found from http://web.cari.net/~nature/breatharian.html

Book: »Diet, Health, & Living On Air« by Morris Krok (97 pgs.) – Chapters include: Laws of Judgment – A Study In Naturalism – Health Disease and Food – Case Histories – Secrets of Living On Air.

Book: »Man's Higher Consciousness« by Hilton Hotema (1962, Hardcover, 300 pgs.) – In his most celebrated work, the great raw-food/fruitarian and contemporary with Dr. Herbert Shelton demonstrates the reason why the cosmic receiver in the human skull fails to respond to cosmic radiation as it did twenty thousand years ago. In 31 lessons the author covers subjects ranging from: breatharianism, cosmic air purifiers, physical perfection, raw foods, body-building material, man's natural home, physical purification, physical immortality, the mysteries of life, secrets of the ancient masters. One of the great classics in the raw-food genre.

Booklet: »Perfect Creation« by Hilton Hotema (32 pgs.) – With all the advances made in technology and communications in the past 50 years, the mysteries of human potential still remain untapped. This booklet demonstrates just how incredible each mind can be. A tremendously inspiring work guaranteed to motivate your hidden potential.

M.A.P.S. – Visions and Agendas

M.A.P.S. ... This »label« simply identifies a movement that is already occurring within society; what the Self Empowerment Academy (S.E.A.) sees as a Movement of an Awakened Positive Society (M.A.P.S.). Maps: Help us find our way; help us relocate from one place to another; are guideposts; can reveal treasure. In light of this, ›M.A.P.S.‹ is a very appropriate label and conceptual umbrella for S.E.A. to present positive personal, global and universal paradigms as pragmatic solutions for many of the challenges that we – as individuals and societies – face as we transit into the new millennium.

As part of our re-education program for people interested in positive personal and planetary progression, S.E.A. also provides the educational website called the Cosmic Internet Academy (C.I.A.): www.selfempowermentacademy.com.au

This site acts as a library, training and network centre to provide both educational and pragmatic information. Jasmuheen through S.E.A. also conducts weekend seminars and »open discussion« evenings globally, which are usually held annually in May/June and November/December. Jasmuheen's travel agenda is also posted on the S.E.A. website and in this newsletter.

Briefly, the focus of M.A.P.S. is to offer a threefold universal model that is potentially easily adaptable, balanced and harmonious to all regardless of their race, religion, age or gender ...

Firstly, we encourage the discovery and/or creation and implementation of a personal paradigm where we, as individuals, create a model of reality that allows us to live our life to our highest maximum potential – physically, emotionally, mentally and spiritually in a manner that honors all life forms. To assist in this, over the last few years we have been laying the foundation for the networking of a massive global re-education program. M.A.P.S. individuals are committed to enhancing life on earth.

Secondly, we recommend that any global paradigm that is created is to bring a positive rebalance within the social, economic, educational, environmental, religious and political arenas. This will be done:

- Socially – by the formation of the M.A.P.S. Ambassadry. Here, by re-education, we seek to encourage the creation of a disease-free society – with solutions to world hunger; the exploration of life purpose issues; abundance in health, wealth, love and happiness; plus how to create and maintain relationships that bring mutual pleasure and mutual empowerment. Many M.A.P.S. individuals now support the idea of a ›sweet transfiguration‹ which is about working for positive and powerful refinement of many of earth's existing systems. This is to be done in a manner that honors all and demonstrates the true synergy of self-mastery and co-operative teamwork. To find out more about the individuals who support M.A.P.S. see the M.A.P.S. Ambassadors section of the C.I.A. site.

- Educationally – one of S.E.A.'s main projects is to present the M.A.P.S. program into the global social system where applicable. This will be done via re-educational programs such as our website library, training programs and networking forums, and via self-empowering books, published articles and select work with the global media. We also wish to promote the M.A.P.S. agenda into the relevant global educational systems such as schools and universities. Our youth are our future and so the conscious, pro-active refinement of the existing education agenda is a major focal point. The M.A.P.S. program can be added to any existing educational curricula.

- Economically – all products and services must promote and support ethical abundance via the new business paradigm of using our heads, hearts and hands. Ethical abundance is also about planetary resource sustainability and environmental awareness. Here we also promote perfect health options via practical lifestyle changes which will eventually eliminate the need for, and the expense of, private and government-funded health care systems. Here we will also look at ways of equitably redistributing resources, disarmament, decreasing pollution and eliminating the slaughter of all life.

- Politically – without forming a specific political party, the M.A.P.S. Ambassadors seek to encourage political programs that recognize the need for holistic education, global ethical abundance, and resource sustainability programs with positive global energy systems that honour the environment and more. Governments are formed to provide community services. M.A.P.S. encourages the Utopian idea of self-mastery, effective self-government and synergistic teamwork on microcosmic and macrocosmic scales.

Thirdly, M.A.P.S. explores and researches further into a universal paradigm that focuses on the following:

- That residing in different vibrational frequency energy bands there are other intelligent life forms in the universe. This model looks at our place in the universe; other life forms now known as extraterrestrial intelligence, beings of light behind the world's religions, and more ...
- That the key to accessing these other energy bands and thus interacting with other life forms, comes from the refinement of a person's consciousness. Personal self-mastery is explored in detail in the training section of our web site.
- That by creating a balance and fine-tuning our physical, emotional, mental and spiritual energy fields, we can easily access and achieve all that we desire personally, globally and universally. This tuning allows us to utilize our natural clairvoyant, telepathic and self-healing abilities.

M.A.P.S. is an unstructured movement of people, it is a label to form an umbrella to hold within it any group or individual, religious or not, political or not, socially active or the yogi in the cave in the cities, the students and their masters. Anyone who supports, in their own way, positive personal and planetary progression.

Background on Jasmuheen
and her work as a M.A.P.S. Ambassador
- Born to Norwegian immigrants in Australia in 1957, Jasmuheen had become an artist and a visionary by the time she was seven. A mother of two adult daughters, she spent over a decade in the business world of finance before establishing the Self Empowerment Academy in 1993 and writing 10 books over the next five years.

- Founder of the international M.A.P.S. AMBASSADRY – The Movement of an Awakened Positive Society – Jasmuheen is probably best known globally for her work in the field of LIVING ON LIGHT. Since 1993, Jasmuheen has been part of a team that has pioneered and successfully implemented a specific process to allow her physical body to be »pranically fed«. As of mid 1993 she has taken her physical nourishment purely from liquid light.
- International lecturer and author, her fourth book »Pranic Nourishment« (also known as »Living on Light«) covers 4 years of her research in this field in great detail. This book has now been translated into the German, Dutch, Italian, Swedish, Croatian and Spanish languages, and will soon be published in French and Hungarian.
- The second book in this series titled »The 21 day Process«, and published also by KOHA Verlag, covers other people's experiences with the process of living on light and includes opening and closing chapters by Jasmuheen.
- Jasmuheen is known as a ›cosmic telepath‹ and is the author of the bestselling »In Resonance« (also available in German, Dutch and Italian), plus the »Inspirations« Trilogy. Her latest trilogy of ›received teachings‹ is called »Streams of Consciousness« Vol. 1 and Vol. 11. Volume 111 is a compilation of selected channelings from the previous 5 books. Jasmuheen has been channeling the Beings of Light, known to her Ascended Ones, since 1993 after many years of receiving telepathic messages from friends and relatives who had passed over. Her new book, »Our Camelot – the Game of DA« was published in English in March 1999 and in German in May 1999. The second and third books in this trilogy, »Wizard's Tool Box« and »Our Progeny – the X-re-Generation« will be published in Divine Time.
- Jasmuheen is also the editor and publisher of the newsletter »The ELRAANIS Voice«. This newsletter is the voice for M.A.P.S. and it focuses primarily on the creation, the discovery and the implementation of social, economic, political and educational brilliance – personally and globally. M.A.P.S. is a voice of social conscience.
- As international lecturer, author and reputable channel, her articles are published regularly in many esoteric magazines globally.
- Jasmuheen has practised mediation and researched metaphysics (the theoretical philosophy of human existence and knowing), Eastern

philosophy and New Age thought for more than 25 years. She is trained in Reiki 1 & 11, Magnified Healing and is an experienced metaphysical counselor/channel. She travels regularly facilitating workshops, with the Ascended Ones, throughout the world.

- As M.A.P.S. Ambassador, Jasmuheen is also the founder of the Self Empowerment Academy (S.E.A.) – which created the website called the »COSMIC INTERNET ACADEMY« (C.I.A.). This site acts as a Cosmic Library and offers many ›Cosmic Intelligence Alternatives‹ for the modern-day challenges of our world, plus 5 forums for global networking.

www.selfempowermentacademy.com.au

Inspired by the Ascended Ones, she now works closely with Mother Mary, Kuthumi and Saint Germain to promote the M.A.P.S. agenda.

Background of the Self Empowerment Academy (S.E.A.)

- A non-religious organization, the aim of S.E.A. is to inform, inspire and illuminate. Via the research, creation and implementation of pragmatic programs, S.E.A. provides information and techniques to empower and motivate individuals in all walks of life.
- From over 2 decades of research – looking at all the world's religions, the ancient wisdoms, the indigenous myths and teachings, plus a basic understanding of quantum physics and alternative healing practices – Jasmuheen has formulated very powerful self-help programs to allow individuals to realize their full potential and create happy, healthy, loving and abundant lives.

Benefits of S.E.A.'s programs:
- Increased clarity of thinking and creativity
- Increased feelings of inner peace
- Awareness of life purpose through opening to inner guidance
- Increased health and vitality
- Enhanced relationships with all
- How to live abundant and meaningful lives
- Learning to live limitlessly and creatively
- Finding and following your joy and passion

252

S.E.A. achieves this by:

- Powerful ancient and modern relaxation techniques
- Meditation using breath, sound, creative visualization
- Powerful programming tools, mind mastery
- Honoring the power of the heart and mind combined
- Understanding the higher light science
- Understanding universal laws of energy.

Jasmuheens favorite Meditation!

Modulation - Set
Personified Transients

Modulation - Set
Personified Transients

Modulation - Set
Personified Transients

Brian Vale   VOL 1

Subconsciousness; MOON Mind
Optical Design; SUN Mind

3 CD's ISBN 3-929512-42-2

Modulation-Set

Brian Vale   3 Volumes

One of Jasmuheens tools for realignement came from the cosmic orchestra channel Brian Vale. Shortly after doing Brian's program of specific frequency modulations she was able to access visions of the Cosmic Sacred geometric patterning. These programs are for the cosmic warrior and if it feels right then perhaps it may be a tool for you.

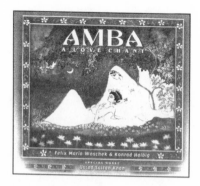

ISBN 3-929512-10-6 CD 60 min

AMBA -
A LOVE CHANT

Jasmuheen said: »As a writer I listen to a great range of esoteric and relaxion music for background ambience as I work. The one that always grabs my attention and gets me to pause, and then listen and enjoy is the wonderful AMBA.«

Living On Light

Jasmuheen

Since 1993, Jasmuheen has been physically nourished by the Universal Life Force of Prana. This book contains the details of her research and of her experiences of this profound process as it reveals a revolutionary form of nourishment for the new millennium. This way of beeing, formerly reserved for saints and sages, is now a possibility for everyone thanks to the information outlined here.

ISBN 3-929512-35-1
Pb 190 Pages

In Resonance

Jasmuheen

»In Resonance« is a manual designed to offer well researched information plus many practical techniques to aid in our personal journey into wholeness with joy!

ISBN 3-929512-36-X
Hardcover 312 Pages

Sensous Spirituality

Angel Meditation

Living On Light
&
Akashic-Records

Jasmuheen

Vol1 ISBN 3-929512-45-9
Vol2 ISBN 3-929512-46-7
Vol3 ISBN 3-929512-55-6

Meditations with Jasmuheen

Vol1
Living on Light
Meditation &
Akashic Records
Meditation

Vol 2
Prana Meditation &
Sensous Spirituality
Meditation

Vol 3
Angel Meditation &
Selfhealing

Music with Jasmuheen

CD 60 min ISBN 3-929512-27-0

The spiritual background of this music is Jasmuheens mantra »One Heart - One Mind«. The first part is filled with love songs and tantric mantras helping you to open up your sexual energies. Part two contains soothing music allowing the listener to tap into their sensual energy.